Editor's Note

Jonathan Wilson, Editor

Even before the astonishing finale, 2011-12 had been voted the best ever Premier League season. After Manchester City had scored two goals in injury-time to win it, there was every reason to support that conclusion. This was a season of superb and unlikely games, of collapses and recoveries, of brilliance and stupidity, of a title race that went to the very last second. This was drama of the very highest order, of the sort that only sport can provide.

It feels churlish to say it, but behind the excitement there must be a doubt and it is this: United collected 89 points and still didn't win the title. Only twice before in a 38-game season have they, by far the most successful side of the Premier League era, surpassed that tally. In the only season that has come close to 2011-12 for drama, 1998-99, they took only 79 points and won the league. This year, United won 28 of 38 games and still didn't win the title. Really, how unpredictable was this season?

True, the champions aren't as far ahead of the rest as in 2005, when Chelsea racked up 95 points, but the trend is obvious. Where 80 points tended to be enough to win the league in the late nineties, now it's 90. City and United finished 19 points ahead of the rest. Admittedly, it's fair to assume Chelsea and Arsenal will improve next season, and Tottenham, Newcastle and Liverpool may do so as well, but still, 19 points is a huge margin — and without significant investment you'd be surprised if Sir Alex Ferguson can coax similar performances from that squad again. The competitive imbalance between top and bottom is vast: the blurb may say that on any given day the bottom can beat the top, but the fact is it happens far less often than 10-15 years ago.

The reason, of course, is money. That's not to denigrate City — plenty of clubs have had vast resources for a variety of reasons — but there is something worrying when even a pundit as cogent as Graeme Souness responds to the final-day drama by saying, "What an advert everyone concerned with the Premier League this year has put out. To have a day like this on the very final day when it's gone right to the wire and taken extra-time for Man City to win it... what an advert for the Premier League."

Maybe a finish like that will drive up TV rights even further, but surely that's a minor footnote. This wasn't an advert: this was the thing itself, indelible sporting drama. Maybe it's unfair to criticise Souness for his first comment after a breathless few minutes, but as Jamie Redknapp went on to speak of the "product", you did wonder whether, as Sid Lowe said, we were witnessing a sporting culture that knows the price of everything and the value of nothing.

June 2012

Contents

The Blizzard, Issue Five

Introduction

03. Editor's Note

⇔ World Cup Bidding

07. James Corbett, The Fall-Out

Significant questions remain unanswered about the World Cup bid process

32. Igor Rabiner, Russia's Victory

Russia's success in the 2018 bid was a triumph over internal as well as external opponents

41. Philippe Auclair, Qatar Hero

Michel Platini is often seen as the ex-pro coming to save Fifa. But why did he vote for Qatar?

⇔ Interview

48. David Tryhorn, Socrates

The former Brazil captain talks about why footballers have a political responsibility

⇔ Theory

59. Philippe Auclair, Roy the Rover

Roy Hodgson explains how his travels have shaped his coaching philosophy

65. Luca Ferrato, Like a Shooting Star

How Ternana soared and then crashed with Corrado Viciani's high-tempo style

68. Steve Bartram, The Skilling Fields

Manchester United are just one of the clubs influenced by the coaching model of Wiel Coerver

● The Asian Market

77. Ben Mabley, The *Gaijin* of Gamba

Fan culture has begun to challenge Japanese hierarchies. The only European Gamba ultra explains how

93. Ian Griffiths, Sing when you're Winning

How the need to appear successful turns fans in Singapore from the S.League to the Premier League

● Photo Essay

98. Misha Domozhilov, The Hard Core

Images of the fans who followed Zenit St Petersburg as they won the Russian championship in 2010

⇨ **Fall**

110. **Lars Sivertsen, The Centre-back and the Kitchen Knife**

Claus Lundekvam opens up on his battle against the addiction that overwhelmed him after retirement

116. **Dominic Sandbrook, My Name is Ally MacLeod and I am a Winner**

How Scotland's humiliation at the 1978 World Cup knocked nationalism off course

121. **Jonathan Wilson, The Lions Sleep Tonight**

Ten years after retaining the Cup of Nations, Cameroon failed to qualify. What went wrong?

⇨ **Polemics**

133. **Brian Phillips, The Real Problem**

Is the 'real fan' being marginalised or is he just a rhetorical tool?

136. **Simon Kuper, Where's Darth Vader Gone?**

Is the age of football as a substitute for war coming to an end?

144. **Sergio Levinsky, The Culture of Violence**

The absence of leadership means there is little hope of Argentina's hooligan problem being solved

⇨ **Fiction**

148. **David Ashton, The Glasses**

A gift from a mysterious visitor changes life for a man on a Scottish estate...

⇨ **Greatest Games**

155. **Vladimir Novak, Romania 4 Yugoslavia 6**

World Cup qualifier, Ghencea Stadium, Bucharest, 13 November 1977

⇨ **Five Rings**

165. **Olympic Stories**

Five tales from the rich history of Olympic football

Information

30. New T-Shirts
186. Contributors
188. Subcriptions
189. About *The Blizzard*
190. T-Shirts

06

World Cup Bidding

"...like walking into a Greenpeace convention wearing a 'DOLPHINS ARE BASTARDS' T-shirt."

WE GO TO NEW LANDS

The Fall-Out

Significant questions remain unanswered about the World Cup bid process

By James Corbett

Zurich, December 2010

It's late on a snowy afternoon, and the Fifa president Sepp Blatter is about to make two short announcements that will shape the future of world football. The unveiling of the hosts of the 2018 and 2022 World Cups will conclude a long, controversial and sometimes acrimonious bid race that has dragged on between nine candidates for two years — longer in some cases.

Inside the conference hall at the cavernous Zurich Messe centre on the outskirts of the city, TV lights burn onto an empty stage and cameras glance across the room, beaming pictures to viewers in every country in the world. A cavalcade of international dignitaries, football royalty and celebrities have descended: Bill Clinton, the Emir of Qatar, Prince William and David Cameron sit among the likes of David Beckham, Zinedine Zidane, Luis Figo, Elle Macpherson and Morgan Freeman.

At the back of the hall, where several hundred journalists and scores of camera crews are situated, a stony faced Gary Lineker appears. He is part of the England bid delegation and has learned his country's fate from its Fifa vice-president, Geoff Thompson. "Two votes," he says, shaking his head, before repeating himself as if he can't quite believe it. "We were out in the first round." He shakes his head again. "Two votes."

In the early hours of the morning I had sat with officials from the England team in the bar of the Steigenberger Hotel, drinking overpriced pilsner and speculating on possible voting permutations. Then there had been a sense that the Russian bid — England's main rivals — might be falling apart after news had broken that Vladimir Putin was not turning up for the final hours of hustings. The Russian Prime Minister had sent out a rambling, paranoid statement, suggesting he wanted no part in what he seemed to say was a flawed process. It appeared to be the work of a man who was staring down his nose at defeat. Among the English the mood was one of cautious optimism. Nobody had anticipated humiliation.

We take our seats at the back of the room with a sense of looming inevitability. The results are supposed to be kept secret by the notary of the city of Zurich, in a sealed envelope to be handed over to Blatter who will announce them. But for 30 minutes Al Jazeera has been reporting victory for Qatar in the 2022 race. Blatter appears on stage and goes through his preamble; he is pugnacious, charming and sly. An Australian journalist mutters about his country needing a miracle. Then my colleague shows me a tweet from Dmitry Chernyshenko, the chief executive of the Winter Olympic Games in Sochi: "Yesss! We are the champions! Hooray!!!!" A couple of minutes later Blatter confirms that Russia will indeed host the 2018 World Cup. There are roars from the Russian bid delegation, who join Blatter on stage to raise the World Cup trophy. Some very pissed-off looking Englishmen watch on morosely.

The room calms as Blatter gets ready to open the envelope with the 2022 winner. Nobody is really taking the Al Jazeera reports too seriously and there's a sense that almost anything could happen. Two of Qatar's bid strategists are sat in front of me and nothing in their manner suggests a stitch up.

Blatter takes the envelope and introduces the five candidates for the 2022 finals. Then opening it, he says: "And the winner, to host the two-twenty-two World Cup is..." The card bearing the name of Qatar appears a fraction of a second before the word leaves Blatter's mouth.

The bid strategists jump up and pump the air with their fists as the room is filled with a mixture of horror and joy. All of us there know that world football will never be the same again.

The race to host the 2018 and 2022 World Cups was a contest in which all of Fifa's mismanagement, vested interests, palace politics and misconceptions were swilled around and then poured into the public sphere. It was a contest that will in years to come be considered emblematic of the Fifa that we know. I

covered every twist and turn as a reporter. It was the most extraordinary story I ever worked on. On the way I met hundreds of people: prime ministers, princes, sheikhs, sport politicians, PR men, lobbyists, technocrats, conmen and an incredible array of hangers on. I even encountered some players, too.

Yet covering the bid race, such as it was, was largely ephemeral. As reporters, we were duty bound to cover all the press releases and puffery from the bid teams, but were never really aware how much of this was filtering through to Fifa's executive committee — the 24 men of destiny who would vote on a winner. Despite the PR coups some bids pulled off (England retaining Paul the Octopus, Australia having Nicole Kidman front its promotional video) these were the only people who ultimately counted.

Nor were we ever sure what they were thinking. We had an idea of what was going on behind the scenes, but only a minority of Exco members were ever willing to speak on the record. Even then they were conspicuous in emphasising their neutrality or pushing the benefits of their own nation's bid. Seven (England, Holland-Belgium, South Korea, Qatar, Russia, Spain-Portugal, USA) of the 10 bids that started out in 2009 had representation on the executive committee, placing those that didn't (Australia, Indonesia and Mexico) at a conspicuous disadvantage.

To understand Fifa one must first understand the extraordinary culture of privileges and luxury afforded to its elected personnel. The professionals who administer it — the multi-lingual marketing men, lawyers, press officers and diplomats — are, on the whole, efficient, businesslike, courteous and a credit to their organisation. But the elected and unelected officials who govern Fifa via its 24-man executive committee and 25 standing committees are — with a few exceptions — utterly wretched: self-serving, grasping and wedded to the lavish hospitality culture that Fifa provides. Some have been proven corrupt. In all cases they enjoy a lifestyle beyond the wildest dreams of most football supporters: five-star hotels, business-class travel, endless banquets and hospitality, VVIP match tickets, *per diems* for themselves and their wives (or mistresses), chauffeur-driven Mercedes. At the top end of the very top table are the 24 executive committee members, who are treated like demigods. As well as all the freebies they get a $10,000 per month honorarium, $500 per day expenses, plus $200 for their travelling companions. No receipts are needed, of course.

In deciding the hosts of the 2018 and 2022 finals, these men were trusted with decisions that would define football's future and have implications, in some cases, beyond their own lifetimes. But before them was a blank sheet. They had no guidance and no agenda. Fifa's bid guidelines didn't stipulate that new territory should be breached, or — given a backdrop of global financial upheaval throughout the bid process — that an existing power be favoured for the sake of a 'safe' World Cup. Fifa offered no advice on TV and commercial markets they wished to corner, legacy aspects, nor what a host nation should offer in terms of football development. Indeed, the process was entirely subjective and down to the whims of

the Fifa Executive Committee. Blatter — as president — held the casting vote if they were unable to come to a majority decision between them. It turned out that wasn't necessary.

Decision day ended with Vladimir Putin — who flew in immediately after the result — taking questions from a roomful of journalists in an impromptu two hour-long press conference. When it was over, as we trudged into the cold Zurich night, we all asked the question that we're still asking: "How did that happen?"

Doha, January 2011

Within minutes of Blatter's announcement in Zurich, the two top trending topics globally on Twitter were "Quatar" and "Katar". The confusion over spelling seemed to embody many of the misconceptions about the tiny desert state and its plans to host the greatest show on earth.

Six weeks later I'm sitting in Blatter's hotel suite in Doha's Four Seasons Hotel, ahead of the opening of the AFC Asian Cup. A day earlier one of his principal enemies and rivals for the Fifa presidency, Chung Mong-joon, had been voted off the Fifa executive committee and replaced by an ally, Jordan's Prince Ali bin Hussein. Blatter is ebullient, taking swipes at his rivals and waving his press officer to sit down when he tries to draw proceedings to a close.

The previous week Franz Beckenbauer had said that the 2022 World Cup should be switched to winter to counter the extremities of Qatar's summer. Blatter, as is his way, picks up on this contentious theme. "Now, look at what players are saying and what people in Fifa are saying," Blatter says. "I personally think now that the decision is taken that we must play at the most adequate period to have a successful World Cup. To have a successful World Cup we have to protect the 'actors' and the 'actors' here are the players. Which means winter — maybe January, or the end of the year... If there is really a will to change the date of the World Cup in 2022 we have enough time."

Qatar, according to all prevailing logic, has no case to be a World Cup host. It is a tiny country with a population of under two million (only around 15% of whom are native Qataris), a climate that can rise well above 35˚ Celsius in summer and no record of footballing accomplishments. Fifa's own inspectors had concluded that parts of its bid proposal were "high risk" and that its plans posed "logistical problems". When it was awarded the tournament the country sat 112th in Fifa's world rankings and had never come close to qualifying for a World Cup. South Africa, about which similar concerns were once voiced, was 39th when Fifa awarded it the 2010 finals.

And yet there was a strange sort of rationale to Fifa's decision to award Qatar the tournament. The "logistical challenges" and "high-risk" factors — the searing heat, the size, the need to build an entire new city, as well as numerous new stadiums and other facilities — were tackled by its well-organised bid campaign. Cooling technologies — essentially outdoor air conditioning — are already successfully used in several of the country's stadiums and the bid proposed to develop a second

generation so that they were powered by the sun. The construction tasks that lie ahead are epic — Lusail, the new city which is hosting the final, is currently a handful of buildings in the desert — but the country's almost unimaginable wealth means that the ambitious and detailed plans they have are feasible. Reimagine the World Cup as an Olympic-style event, and the size of the country becomes less of an issue too.

Above all, Fifa under Blatter is an organisation fixated both with its own legacy and the notion of making football mankind's central cultural activity. Giving the World Cup to Qatar — one of the few places in the region with the political stability and cultural liberalism to host such an event — at once opens up the Middle East to football and changes perceptions of a misunderstood part of the world in a way that nothing else could.

Yet the howls of outrage at Qatar's candidacy were as immediate as they were inevitable. Brian Glanville described it as a "wretched little anonymity of a football country" and "Bin Hammam's dismal desert state". The Australian broadcaster Les Murray added that it was "ludicrous". "Fifa is in big trouble," he warned. "Nobody will believe that Qatar won this process legitimately." Murray's criticisms were significant, for he is also a member of Fifa's well-fed but largely impotent ethics committee.

A day after meeting Blatter, I meet Hassan Al Thawadi, the successful bid's chief executive, in the lobby of the same hotel. Still only in his early thirties, a graduate of Sheffield University who sat his A-Levels in Scunthorpe, Al Thawadi is immediately likeable, charming and persuasive. His American-inflected pronouncements are rapid fire and he apologises, self-deprecatingly, for his "verbal diarrhoea". He speaks with candour, pride and humility about winning the World Cup. Off mic there is a genuine sense of hurt at some of the insinuations already made about his country. Yet beneath the charm lies an obvious intent. A former colleague of his once told me, "He can be ruthless. He'll do anything it takes to get what he wants." An agent from the PR firm Brown Lloyd James sits in with us. She speaks only to order the three of us water.

I ask him about the prospect of a winter World Cup. Outside the sun is dropping and it's a steady 24°. The prospect of football in such a climate seems enticing. "We're ready to host the World Cup whenever it's meant to be hosted," he says. Then he neatly throws the ball back into Blatter and Beckenbauer's court. "If Fifa takes the path that it is hosted in the winter time, we are ready to host it in the winter time. We're looking to host the World Cup as we submitted, as per our bid book, during the required times by Fifa. At this moment in time we're looking at the summer period for 2022."

But the questions about Qatar's suitability won't go away. Al Thawadi's comments are largely ignored and the presumption remains that Qatar intends to change a summer event to suit its climate. Every time, it seems, that there's a Fifa gathering, Blatter or some other Exco member are asked about Qatar, and the winter World Cup issue comes up. In March scientists at Qatar University claim to have developed artificial clouds to provide shade for stadiums and training grounds at the 2022 World Cup. The story is ludicrous

and becomes another stick with which to beat Qatar 2022. Al Thawadi's team are deluged with calls. They claim to know nothing about the prototypes.

By then troubling questions are also raised in the British and US media about the methods used to gain Qatar's victory. A former media officer who left the bid in March 2010 has turned on her former employers and begun passing on documents and allegations to journalists. The *Wall Street Journal* claims that a payment of $78.4 million from Qatar to help the Argentinian Football Association (AFA) was considered by bid officials to earn the favour of the AFA boss Julio Grondona, an Exco member. Various allegations about the reach of the country's influential Aspire sporting academy are raised. There are even tales of an unseemly bidding war with Australia to gain the favour of Archbishop Desmond Tutu. Quite how this would win a World Cup bid is unclear.

Everyone on the old bid circuit seems to know who the whistleblower is. There doesn't appear to be a smoking gun but the allegations and drips of innuendo are troubling. The Qataris turn in on themselves, seemingly powerless to silence her. They become reluctant to speak to the press but can't quite cut all lines of communication. As spring comes and the heat starts to rise in Doha, it seems that barely a day goes by without a bid official or source calling me to sound off about my colleagues in the British media or complain about the whistleblower. I'm never sure if I'm being briefed or am merely there to listen to their mounting frustration.
We talk about how Qatar won the World Cup over and over. Officials insist, again

and again, that they think it was the final presentation that ultimately made their bid a winner. And it was brilliant. But then so was England's. The Qataris rehash the virtues of their bid. I was one of the few observers who thought they had a plausible case. But when I think of their innovative and ambitious bid, their youthful leaders, their idealistic concept of World Cup for "the entire Middle East", I then think of some of the Fifa Exco members who were meant to vote for them — old, conservative, corrupt in some cases, racist in a few as well — and wonder *how can this be*?

Of course the bid game was never just about football, and the bid committee were just part of a multi-fronted effort to win the World Cup. Qatar's government has used football and sport in general to assert itself on a global stage for many years. All governments who took the bid process seriously exerted some level of diplomatic or trade pressure. This could certainly impact some if not many of the Exco.

Take Jacques Anouma of Côte d'Ivoire. His home country has suffered years of civil unrest, secessionist movements and failed elections. The modus operandi of Laurent Gbagbo, its president from 2000 to 2011, was to cancel elections and to send out death squads to terrify and murder his opponents, including many women and children.

Anouma was not only a "very close associate" of the president, but his "personal financial adviser" too. According to Lord Triesman, the former chief executive of the Football Association, "there was not a prayer" that Anouma would do anything that President Gbagbo did not want him to do. "You could take him to see

Old Trafford and Wembley; you could talk to him about football until the cows came home, but the reality was that that would be something that was much more likely to be directed by a ruthless dictator in charge of that country," said Triesman.

Nor was Anouma alone in his links to questionable regimes. At Fifa events, Egypt's Hany Abu Rida was conspicuous in his light-coloured suits and oversized aviator shades resembling, as one FA official put it to me, "a 1980s Middle East dictator". Perhaps he took inspiration from his friends, the Mubaraks, who had ruled Egypt with an iron fist since 1981, pillaging the country's wealth and ruthlessly suppressing their opponents. According to Triesman, Abu Rida was a "very close associate" of the Mubarak family. He said that it was pointless seeking favour with Abu Rida "unless there was some agreement at a more senior level". Abu Rida, like Anouma, was in his view merely the puppet of a dictatorship. "These were regimes that were not only capable of deciding who should be in all of these key positions but determining their behaviour," he said. Including, it seems, their World Cup votes.

Then there were the trade deals between Qatar and home nations of Exco members. Throughout 2010, Qatar's state-owned airline unveiled massively subsidised routes to Argentina and Brazil. In August, the Emir of Qatar made an official state visit to Paraguay to finalise one of the biggest trade deals in the country's history. Of course all this may just be coincidence but all three South American Exco members — an Argentinian, a Brazilian and a Paraguayan — all apparently voted for Qatar. So it seems did Michel Platini, who was allegedly asked to vote for Qatar by the French President, Nicolas Sarkozy, as completion of a deal to buy French aircraft by Qatar Airways neared [see Philippe Auclair's piece for more details on the relationship between Platini and Qatar].

Qatar played the Fifa development game as well. Fifa was always keen on legacy aspects of all bid proposals, a desire that was largely undefined. England would send John Barnes or David Beckham to carry out coaching clinics in the developing world, but Qatar had grander plans. It unveiled a scheme to construct modular stadiums for the World Cup and donate them to the developing world after the finals. Aspire — Doha's sports science institute and arena — also opened offshoots in Guatemala and Thailand. Conveniently those countries also have Exco members, Rafael Salguero and Worawi Makudi.

All this was perfectly legitimate according to Fifa's rather loose bid guidelines. Qatar was just better able to exploit their ambiguities than some of their rivals. You wonder whether Fifa deliberately left the guidelines lax so that bid teams could exploit them to Exco members' benefit or whether they were simply incompetent.

A few weeks later I get an unexpected email from an old acquaintance asking me to call her. Like the rest of the world I'd heard much about Phaedra Al Majid, now notorious as the backtracking 'Qatari whistleblower', but had neither seen nor heard from her since she unexpectedly left what was then the Qatar bid in March 2010. A US citizen of Iraqi descent, Al Majid was an experienced media manager, rewarded with a senior position

on the Qatar bid after impressing on the local organising committee staff at the 2006 Asian Games. She was effectively second in command to the bid's director of communications, Nasser al-Khater.

The narrative of bid politics tended to cast its protagonists as somewhat faceless participants in a game of international power politics but Phaedra was very real: passionate, committed and liked by those who worked with her. The circuit also set up all sorts of unlikely encounters and while she was working for the Qataris we met at a bid expo in the shadow of Cape Town's Table Mountain, with the Emir's son in the backroom of a Johannesburg conference hall and in a Soho basement with Gabriel Batistuta. We also spent an amusing 40 minutes unsuccessfully traipsing around a Doha car park after she forgot where her car was parked following a friendly between England and Brazil in November 2009. I tell her that I saw a dusty, rotting shell of a car in the Khalifa Stadium car park on my last visit and she laughs that it was probably hers.

We talk about what's happened since she left the bid and she says that she was unsurprised that Qatar won in the end and believes, that despite everything, the Arab world should host the World Cup. She says that despite the question marks over Qatar's infrastructure and the searing heat that she has no doubt it will host an amazing tournament.

The conversation turns to the affidavit. I tell her that the circumstances seem strange, that in some minds the whole thing smacks of a conspiracy. She says she can't talk about it, that I must speak to her lawyer at Troutman Sanders (who subsequently says, beguilingly, "the affidavit is far from the whole truth").

Neither he, nor Phaedra, say any more. The sense that nothing is ever as it seems with Qatar is heightened once again.

In May we trudge up to the Palace of Westminster for a parliamentary select committee hearing into the governance of football. A session has been specially convened to hear about England's World Cup bid and Fifa. Rumours abound about shock revelations in store.

Lord Triesman, ousted as head of England's World Cup bid mid-campaign after a tabloid newspaper sting that prompted suspicions of a stitch-up by rivals, is the star turn. He speaks candidly about the demands of some of the Fifa Exco members, claiming that the Paraguayan, Nicolás Leoz, asked for a knighthood in return for his vote.

Then comes Mike Lee, a bid consultant for Qatar. Lee is one of the smoothest operators in sport politics, a brilliant PR man who has worked on successful Olympic bids for London, Rio di Janeiro and Pyeongchang, as well as Qatar 2022. He is here to talk about England's shortcomings, a favourite subject of his. But midway through his evidence session, he is hijacked by Louise Bagshawe MP, who provides a written statement from the *Sunday Times*. It alleges Qatar paid $1.5million bribes to Jacques Anouma and Issa Hayatou.

Smirks light up the faces of a roomful of journalists as Lee is left to squirm in

his chair. "I thought we were discussing 2018," he says.

The statements are based on evidence provided by the Qatari whistleblower, and so Bagshawe has used Parliamentary privilege to float the allegations. Libel laws mean that it would never otherwise have seen the light of day. The Qataris are furious. Their World Cup is tainted again. But nothing further comes out.

A name circulates of an alleged bagman, a Guinean called Amadou Diallo, about whom rumours have been floating for almost a year without any firm allegation being made. Diallo is a former Fifa development officer and now part of the entourage of the AFC president Mohamed Bin Hammam. Someone who worked with him at Fifa described him to me as a "cockroach."

Bin Hammam is fighting Sepp Blatter for the Fifa presidency. It seems, at times, as if this tiny gulf kingdom is taking over world football. Bin Hammam has been on the Fifa Exco since 1996 and was formerly a close ally of Blatter. He is one of the most powerful men in the game and also has the ear of the Emir of Qatar. It has been claimed that he used his wealth and influence to help Blatter win the Fifa presidency in 1998.

For the World Cup bid Bin Hammam was the third strand — along with the Qatari government and the bid team itself — operating to secure its success. He was the Exco arch-strategist, a man who cleverly built up a platform — via a secret deal with Spain-Portugal, who were bidding for the 2018 finals —that formed the basis of its victory. The pact was a symptom of the ludicrous decision to have a dual bid process and it gave Qatar seven votes to start, a formidable number when just 13 were needed to win.

Yet Bin Hammam's Fifa presidential ambitions are to come crashing down dramatically, calling into question the World Cup victory. Ahead of the June vote he criss-crosses the globe trying to get the support of Fifa's 208 federations who will decide between him and Sepp Blatter. As the campaign progresses he keeps a low profile as Blatter seemed increasingly desperate for votes. "The election is hard to predict," Bin Hammam wrote in an email to me on 5 May. "I remain in the same optimism of 50% chances, although I am doing reasonably okay."

He granted me one of the few interviews he gave on the campaign trail. "Most of Fifa's challenges lie with its image," he said. "Being the most popular game played every day by millions of people, football attracts massive attention from the fans and media worldwide. As a result, all of Fifa's actions and decisions, even at the minute level, will be under microscopic scrutiny and a problem in Fifa will be magnified a thousand times over compared to a similar problem in another organisation. For this reason, people working within Fifa must be extra careful and more cautious in their acts as their behaviour will be analysed, watched and monitored closely."

His words proved prescient. Unfortunately for Bin Hammam events intervened and the interview was never published. On 24 May, just a week after the British parliamentary hearing, Bin Hammam was accused of distributing $40,000 cash bribes at a meeting of Caribbean federation chiefs. Video footage later

emerged of the Concacaf president Jack Warner urging delegates to take the money. Bin Hammam withdrew from the Fifa presidential race. Fifa subsequently banned him from football for life. The stench of sulphur rose.

Among the Qatari organisers, tensions rose to breaking point. There was talk of the Emir's direct involvement. The mood was thick with paranoia and a paralysis crept over the team, heightened when the Fifa general secretary Jérôme Valcke said in a leaked email that Qatar had "bought" the World Cup, a reference he claimed was to their astronomical bid budget rather than other forms of inducement. Again the headlines went global.

Nothing seemed to go right for Qatar 2022. In July, as Doha sweltered, several prominent British journalists visited the desert kingdom. While they were there, the whistleblower outed herself. Phaedra Al Majid was a feisty media manager who had worked on the bid until March 2010. She had "wanted revenge after losing her job" but her "lies had gone too far" and in a sworn affidavit retracted the allegations she had passed on to journalists and, indirectly, the British parliament. It was a sensational development, seemingly defying all credibility. Privately the Qataris claimed that with the journalists in town, it provided more problems than solutions as it appeared stage-managed. From afar, the whole thing smacked of a conspiracy.

Ten weeks later I caught up with Hassan Al Thawadi again. One of the first things I asked him about was the circumstances surrounding Al Majid's affidavit. "It seems as if we're living in a damned if you do damned if you don't scenario," he sighed. "What had happened was that she contacted a member of the bid team. During the course of the conversation she wanted to make amends. She admitted to lying. She wanted to find the best way of making amends. For us we wanted to make sure that everything was above board to avoid any of these views that we might have in any way insinuated anything or forced anything and accordingly we made our lawyers aware of the conversation and the fact that were would be an affidavit signed. Accordingly the lawyers were on board — three different law firms — in taking the affidavit in ensuring there was nothing suspicious in the matter."

Al Thawadi insists that any public statements were made of Al Majid's own volition. I ask if there was any pressure put upon her. "None whatsoever," he replies. Was she offered any financial inducements? "None whatsoever."

It's early October and we're in London for the Leaders in Football conference at Stamford Bridge, where he's giving the keynote speech. A hitherto low key visit has evolved into something more and the Qatari delegation of three has quadrupled. In an executive box a harassed aide tries to juggle the logistics of the VIPs and the demands of the British press pack. A hyperactive reporter from a Sunday newspaper calls every five minutes, demanding an exclusive interview with "the Sheikh" [sic]. Mohamed Awada, Bin Hammam's former PR man, loiters in the background. Awada once accused one of Bin Hammam's enemies of engaging in "black magic"; I wonder to myself what would happen if he were unleashed on the British press corps.

I ask Al Thawadi if the reporting on Qatar has always been fair. "That's a loaded question," he laughs. "Without criticising anyone in particular the reporting took on board one perspective and maybe didn't consider another perspective on other matters. So, to give a simple answer, I think it was unfair."

But don't people have a right to question given what we know about the conduct of some Fifa members? "I don't see that," he says "With all due respect... there's been criticism for a significant number of years and a significant number of bids. My simple question is, had the United States or Australia won, would the same questions have arisen? I don't know. The way the whole campaign started against Qatar it makes me wonder if the same questions might not have been asked, or asked as passionately. All I can say from our side is that we did not break any of Fifa's rules. We did not compromise any of our principles. We knew what was at stake and if we compromised these principles or these rules it was not just going to be the embarrassment of the bid, it was going to be the embarrassment of the country and with the country striving to achieve so much, there was no way we were going to compromise it with a stupid action."

I ask if anyone ever asked for inappropriate inducements. His answer is monosyllabic but emphatic: "No."

He seems unusually weary. He'd told me in January that the first thing he did after the host announcement was sleep. The bid race was exhausting for everyone involved but little could he have imagined on 2 December that the spotlight was still to be cranked up to full beam. I ask if he thinks the questions and insinuations about Qatar's conduct will ever end. "I think we'll work very very hard towards achieving the dreams about the Middle East," he says. "Whether these questions stop or not I don't know, in all honesty. I do hope so. People can be cynical, fair enough. But we will dispel all cynicism on the ground when they see our actions: when people see that every promise we have made, every ambition we've put towards this World Cup, every dream that is hanging on this World Cup will be achieved - we'll put those cynical thoughts to rest."

London, May 2011

In a hotel suite in the west end of London, the Australian documentary maker Quentin McDermott from the Australian Broadcasting Corporation's *Four Corners* programme is interviewing the controversial football consultant, Peter Hargitay. It's for his latest film, about Australia's failed World Cup bid. Despite blowing Aus$46.7 million of taxpayers' money on their bid, nobody from Football Federation Australia (FFA) has seen fit to give an account of what went wrong. Flanked by his lawyer and even his own camera crew, Hargitay, a 60-year-old Swiss-Hungarian, is doing what no other representative of the lavishly funded bid has been willing to do.

"So we lost," says Hargitay. "Now are we proud of it? Of course not. Could we have avoided it? Maybe not. In hindsight, maybe not. But hindsight doesn't help. To go on and on about it, you spent 0.00045% of your GDP on this bid but you would have earned 10 to 15% of your GDP [these figures are highly contentious;

most observers suggest even a best case scenario the boost to GDP would be no more than 2%] had you won. Isn't that a risk worth taking?"

Many in Australia say that it was.

Of the nine nations bidding for the World Cup, Australia's fared worst, gaining just one of 22 possible votes in the election for the 2022 finals, and being eliminated in the first round. In its final stages Australia's bid was toxic: flaccid, badly thought out, supremely arrogant, lacking empathy with grassroots football in its own country. It was epitomised by an atrocious final presentation: a film involving an animated kangaroo and a score of Australian celebrities; then the country's football idol, Tim Cahill, left silently to stand on stage in Zurich as a mere adornment while Elle Mcpherson and Australia's bid chairman, Frank Lowy, took charge of proceedings. It seemed indicative of the bid's lack of understanding of the game.

And yet Australia is important because it tells us much about Fifa and the way that many countries went about their bid business.

The Australian World Cup bid had its origins almost a decade ago, when state and federal governments identified it as an aspiration. It gathered momentum during the 2006 World Cup finals, which saw Australia's first appearance in a generation and the FFA chairman Frank Lowy deeply impressed by Germany's party atmosphere. Lowy announced in October the following year that Australia intended to bid and soon extracted from their new prime minister, Kevin Rudd, a pledge of government support.

When putting together a bid team, there was an acknowledgement that Australia was a minnow in the murky waters of football politics. It had no Fifa Exco representation and had only joined the AFC in 2006. Many in Asia still consider it an outsider. "We would be naive to think that we, as a relative newcomer on the international football stage, had all the expertise to deliver the best outcome," the FFA chief executive Ben Buckley admitted in an interview with the *Australian Financial Review* in 2010. He spoke of the need to engage "international organisations to assist with the bid." In Australia's case this meant a team of three controversial European consultants.

One of these was Fedor Radmann, an Austrian veteran of the collapsed sports marketing company ISL, who had gone on to play a key role in Germany's successful bid to host the 2006 World Cup. Germany arguably put on the greatest finals in the history of the tournament. But the decision to award the finals to Germany ahead of South Africa in 2000 was described to me by a Blatter aide as "the greatest scandal in the history of Fifa". A nexus of hidden payments, secret deals and alleged threats secured Germany's victory at the last — but only after Oceania's Charlie Dempsey mysteriously absconded from the vote, leaving Germany to win by 12 votes to 11. Germany's *Manager Magazin,* which in 2003 meticulously unravelled the German bid, described Radmann as Germany's "puppet master". Radmann, who subsequently worked for South Africa's successful World Cup bid and briefly served as chief executive of Salzburg's 2014 Olympic bid, was hired along with his long term associate, Andreas Abold.

The other notable appointment was Hargitay, a man for whom the journalistic euphemism "colourful" seems to have been invented. In the 1980s he worked as a spin doctor for Union Carbide, the US chemicals company whose plant in Bhopal was responsible for a leak that Greenpeace estimates caused the deaths of 20,000 people. Hargitay was hired to gloss up the company's image; almost three decades later many of the disaster's victims await justice. He moved on to work for Marc Rich, America's greatest tax-dodger and an apartheid sanctions-buster who appears on the US's top 10 most wanted list. Later there were other business interests in film and, curiously, a Zurich-based private investigation agency.

There were also his own brushes with the law. In 1995 Jamaican detectives seized cocaine on a ship belonging to a Hargitay company. He was arrested, tried and cleared. Two years later he was arrested in Miami en route to Europe and detained on suspicion of cocaine trafficking. Again, he was cleared and freed, but only after serving seven months behind bars.

Despite this interesting past, Sepp Blatter saw fit to hire him as a special adviser around the time of the 2002 World Cup. The decision followed the collapse of ISL, a presidential challenge from Issa Hayatou and the rebellion of his general secretary, Michel Zen Ruffinen, along with several of his executive committee. Blatter was no Marc Rich, but his reputation had taken a beating. For the next five years Hargitay was frequently seen at the Fifa president's side. Such access purportedly made him one of the best connected operators in football. He briefly worked for England's nascent World Cup bid before taking on a well-paid consultancy with the Australian bid. What could possibly go wrong?

Large aspects of the consultants' briefs were to engage with the members of the Fifa Executive Committee. This would mean meeting, presenting, persuading and, invariably, entertaining and using Australian taxpayers' money to partake in the lavish hospitality culture for which Fifa is renowned. "I happen to have the access so our team has the access," Hargitay bragged to the *Sydney Morning Herald* in June 2010. "I believe it is unparalleled access. Access means there is trust. I can say that Mr Blatter gives me his trust, so does the secretary-general [Valcke] who shapes opinions. All the key [executive committee] members who have been long-serving, I know them personally and there is a level of trust that I am proud to enjoy."

Even before the consultants came on board, the Exco had had a taste of Australian largesse. When the Fifa Congress was hosted in Sydney in May 2008, Frank Lowy held a private dinner at his residence for the Exco at which the men from Fifa received gifts of Paspaley pearl cufflinks. Their partners received pearl pendants. The jewellery, paid for by the FFA, was worth close to $100,000. Australia was still to formally lodge its bid and thus was not bound by its rules. These stated that anything given during the World Cup bidding process should be no more than "occasional gifts that are generally regarded as having symbolic or incidental value".

Yet when the bid process started the stakes were raised even higher. At meetings held in April 2008 and March 2009 between Frank Lowy, Ben Buckley

and the OFC president and Fifa Exco member Reynald Temarii, the Australians were handed a shopping list. This included Hyundai vehicles for each of its associations apart from New Zealand and TV rights for the broadcast of A-League and Australia games in Oceania. Because they had no Exco member of their own, Temarii's vote was absolutely fundamental to their bid strategy. An internal bid team document resolved to "work with AusAID [Australia's international development agency] and commercial partners to deliver on OFC's request." The FFA went back to the Australian government and requested additional money for international football development in Oceania. Surprisingly they agreed. In August 2009, Temarii, Buckley and the Australian prime minister Kevin Rudd signed a partnership agreement with Oceania promising funding of "up to Aus $4 million over three years".

Nor was Oceania alone in benefitting from Australian taxpayer-funded generosity. Five days after the agreement with Temarii, a memorandum of understanding was signed with the AFC president Mohamed Bin Hammam, pledging Aus $5.1million to its Vision Asia football development programme. Bin Hammam was so grateful for this donation that he announced the following June that his confederation — of which Australia was, of course, a member — would be backing a European candidate for the 2018 finals.

A further cooperation agreement was signed with the Indonesian FA (PSSI), at a time when the archipelago was still a host candidate. Its federation president then, Nurdin Halid, is a fraudster who twice ran the PSSI from a prison cell, once while serving custodial sentences for stealing food aid from tsunami victims. He is reviled in his own country but this didn't stop Lowy from being photographed with him and describing their friendship as "strong". The Bakrie family, to whom Halid is closely associated, subsequently bought the Brisbane Lions A League franchise. Such are the prices you have to pay if hosting the World Cup.

Australia's money went far and wide and was spent in little ways and large. Everybody was desperate to court the nefarious Concacaf president Jack Warner and the bloc of three Exco votes he carried even though they were committed to the USA bid, which fell within his confederation and was favourite for the 2022 finals. No matter. When he complained, more than a year after the Sydney Fifa Congress, that his wife Maureen hadn't received her pearls, an FFA official was immediately dispatched to buy her a $2000 necklace.

Far larger favours were spread to the Caribbean, despite the slim chances of a return. When, in September 2009, Trinidad and Tobago's under-20 team went to a training camp in Cyprus, the FFA picked up the tab. "As a developed nation within football, FFA has a responsibility to promote football and social development among less developed nations," Buckley explained when the news broke the following year. "Commitment to furthering international relations and football and social development is also a critical requirement within the bidding process." A further memorandum of understanding was signed with the Jamaican federation in October 2010 worth $2.5million of funding. Hargitay, who has a home in Jamaica, was photographed looking on as the document was signed.

Almost a year after the hosts were decided, I catch up with Bonita Mersiades, the former head of corporate affairs at the FFA. For years Mersiades has had a formidable reputation both within Australian football and beyond. She is someone simultaneously in tune with football's grassroots and its corridors of power, rare qualities that set her apart from most other administrators, particularly in Australia. For a long time she was a confidante of Frank Lowy and was part of the movement that cleaned up the cesspit of Australian football in the early 2000s. Mersiades left the bid and the FFA in January 2010 after falling foul of Hargitay. Some say that she was sacked for being too honest.

I asked her about life on the bid circuit and what it told her about Fifa. "The bid process in terms of them saying, 'We're going to send out this document on a certain date and you'll respond by this day, etc' worked like clockwork," she says. "But beyond the actual process and the bureaucracy of Fifa, it was very haphazard. There was too much focus put on those 24 individuals and there would sometimes be unwelcome demands from some of them. I think inserting the Fifa Exco into the bid process was part of a flawed environment."

Was the bid designed to appeal to the best interests of football, or the 24 men, or was it a two-tracked approach also aimed at the wider world? "I think that was probably one of the mistakes we made," she admits. "From my perspective it was always about what was best for football and particularly what was best for Australian football because you have to have a legacy for football within your own country as well as more broadly for the game.

"I think there was a view within some in the bidding team that it was only the 24 individuals. There are many things that went wrong with the Australian bid. But certainly in 2010 we lost sight of what the actual World Cup was about — the football, fans and players. We lost a closeness with what we were trying to achieve by focusing on those 24 men to our detriment."

Indeed, it soon became clear that she was the glue that stuck together the public image of the Australian bid. Without her it quickly collapsed into acrimony. There was a bitter falling out with rival codes of domestic football that almost brought the bid crashing down. There were numerous PR gaffes and missed opportunities. There was unbridled paranoia towards the domestic media which even led to the public service broadcaster, SBS, dropping web-based articles critical of the bid. On the bidding circuit Australia's opponents described them as aloof, arrogant and unpleasant; qualities they carried into their daily conduct with the international media.

All the while astronomical amounts of taxpayers' money continued to be spent. According to the bid team's audited accounts, the bid book, technical inspection and final presentation cost a staggering Aus $10.3 million. This was a sum roughly equivalent to the USA's entire bid budget. For the final bid presentation film they hired the Hollywood director Philip Noyce, an 80-man crew and 300 extras. The CGI kangaroo took 6,000 hours to animate. The bill was added to the taxpayers' tab.

Of the Aus $42.7million spent by Australia, the bid consultants were paid a total of Aus $5.1million — a sum that would have risen considerably with win bonuses. Hargitay's company received Aus $1.45m of this. In most eyes this is not bad going for 18 months work. Hargitay, however, described it as a "pittance".

"Our objectives are understood very well in Concacaf despite the fact that the US are a competitor," he had boasted in June 2010. "We are even better understood in South America. Eventually, one, two or three will drop by the wayside and that's when phase two will kick in. I am absolutely confident that if there is only one Asian bidder left then all four votes from Asia will go to them. That I am sure of."

And yet Australia's consultants brought them just a single vote, apparently from Franz Beckenbauer — a close friend of Radmann, but a vote the FFA had been confident of securing even before the consultants' engagement. Even that had a heavy price. A 2007 cooperation agreement between the FFA and the German football federation saw Australia stand aside in the race to host the Women's World Cup. Surely that prize wasn't given up to win a measly vote towards the men's tournament?

"The evidence suggests the consultants were not value for money," says Mersiades. "If we had won, it is unlikely that anyone would have raised questions about the value for money of the consultants or how the bid was won. There was — and still is — a view from many that winning the bid was such a valuable end in itself for football in Australia that the means was irrelevant. While some people involved in the bid held their collective breaths at the engagement of Australia's international consultants, they were also tolerated because it was understood they would put us in the milieu of whatever it is that goes on behind closed doors with Fifa Executive Committee members and they could win it for us.

"Funnily enough, the same people who accepted the international consultants unquestioningly, and all that they brought to the Australian bid team, also cried foul about Qatar's win. They made the somewhat hypocritical assumption that, if we had won, it would have been okay; but for Qatar to win, there must be corruption as a Qatar win in their view — to quote Les Murray — was '...so absurd, it was just about unthinkable.'"

There is no shame in losing a World Cup bid but Australia's abjection was no less than they deserved. Ultimately the FFA betrayed their countrymen who paid for this vainglorious ego trip but weren't in any way represented by its sales pitch. Australia is, in many respects, the greatest sporting nation on earth. Seldom did the world get to see that reality meaningfully articulated.

I ask Mersiades whether she thinks that, like England, Australia was never going to win, no matter how good a bid proposal it came up with. "The funny thing," she says, "is that while the process was flawed, maybe the outcome is actually right in terms of what is best for the game — taking the game to different parts of the world, such as Russia and the

Middle East. Maybe it's not a bad decision in the end."

Yaroslavl, September 2011

Even hours after crashing, the fuselage of the medium-range Yak-42 jet smoulders in the Volga River as rescuers look forlornly amidst the floating wreckage for survivors. They find only dead bodies. The Lokomotiv Yaroslavl ice hockey team which had been travelling for a match in the Belarusian capital Minsk has been wiped out almost in its entirety. Seven crew and 36 members of the team and coaching staff of the three-times Russian champions are dead.

In its technical reports prior to the vote, Fifa had highlighted the transport situation in the Russia as a "high-risk" factor. The size of the country and inadequacy of its roads make air travel a necessity. No matter for the Fifa Exco. Only two days after they vote the Russian bid the winner, a Dagestan Airlines jet was forced to crash land at Moscow's Domodedovo airport whereupon it broke up on the runway, somehow only killing two of the 169 people on board. As well as the Yaroslavl crash, there were major air accidents in Russia in January and June and a suicide bomb attack at Domodedovo that killed 35 people.

During the bid race, Russia's infrastructural shortcomings were a constant line of attack from England's bid team. So too was the state of Russian football which is beset by crowd violence, racism and match fixing. Little has improved with the greatest show on earth now guaranteed. In the past year, Roberto Carlos and

Chris Samba have had bananas thrown at them by fans of their own club, Anzhi Makhachkala, while police in Grozny attacked the Krasnodar striker Spartak Gogniev on the pitch.

In bidding to host the 2018 World Cup, Russia touted a different concept to their rivals, seeking virtue in their status as a new World Cup territory and offering an ambitious domestic legacy focused on building new stadiums and extensive football infrastructure for their domestic game. I met its bid chief executive, Alexey Sorokin, a former diplomat, on many occasions through the bid process and he was always open about the challenges facing Russian football. He said that Russia needed the World Cup in order to transform itself.

"Right now we have come to the point where we are impeded by our own infrastructure and it needs to be modernised," he told me in December 2009. "We think that if we have good stadiums, more people will come and there will be a better climate for matches. Our football will benefit from better stadiums for sure."

But surely, in a competitive bidding environment, the World Cup should be a reward for excellence, rather than a catalyst to achieve it? Perhaps if Fifa had provided adequate bid guidelines that question may have been resolved before established football powers, such as England and Spain, entered the fray.

Murky rumours and insinuations about the nature of Russia's win have proliferated since Zurich. Certainly some skulduggery went on to secure the exit of England's bid in the first round of voting. The

Holland-Belgium bid president Ruud Gullit said in Zurich that he was "stunned" when Holland-Belgium got four votes in the first round of voting. "And when England had gone out after the first round, we only got two! One day I will find out which game was being played in Zurich." But do such shenanigans constitute corruption? Certainly there was something predestined about the 2018 result. Citing the influential Russian political analyst, Stanislav Belkovsky, the *Guardian*'s Russia correspondent Luke Harding claims that the Kremlin and the Russian bid knew a week before the secret ballot that Russia had already won.

England, for its part, was privately never in doubt about how Russia won. "Off off off record," one of their PR men texted me hours after the vote, "It must have been paid for." Some journalists bought this line. The next day, the *Sun* led with the headline "Fifa Bungs Russia the World Cup." Yet when there was a parliamentary inquiry session on Fifa the following May, none of the bid's senior management consented to give evidence in a haven in which they would be protected by parliamentary privilege. Only Lord Triesman — who had left the bid in May — saw fit to answer questions and when he called into question the conduct of some Fifa Exco members, he was derided by some former colleagues who bitched that he knew nothing.

Within weeks of being awarded the tournament, work got under way on preparations for Russia 2018. It had to, for there is much to be done. "It is no secret that we have a lot to construct and infrastructure to be prepare. It is a huge task," Sorokin said in August 2011. "We are coming to an understanding of the scope of this event. The basic lesson is we need to start right away. We need to start right now in order to be fully prepared for the 2017 Confederations Cup and the World Cup in 2018."

I have no doubt that the magnificent stadium plans in Russia's bid proposal will be realised. The World Cup may also change global perceptions of the country, as it altered the image of Germany. It's the less glamorous things I worry about, like security, accommodation, and yes, airports. But certainly there will be plenty of people wishing to put their name to a great vanity project, like a stadium. Supporting this construction programme is an unparalleled nexus of private wealth. In Zurich, as Vladimir Putin gave a press conference hours after the vote, he effectively told Roman Abramovich, who was sitting with journalists, that he would be picking up the tab for one of the stadiums. Abramovich met the order with a slight shrug of his shoulders and a grin. How could he possibly refuse?

Cologne, October 2011

In the refectory of the German Sports University in Cologne, delegates of the Play the Game Conference are sipping Kölsch beer and swapping stories, conspiracy theories, intelligence and gossip. Run by the Danish Institute of Sport Studies, Play The Game is an initiative to promote democracy, transparency and freedom of expression in international sport. Its biannual conference brings together stakeholders from across the world, a collection of administrators, academics, journalists and a few curious onlookers, too. It

is leftish, radical and provocative; a state-sponsored exposition of the ills of modern sport.

It's the first Play The Game conference since the World Cup bid race drew to its unsatisfactory conclusion and although other sports, such as handball and volleyball, are given a prominence here that would be lacking at other such symposiums, football is for many the main draw. And Fifa, after its *annus horribilis*, is the main talking point.

"I think the World Cup bid race made it completely clear that Fifa and — potentially other international sport federations — are completely unprotected to people who want to abuse the wealth of sport, the popularity of sport, the astronomical revenue of sport for their own personal gain," Jens Sejer Andersen, Play The Game's international director tells me. "Thanks to investigative journalists, basically from the UK — I'm referring to the *Sunday Times*, Andrew Jennings and the BBC — it was finally documented in a way that nobody could ignore: that Fifa is based on a system of corruption, not only some greedy individuals here and there, which you will always find in this world. It also became scarily clear that Fifa had no tools to fight this kind of internal corruption and perhaps no interest in really doing it."

Jennings, one of the most brilliant and forensic sports journalists at work today, is invariably in the thick of the action in Cologne. Now in his late sixties and with a shock of white hair, he maintains an energy and verve that masks his age. His natural ebullience and showmanship also disguise the meticulousness of his work and the hours he spends at his home in Cumbria poring over file after file of leaked documents. He's refreshingly self-deprecating. "I used to deal with real criminals," he says. "The Chechen mafia, the mob in Palermo, bent coppers. Fifa are a bunch of clowns by comparison — but they've been very effective in concealing their corruption."

Invariably he's a controversial figure and has been banned from Fifa press conferences for years. Many despise him, although mostly it seems for doing his job rather too well. When a BBC Panorama investigation he led into the ISL bribery scandal was broadcast on the eve of the World Cup vote, naming the former Fifa president, João Havelange, and the Exco members Ricardo Teixiera and Nicolás Leoz, as taking a $10million bribe booty from the collapsed sports marketing company ISL, England's World Cup bid team described it as an "embarrassment" to the BBC. Claiming that it merely raked over old allegations, they said it belonged on the History Channel. Fortunately the IOC took the claims rather more seriously and their investigation effectively forced Havelange's resignation at the age of 95, thus ending one of the longest and most high-profile sports administration careers of all time. Teixiera may well be next, although Fifa — as is their way — dismissed the allegations.

For now a Swiss court protects the other recipients of bribes. A secret document details more than 160 other payments to high-ranking Fifa officials. Fifa has said publicly that it will release the document, while at the same time trying to suppress it legally. Such are its strange ways.

The next day in Cologne, Jennings says that Fifa meets all the definitions of the mafia, with an all-powerful don surrounded by "greedy crooks", who are protected by a code of "omerta" that silences whistleblowers. Across the conference hall is Fifa's new director of communications, Walter de Gregorio, a towering Swiss former newspaper editor of Italian stock. As Jennings continues, you can see the anger building on de Gregorio's face. Taking the microphone he tells Jennings, "The Mafia killed and raped thousands of people. It's disrespectful to Fifa and to people who lost their lives." Jennings smiles, and unbuttons his shirt to reveal a blue T-shirt provocatively bearing the slogan, "Fuck Fifa."

Afterwards, amid a scramble of TV cameras and other journalists, they continue arguing outside the auditorium. It's pure theatre, not unlike a staged confrontation at a wrestling match. Indeed one wonders why De Gregorio, just a few days into his job, gets so impassioned about something that hasn't happened on his watch. "Why are Fifa spending money on expensive lawyers to suppress documents?" demands Jennings, waving a paper at De Gregorio, which purportedly lists the suppressed ISL bribe payments. "There is more coming!"

Jennings has been pursuing the ISL bribery case for more than a decade, but the end is almost in sight. A Swiss regional court in the canton of Zug has overturned objections to the release of the files and it will now be referred to the Swiss Supreme Court. 2012 may be the year that the ISL scandal brings the house of Fifa crashing down. Jennings believes the current crises mean the truth about the World Cup host decisions won't be so long coming out. "Despite Blatter's attempts to kick allegations into the long grass with his bogus reform process, Fifa is becoming destablilised," he says. "He's very isolated and as they turn against each other, everyone looking after themselves, an organisation disintegrates. That's when the leaking comes. It happened in 2002 and I think it'll happen again. I don't think Blatter can win this one."

The end of the ISL case will mark the end of a long and often lonely struggle to suppress the truth. In Britain, Jennings has largely worked alone on the case and is dismissive of most of his colleagues in the British press. "They have a self-imposed isolation from the story," he says. "They don't talk to anyone, they don't have the sources. They pontificate but they don't get the documents."

One of his principal collaborators is the Berlin-based journalist and blogger, Jens Weinreich. Born in East Germany in 1965, Weinreich has been on the case of Fifa and the IOC for almost his entire career. Ostensibly he seems as unlike the hell-raising Jennings as is possible; softly-spoken, baby-faced, disarmingly modest. But they share the same meticulousness in their work and an unstinting commitment to finding the truth and unravelling corruption.

In Cologne he shares a platform with Jennings and speaks on the bid decisions. "The meaning of the word corruption is a wonderful playing field for language artists, but it is very simple," he explains. "Corruption is the misuse of entrusted power for private gain. That's it. It is not a rocket science. It should be understandable even for senior FIFA officials, for lawyers, for academics, and journalists who still have problem using the right word – corruption." But football,

he says, is a "parallel society... with its own jurisdictions." In this strange world "stealing money is not stealing money, crime is not crime, misusing funds is not misusing funds, bribery is not bribery — it is, for instance, development aid, or something like that."

Based on information provided to him by several whistleblowers, Weinreich alleges that the amount of money paid to World Cup voters was "much higher than in any corruption case before, even higher than the amount of money paid in the ISL case." Indeed the cost of one of the 24 votes, claims Weinreich, is higher than anybody had ever imagined. "The working thesis based on World Cup scandals is that one vote is allegedly worth up to and over $20million — partly paid in euros, partly paid in dollars, partly paid in cash, in most cases paid into secret bank accounts and tax havens," he says.

"During my research I found new words, new vocabulary. I give you just a few examples. I have heard a lot about 'one-day companies', I have heard a lot of 'one-day accounts'. It is more complicated than just to give the money in brown envelopes. What does it mean? The money transferred was arranged in quite a sophisticated way by financial experts. Can we prove it? Not right now."

Weinreich says that the task of finding the truth has been made harder by a "big cover up" that transcends sport. "I'm not only talking about Fifa and its propaganda and its newly hired spin doctors and PR agents; people who are paid well to tell lies and influence journalists," he says. "I am talking about private intelligence companies and services in different countries. They are all busy covering up all that has happened the last few years."

He says there is a need for an independent investigation commission, sentiments echoed by Jens Sejer Andersen. "For me there is no doubt that Fifa needs an open investigation into many aspects of its governance," the Dane tells me. "There should be an independent forensic investigation, with police expertise, into relations between Fifa, its marketing partners, where we would get a public map of the corruption patterns in football. And there should be an independent investigation into how the World Cup of 2018 and 2022 were actually handed out."

"There is a need for total transparency," adds Weinreich. "At the moment I don't see any transparency from Fifa." He acknowledges that despite oral testimony, "there is almost no proof of corruption so far" in the decision to award the World Cup to Russia and Qatar.

"But it will change, no worries. It's just a matter of time."

Planet Fifa, January 2012

Global football finds itself in a severe state of crisis. Fifa continues to be plagued by repeated and unresolved allegations of corruption and mismanagement. The complexion of the Fifa Executive committee has changed inexorably since bid D-day — Chung Mong-joon, Mohamed Bin Hammam and Jack Warner have all been ousted, Franz Beckenbauer has gone of his own accord — but no one

seems to have noticed. Blatter, the man who symbolises the organisation, still sits in his throne, crown slightly tipped after his bruising and flawed election for a fourth term as president. All over the world, Fifa is considered corrupt and, in many eyes, has lost all credibility to lead. Anger at Fifa has united an incongruous cast of global figures. David Cameron has described the organisation as "murky". Henry Kissinger said that the cesspit of Fifa politics made him "nostalgic for the Middle East". Mahmoud Ahmadinejad described Fifa as "dictators and colonialists".

Blatter repeatedly promises to release the ISL documents, but it's past the point where anyone believes him any more. While he makes these pledges, Fifa continues to lead the pursuers of truth a merry dance through the Swiss courts. A bribery scandal of staggering proportions has become bogged down in legal minutiae. The story loses a little bit more of its resonance with every month of obfuscation.

Troubling and unanswered questions remain about the serially flawed dual World Cup bid race. This story won't go away either. Rumours abound of plots to take the 2022 finals away from Qatar. One story is that a crack team of private investigators and lawyers, paid for by a failed bid, are scouring the planet for a smoking gun. Bid insiders report inquiries from investigators whose paymasters remain shrouded in mystery. At least two contacts have received threats, one serious enough to involve a law enforcement agency. It is understood that the national criminal investigative body of one of the defeated bid nations is investigating corrupt football officials. We shall have to wait and see if these relate to the host decisions.

Red herrings abound too and disinformation and smears are tools in the armoury of those who want to discredit the host nations and Fifa. Someone purporting to be a private detective claims to be in the possession of a "top-secret 865-page report alleging massive corruption in the 2022 World Cup bid process". The report that "for the first time unmasks the powerful figures involved and the subsequent betrayal and backstabbing following the Qatar 'win'" is offered to certain journalists for the small sum of €15,000. A taster sent through reveals it to be a totally unconvincing fake — probably authored by the same person who set up a bogus website during the bid process to discredit Qatar and Russia. It is believed that the person behind that site worked with one of the vanquished bids.

But despite the stream of gossip, innuendo and rumours, substantive allegations about the conduct of the two successful bids are still to emerge. My dealings with the Qataris and the Russians have shown the personnel of these teams to be essentially honest. But on Planet Fifa little is ever as it seems and you can't vouch for anyone when so much business is conducted behind closed doors. The conduct of certain Fifa Exco members has done so much to discredit the entire process that you can't help but be suspicious.

If the truth ever emerges about what happened in Zurich, Fifa's ability to deal with serious allegations about the conduct of its elected officials remains deeply questionable. In October 2010, six weeks before the decision on the bid was announced, the *Sunday Times*

exposed two Fifa Exco members, Amos Adamu and Reynald Temarii, asking undercover reporters posing as US bid lobbyists for inducements in exchange for their votes. In Adamu's case he wanted $800,000 paid directly to his bank account. Another six officials, including the former Exco members Slim Aloulou and Amadou Diakité and a former Fifa general secretary, Michel Zen Ruffinen, were implicated by the investigation, which included allegations about the Qatar bid. Fifa's ethics committee moved quickly and handed out several bans from football, including Adamu and Temarii, who were excluded from the vote. Yet Fifa's investigation was cursory at best. The wider issues raised by the *Sunday Times* were not probed nor was evidence provided by the paper considered by the ethics committee. Neither of the reporters who carried out the sting were ever asked to give evidence. In fact they were roundly condemned by the chairman of the ethics committee, Claudio Sulser, for having the temerity to expose the organisation.

In a chain restaurant near London's Tower Bridge, I meet Jonathan Calvert, one of the reporters who carried out the sting. The ease with which he infiltrated the hidden world of federation chiefs and Exco members is staggering. In essence his operation required only a company registered at a mailbox address, some business cards, a hidden camera and the whiff of cash to get people falling over themselves to talk. His exposés almost brought the entire bid process — with its multi-billion prize at the end — crashing down.

Calvert believes that Fifa's inquiry was completely inadequate and while several officials were banned it ignored serious allegations about cash changing hands ahead of the World Cup vote. "I probably wasn't surprised that Fifa went ahead with the vote, because they would have done so come what may," he tells me. "They very quickly investigated our allegations and suspended anybody who was vaguely connected with them. As far as they were concerned that was an end to the matter, but I don't think it was anything like an end to the matter. In our tape recordings of the various officials that we spoke to there were several allegations that related to specific contests to the 2018 and 2022 World Cups that were there for them to investigate, but they just ignored them."

Fifa, he says, "didn't do anything to investigate the claims that money was changing hands in return for votes." He adds, "A normal corporate entity which had such big allegations about its processes would have endeavoured to bring in an outside body to see if there was any truth in them."

I ask him what Fifa should do next and Calvert says that the opportunity is still there for them to reinvestigate how the bids were won. "They've got a lot of allegations, there were a lot of people they can talk to, they could get an outside body in to investigate. That would at least set peoples' minds to rest that they have at least done something about it. On the other hand I don't think they will, because I don't think it's in Sepp Blatter's interests to do that."

New T-Shirts

The latest additions to our range of top-quality fitted t-shirts have arrived – perfect for lazing on the beach this summer, or as a gift for the footy-geek in your life.

The Seconds of the Greats

From David Winner's interview with the Dutchman in Issue One, we've re-created his St James' Park masterpiece in tableau form.

Available in both black and white, much like Newcastle United.

Dolphins are Bastards

We've got nothing against Flipper and his chums, just don't question Platini for God's sake. Or wear this to a Greenpeace meeting.

Available in light blue.

Blizzard Tree

The seeds of the Blizzard were first planted a little over a year ago, and have now grown into our new cover illustration for our second year. The dog is gone, long live the tree.

Available in grey.

Order Online at
www.theblizzard.co.uk

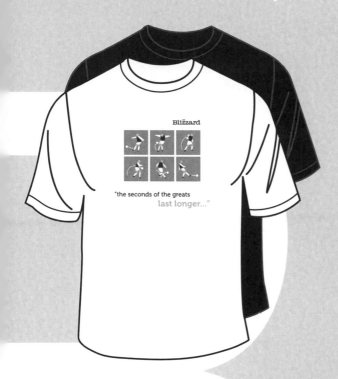

Product Details

All t-shirts are available for **£16 + (£1.45 P&P - UK)**. Shipping prices vary dependent on location — see **www. theblizzard.co.uk** for more details.

Subscribers get a £2 discount off all Blizzard clothing.

- 180 gsm 100% cotton t-shirts
- Fitted body shape
- Tubular constructed body for shape retention
- Extra-reinforced shoulder seams
- Available in S (36/38), M (38/40), L (40/42), XL (42/44), XXL (44/46)

Russia's Victory

Russia's success in the 2018 bid was a triumph over internal as well as external opponents

By Igor Rabiner

It all started on 5 May 2009. Watching evening television news, Russian viewers saw a clip from a weekly government meeting in which the prime minister Vladimir Putin addressed the minister of sports, tourism and youth policy, the Fifa Exco member Vitaly Mutko. "I entrust you with the task of preparing a bid in the name of the Russian Federation to host the Fifa World Cup 2018 or 2022." Soon after, he added the most important words: "I'll sign all guarantees."

That was vital. "The handful of dreamers", as Alexei Sorokin, the CEO of the Russian bid committee called them, wouldn't have been able to do anything without an order from the very top. With the world in financial crisis, Russia had enough problems to deal with without a World Cup. It was the sports minister Vitaly Mutko who first decided to mount a bid to host the tournament, something acknowledged even by the former Fifa vice-president Vyacheslav Koloskov, a man whose relationship with Mutko is distinctly frosty. "He's well received at the place where such a project could be approved," Koloskov said. "Nobody else could have initiated this."

There was plenty of opposition. I've asked many well-informed people who was against the bidding process and received a number of different answers: the presidential administration, the FSB (the former KGB), the Ministry of Justice... Mutko was treading through a minefield, but he made it to the other side because once Putin had said something in public there was no going back.

Mutko has a lot of enemies at a high level, but his bluntness of speech suggests that doesn't bother him too much. In 2005, for instance, shortly after he'd become president of the Russian Football Union (RFS), he was approached by Boris Gryzlov, chairman of the Gosduma (the Russian parliament), chairman of the supreme council of the United Russia governing party and a former minister of internal affairs, who reportedly gave him a list of the people he wanted appointed in various key posts within the RFS. Mutko looked him in the eye and replied, "Have you mixed me up with somebody else? There's *one* person who can tell me to do things — and if he asked I'd appoint the Pope as vice-president — but I won't listen to anybody else." Gryzlov didn't take the snub well; being friends with Putin has its drawbacks.

That connection goes back to the early part of the nineties when Mutko and Putin were deputy mayors of St Petersburg under Anatoly Sobchak. Mutko was cautious, though, when I asked if he and Putin had been friends since then. "Friendship is a sacred concept," he said, shaking his head. "So I wouldn't risk saying that I was a 'friend' of one of the country's great leaders. In our state hierarchy there is a big distance between us and I try to observe that. But we have good, warm relations that are underpinned by decades of working together in a difficult period. The period from 1991 to 1996 was very difficult for St Petersburg. We went through two putsches together and the economic situation was tough. We handled all that and that united us to some extent."

Crucially, Mutko was able to persuade Putin to make two key decisions that set the bid apart from the others: entry for all World Cup ticket-holders to Russia without the need for a visa, and free transport for all ticket-holders throughout the country during the tournament. Some ministers insisted that would lead to huge financial losses, but Mutko was adamant that without concessions large numbers of tourists simply wouldn't come to Russia. Putin accepted Mutko's view.

When Mutko first mentioned to Putin the idea of bidding for the World Cup, the prime minister asked what Russia's chances were of winning. "20-25%," he replied. He believed between 30 and 40% of the votes were already committed to Spain-Portugal and insisted Russia had no chance unless Putin became actively involved, meeting "more than half" of the Fifa Exco members personally before the vote. That marked a significant change from his tactics for the 2014 Winter

Olympic bidding, when he had merely turned up at the last in Guatemala, where the vote took place, to speak to IOC delegates. This time, he could arrive in Zurich after the vote with the crown already on his head.

The British prime minister David Cameron, by contrast, went to Zurich the evening before the vote. By coincidence, he was on the same flight from London as Andrei Arshavin, who gave a speech at the final presentation, and Alexander Chernov, a member of the Russian bid committees for Euro 2008 and the 2012 Summer Olympics, who was working with Arshavin on his delivery. "We were boarding the plane in Heathrow, rehearsing Andrei's speech," Chernov said. "Andrei was a little ahead of me and there were two men behind me. Suddenly he glanced back and said in English, 'Hello!' I turned round and saw David Cameron. He also said hello and they smiled at each other. I couldn't stay silent. So I joked, 'You know, we are rehearsing the speech. You speak good English: could you check it for us?'

"A little later, Cameron slapped me on the shoulder and exclaimed, 'Oh, Putin is not flying!'

"I said, 'I know'. It seemed normal — but then I thought: the prime minister of a great country says to somebody he doesn't know, not even trying to hide his delight, that Putin is not flying. He obviously thinks this means a victory for England. They were so scared by the thought of Putin's speech that he says this to me at the front of the plane."

One of Cameron's security guards, an Arsenal fan, exchanged phone numbers with Arshavin and arranged for him to sign some shirts and balls for him. This, Arshavin said, was typical; nobody blamed him for backing the Russian bid and the criticism he received from some Arsenal fans before his return to Russia on loan at Zenit "was about my form, nothing else."

"When I got back after the vote, I said to Jack Wilshere and Samir Nasri, 'You are young and in 2018 I'll sit in a jacket and tie in the VIP zone and you'll shake hands on the pitch in front of me. And if you play in St Petersburg I'll show you the city in all its brilliance.'"

Putin's work on the Exco members wasn't all he did. In 2006, he received Sepp Blatter at his official residence outside Moscow, perhaps already calculating the future dividends that warm relations with the head of world football might yield. Setting up that meeting was a triumph for Mutko who, at the time, had been at the RFS less than a year and wasn't even an Exco member.

There are a lot of photos on the wall of the office of Vyacheslav Koloskov at the headquarters of the Russian Olympic Committee. Two are bigger than the others. Not, as you might expect, those of Putin and Dmitri Medvedev, but those of Nikolai Starostin, the patriarch of Russian football, and João Havelange, the Brazilian former president of Fifa. They, effectively, were his mentors and Koloskov, at 70, doesn't change his portraits according to the prevailing political situation.

For Koloskov, Putin remained always slightly out of reach. "After the USSR collapsed, we organised the CIS Cup to maintain the football relations of former Soviet republics," he wrote in his book, *Onside and Offside*. "Our initiative was supported by Sepp Blatter. Despite being busy, he visited this tournament every year, pointing out its importance for football development. I thought that the country's leadership also understood this and it would be good if during such a tournament Blatter was received by President Putin. I expressed this idea to the president's administration but got the answer, 'Wrong scale.'"

Koloskov explained to me that the problem was that he didn't know anybody in the Putin administration personally and so could only send written notes. At the time, Michel Platini was working as an advisor to Blatter. Finally, Putin's administration agreed to organise a meeting with Blatter, but only if Platini was there as well. Platini, though, had to return to France for the congress of the French football federation and so the meeting never happened. "In their logic, Blatter became too familiar," Koloskov explained. "He is a functionary and Platini was an outstanding player. So, a photo with him in the papers, in the administration's opinion, would mean more in PR terms."

So when did Blatter's "scale" become right? "It's about administrative resource [a term used idiomatically in Russian to describe closeness to power]," Koloskov said. "When Mutko became RFS president and had direct access to Putin, he was able to explain to him that he is the key figure in world football and that a lot of things depend on his attitude towards us." Koloskov, fortunately, did not tell Blatter why the meeting with Putin at the

CIS Cup didn't happen; if he had done so, the warm relations Putin and Blatter enjoy may never have developed.

Koloskov believes Putin gave Russia one other great advantage over its competitors. "I'm not a politician or an economist," he said, "but the other big factor in our favour is the stable political situation in the country. There is no doubt that the duo of Putin and Medvedev will lead Russia for a pretty long time. And that in turn guarantees stability in terms of fulfilling obligations. It's not going to happen that Putin signs the documents then somebody else replaces him and isn't interested in the project."

There may be practical advantages, of course, but such political predictability comes at the cost of real freedom of choice. Perhaps even the leaders have begun to take their positions for granted. At the press conference he gave in Zurich a few hours after Russia's victory, Putin was asked whether he would stand in the next presidential elections (for the term ending in 2018). Putin smiled and said that he and President Medvedev were old friends and would decide between them which would be president and which prime minister. That the people might not vote for him didn't seem a concern; it wasn't mentioned even for the sake of propriety. A year later, hundreds of thousands of Russians took to the streets in protest at the lack of democracy.

Blatter's fondness for Russia predates his meeting with Putin. Koloskov spoke of taking him to visit Sergiev Posad, the holiest site of the Russian Orthodox Church, in the nineties where a

metropolitan bishop showed him some of the shrine's secrets.

On another occasion, when Russian hosted an IOC meeting, Koloskov took all the football delegates to a private concert outside Moscow. As they returned to the capital late at night, their bus broke down and pulled over by the side of the road. Two elderly women from a nearby house came to see what the problem was; Koloskov explained and asked if they could bring some water for the delegates. They returned a few minutes later not with water but with a tray of vodka and some food. Blatter was touched by the hospitality and got off the bus to drink with locals. He asked if the stop had been pre-planned. Koloskov insisted it hadn't and asked why Blatter would think such a thing. "Because these ladies are so kind and the men know so much about football," Blatter replied. "And they want Russia to be a great football power. If people in the provinces worry so much about football, the sport has a great future in Russia."

Koloskov and Blatter had become friends in the early eighties when, as a Soviet representative on Fifa's Exco and Fifa's general secretary respectively, they played tennis together. The former Uefa president Lennart Johansson told me that Koloskov was not just a colleague but a close friend of many Fifa and Uefa officials.

After Blatter had beaten Johansson in the 1998 election for the Fifa presidency, relations between them were strained. "There were a lot of negative feelings after the elections," Koloskov explained. "It happened that they both were in Moscow and we went to my friends' house in the Moscow region. So, I shut them in a private room, put a big bottle of vodka on the table and some good food. And I told them, 'Don't come out until you find a common language.' They came out after 30 minutes, the bottle half-empty. They said, 'All our difficulties are over.'"

That sort of experience made Koloskov valuable. He had been asked to stand down from the RFS presidency to make way for Mutko in 2005 and only learned about the decision to bid for the World Cup from the newspapers. A bitterness lingered between the two but one day Mutko came to Koloskov's office at the Russian Olympic Committee and asked him to work with the bid committee.

It is believed his participation was sealed on 22 January 2010 when Blatter met Russia's president, Dmitry Medvedev, at the Kremlin (Putin by then had been forced by Russia's constitution to relinquish the presidency to become prime minister). That showed there was no disagreement in the Russian leadership about the World Cup bid. Medvedev took Blatter round the Kremlin and they met with other officials including Mutko and the deputy prime minister Igor Shuvalov. It is said that at that meeting Medvedev asked Blatter how to make the Russian campaign the most effective it could be. Blatter replied that involving Koloskov could only help.

Even Koloskov's birthday became part of Russia's campaign. It fell during the World Cup in South Africa, on 15 June 2010. Koloskov and his friend Alexander Chernov, whose idea it was, brought vodka, caviar and other Russian food to a hotel in Johannesburg and arranged a great party at which Koloskov's wife,

Tatiana, who speaks excellent English, acted as toastmaster. Koloskov invited all the Exco members and former Exco members who were in South Africa, not expecting many to come. But the majority did turn up: Blatter and his family, Johansson, Villar, Hayatou, Erzik, Bin Hammam, Warner... it was the perfect environment for low-level promotion of the Russian bid.

There were Russian tricolours on the walls and Russian music to which, it's said, everybody, including Blatter, was dancing when the president of the Mexican federation introduced a mariachi band who played for an hour. Even Angel Villar, the president of the Spanish federation and so the head of a rival bid, danced along.

Alexei Sorokin, the CEO of the Russian bid, was in Angola in 2010 for the Confederation of African Football Congress that preceded the African Cup of Nations. It was part of a long programme of trips and, when he got back to Moscow, he fell ill. "My temperature went up to 40°C," he said. "I thought it was normal flu and the doctors told me the same. But it didn't drop for several days and I was delirious. Finally the third doctor I saw asked if I'd been in any tropical countries recently. When I said Angola she arranged a blood test straightaway."

It confirmed that he had malaria, which had progressed so far that he almost lost a kidney. The trip wasn't even worthwhile. "That congress and all the presentation possibilities at it were taken up by Qatar," he said. "They didn't let any of the candidates for 2018 speak, even though they were only bidding for 2022. There were rumours they'd paid the Africans three or four million dollars so that nobody else got the chance to speak. Many journalists hammered the organisers of the congress for that. Fifa didn't interfere in the presentation process before then but after that it started to observe it more closely."

At around the same time, there was a change of leadership at the RFS as Medvedev ordered that all state ministers had to leave their positions as heads of sports federations. Mutko stood down and was replaced by Sergei Fursenko, the former president of Zenit St Petersburg, who seemed indifferent to the World Cup bid. Putin stepped in and ensured that the bid committee could continue its work separately from the RFS, which was probably just as well.

At a Concacaf congress in New York, for instance, Fursenko, eager to be seen to be working for Russia, buttonholed a man and started explaining to him how strong the Russian bid was. Only after 10 minutes was he persuaded to stop; he'd mistaken a waiter for Jack Warner, the then-president of Concacaf.

Yet at other times Fursenko seemed to be working directly against the Russian bid. As soon as he became head of the RFS, he demanded that the bid committee leave their office on the sixth floor of the House of Football in Moscow, supposedly to clear it for Dick Advocaat, the manager of the national side. Every other day one of Fursenko's assistants would come in and ask when they'd be leaving. That was at just the time that Sorokin was recovering from

malaria, but there was little sympathy, with Fursenko's people allegedly telling the bid team that they had no leader and that even if Sorokin survived he'd be crippled. Eventually, just as the Russian team completed its bid book - the hardest stage of the process - it had to find new offices.

Yet Fursenko was among those who went to Zurich Messe to collect the certificate that confirmed Russia as the hosts in 2018. Sorokin is diplomatic about their relationship. I asked him if he shook hands with Fursenko after that. "Why not?" he asked. "He personally didn't do anything bad to us. The representative who came in and spoke to my assistants about my disability may have been acting on his own initiative. Most likely Fursenko didn't know."

In July 2011, I talked to Franz Beckenbauer, who was an Exco member at the time of the vote. He was enthusiastic about Russia's success. "I think they will be perfect hosts," he said. "All of the European candidates were strong but I think England lost out to bad press. They were complaining about Fifa and the Exco members. The Exco members are human beings, after all. Maybe they didn't like being asked to vote for England after being told they are corrupt. And the joint-bids (Spain-Portugal and Belgium-Holland) possibly weren't very popular with the voters. So Russia had the best chance from the very beginning. For me, they are a wonderful host."

Arshavin agreed the press had a major role. "It's a paradox of the freedom of speech," he said. "It's the occasion when this freedom in your country suddenly plays against you. English people promote tolerance, freedom of speech and plenty of other freedoms. But when there is too much of it, maybe it's not so good."

Koloskov was scathing about the *Sunday Times* investigation that led to Amos Adamu and Reynald Temarii being excluded from the Exco, having been found guilty of corruption. "It was an absolute provocation, which caused a furious reaction of Exco members," he said. "They judged the story an abuse. It's a family which had got used to being responsible for each other and all together. With the help of faulty methods, two members of Exco were blamed dishonestly, which put a stain on the Exco's reputation in general. I was an Exco member for almost 30 years and there was no question how I would have reacted to such an incident if I were still on it."

Given Fifa acknowledged the pair's guilt and punished them accordingly, it's an extraordinary stance to take. "Fifa reacted to the situation very efficiently," Koloskov went on. "It quickly and clearly pointed out that it wouldn't tolerate a violation of its ethical code. But that doesn't cancel the provocative essence of the methods used by British press."

Not surprisingly, Mark Franchetti, the Moscow correspondent of the *Sunday Times*, has a very different view. "All this talk of an offended family in which everybody defends each other is a mafia mentality," he said. "When you see the video there's concrete proof of an Exco member being prepared to take money for his vote. It's brilliant, very strong journalistic work. After this story Fifa,

rather than uniting against England, should have said to the *Sunday Times*, 'Thank you very much, guys, for what you have done. We didn't know that and we found out thanks to you. It's terrible, but thanks again for helping up remove corruption from our organisation.'"

So was Franchetti asked to investigate the Russian bid? "I only had a request from the *Sunday Times* to write a story about the scandal concerning Muto at the Winter Olympics in Vancouver [when he claimed 97 breakfasts on expenses at a cost to the Russian state of $4500 for a two-week stay]. It had nothing to do with football and I didn't investigate anything to do with the World Cup."

That wasn't the end of it. A little while later, Franchetti was asked to call Koloskov. "My colleagues in London had information that he, as an advisor to the Russian bid, presented paintings during the campaign to Blatter, Platini and the Belgian Exco member Michel D'Houge, who's a friend of Koloskov," Franchetti said. "D'Houge himself said he'd been presented with a painting.

"I called Koloskov and he denied everything, saying it was nonsense and a lie. He said that he didn't meet personally with Blatter during the bidding campaign, that he has a bad relationship with Platini. He confirmed that he is friends with D'Houge, but said he didn't present with him any painting, only with a Russian casket as a souvenir. But D'Houge, whom my colleagues reached later, repeated, 'No, he presented me with a painting!'

"Of course, that doesn't mean Koloskov bribed D'Houge — particularly given D'Houge talks openly about the painting.

They're friendly and maybe Koloskov just gave him a cheap picture as a souvenir from Russia. He has a right to do that. But the fact their stories are so different makes you suspicious. But that's not my business; I sent Koloskov's quotes to the paper and the rest of the work was done in London."

To my surprise, Koloskov was quite happy to discuss the issue. "I was on vacation in my father's homeland in the Ryazan region, when a correspondent of the *Sunday Times* called me. 'Vyacheslav Ivanovich,' he said, 'I have an urgent question. I got a call from the paper and they told me that you presented Blatter and Platini paintings by Picasso.'

"I was shocked and replied, 'First of all, during the bidding campaign I never met Blatter personally. The president of our country met him, and there was no need to duplicate that. Second, my relations with Platini are far from friendly. I talked with him, but formally and briefly. And the last time I've seen Picassos was in 1982 when I visited an art exhibition during the World Cup in Spain. So, I regarded the story as a joke.'

"The journalist went on to ask about D'Houge. I said that I gave nothing to D'Houge apart from a casket for his wife. Sorokin and I flew to see D'Houge. Of course we knew he'd vote for Belgium-Netherlands but I thought if they went out in the first round of voting, we had an opportunity to get him on our side in the second round.

"We had a very good dinner in a restaurant near the airport. Sorokin had some picture with him. I had a casket for his wife. I didn't ask how much the painting cost, but there was no way it could be expensive: first, we observed all the Fifa rules, and second, the bid committee had very little money. I didn't see this painting unwrapped. But the fact that Sorokin freely brought it through customs both in Russia and Belgium made clear that it was far from a masterpiece.

"I gave D'Houge the casket in the restaurant, and the painting was also given through me, but I immediately forgot about it. If D'Houge called me and said, 'Slava, the press has information that you presented me a painting,' of course, I would have confirmed that. But there were no calls, so I decided not to say anything, thinking that the media want to make a scandal out of it. In fact, it was true I didn't present it myself: it was a souvenir from the bidding committee.

"The final act of this fabricated story was in Monaco at the Uefa Super Cup in August 2011. We met with D'Houge there, and he said, 'Slava, you cannot imagine what was going on with that painting. The press called me every other day. I had to hire an expert. He looked at it and said it was an ordinary picture without value, that its cost is minimal. We gave the media an official statement about that and finally they left me alone.'"

Other issues might not be so simply resolved, but for Russia phase one is complete. The next stage is to do what Germany did in 2006 and put on a tournament so good nobody remembers anything about the bid process. And most important of all, Russia has to try to ensure the World Cup doesn't become another Potemkin village, as we call it — a shining showcase built for naive foreigners to hide the depressing reality, as the Russian minister Grigory Potemkin is supposed to have built facades along the banks of the Dnipr River to impress the empress Catherine II.

The Russian bid committee worked extremely hard and achieved a great result but what is important now is the outcome. Russia has a unique opportunity to change not only its football and the stadiums but also the whole country and its mentality, its willingness to learn foreign languages and accept different cultures. That will take a lot of effort but it can't just be proud to have won the bid; that is just the beginning.

Igor Rabiner's book, Как Россия получила чемпионат мира по футболу-2018. Спортивно-политическое расследование, [How Russia got the 2018 World Cup: A Sporting and Political Investigation] *is published by Astrel.* Ⓑ

Qatar Hero

Michel Platini is often seen as the ex-pro coming to save Fifa. But why did he vote for Qatar?

By Philippe Auclair

"Let me tell you a tale," my friend said, "a tale in the Oriental style."

This friend will remain anonymous, for two reasons: firstly, while he won't mind my re-telling the tale in question he would probably prefer not to see his own name in print; secondly, his name wouldn't mean much to most readers anyway. This friend could adopt Descartes's *larvatus prodeo* [masked, I proceed] as his motto, as the path he's followed in football, which took him to very high places indeed, remains largely uncharted. He wouldn't have it any other way.

This conversation took place at his (unmarked, unlisted) London office, six weeks before Fifa chose Russia and Qatar to be the respective hosts of the 2018 and 2022 World Cups. To say that these decisions came as a surprise to my interlocutor would be a wild exaggeration, as, that afternoon, after fielding calls from Sepp Blatter and Mohammed Bin Hammam, he assured me that the Russians would walk it, that England would be lucky to get more than a solitary vote and that it was touch and go for the Qataris to bag the prize in the first round. I passed on the information to my contacts at England 2018, who clearly thought that my source had offered me something stronger than

espresso at our meeting. We all know what happened in the end. But let's go back to the tale itself.

"Once, there was a French president whom we shall call Nicolas. He didn't have much money. In fact, he was desperate for some but, thankfully, his good friend the emir had plenty of it. The emir told him that he'd buy all sorts of things from France, expensive things like planes and nuclear power stations and Nicolas was very happy. But then the emir said, 'There's one condition, though, just a little thing.'

"'What could it be?' Nicolas asked.

"'Just tell Michel to give us the World Cup,' the emir replied.

"Nicolas didn't have much of a choice. He needed the money. So he asked Michel to do what he was told, and Michel said he'd do it."

This is only a tale, of course. Maybe it's true and maybe it's not. I pass it on it as it was given to me, minus some details related to the way the Qataris used their huge campaign budget to promote their bid. I was troubled, though. It was true that Sheikh Hamad bin Khalifa Al Thani, ruler of Qatar, had travelled incognito to Paris a few days before this conversation took place — 'incognito', in this case, meant not staying at the Hôtel Lambert, his palatial residence on the Île Saint-Louis, but instead taking over a whole floor at the Royal-Monceau hotel, which he, or his country, or his country's sovereign fund, which is pretty much the same thing, happened to own as well

The aim of that visit was not to secure a vote at the forthcoming Fifa Congress, not primarily anyway. The French government was thinking of selling a significant stake of Areva, a state-owned body which controls the country's nuclear industry from uranium mines to power stations, to the gas-rich emirate. The transaction didn't take place in the end, partly because of an almighty uproar in the French media. But it demonstrated the strength of the links between France and the minuscule Gulf state, three-quarters of whose 1.7m residents are 'guest workers', mostly shipped in from the Indian sub-continent, who enjoy no civic rights and are treated in such a shocking way by their employers that, in November 2011, the International Trade Union Confederation (ITUC) asked Fifa to re-consider their choice of Qatar as World Cup-hosting country. Good luck to them.

Who was the first head of state to make an official visit to the Élysée palace after Nicolas Sarkozy's election to the presidency in 2007? Sheikh Hamad bin Khalifa Al Thani. That was good business

for la République. France sold Qatar £208m worth of defence equipment on that occasion, as well as a fleet of sixty Airbus 350s. And if Nicolas and Hamad like each other, the same can be said of Carla and Moza, that is Carla Bruni, the pop-singing wife of Nicolas, a regular guest in Doha, and Sheikha Moza al-Misned, the wife of Sheikh Hamad, the figurehead of the Qatar 2022 bid and president of the Qatar Foundation, the 'charity' which disburses £25m each year to make sure Barcelona don't have to lower themselves to endorsing a commercial shirt sponsor[1].

In the context of geopolitics, the Uefa president and Fifa vice-president Michel Platini, whether he says tu to Nicolas Sarkozy or not (he does — they go back a long way), is a prestigious but not overly significant cog in the wheel of the Franco-Qatari 'special relationship', which is not to say he is without consequence from a football perspective. One of his greatest assets must be that, as a recognised great of the game, his views carry far more weight than those of the Swiss former amateur goalkeeper Sepp Blatter. To question him is, somehow, to question the near-genius of Juventus and Les Bleus — something like walking into a Greenpeace convention wearing a 'DOLPHINS ARE BASTARDS' T-shirt or finding out that the ethereal Isolde you were in love with had an inch-thick dossier at the local VD clinic.

This might explain why I was met with a rather cool reaction when I suggested

---

[1] *Pep Guardiola banked £350,000 to endorse the Qatari bid; a pittance, true, when compared to what Zinedine Zidane got. Zidane, who had initially refused to lend his name to their campaign, finally relented when he was offered a deal worth £14m.*

to a few people back in France that my tale at least provided us with a lead worth following. We French tend to be very protective of the powerful, especially when they hold a prestigious position in an international organisation and contribute to the grandeur of our nation. Even Dominique Strauss-Kahn. A pity, in that case, as Michel Platini himself confirmed in March 2012 that Sarkozy had told him over lunch that "it would be a good thing if I did it" — that is, vote for Qatar. But, of course, this didn't mean the president had specifically asked him to do so, as he knew "that I am free and independent." Honesty or impudence? Or both? The man who can keep a straight face when describing himself as "a player at heart, not a politician" has developed a remarkable gift for presenting the indefensible as if it were dictated by self-evident common sense.

How on earth does he get away with it? Take his proposal to hold the 2022 World Cup in winter, an option that neither Fifa nor the Qatari organisers themselves had studied or were in favour of, and which he made without having consulted any of his experts about the impact this might have on club football. "I thought, after South Africa 2010", he said, "where it was 0° at 5pm and there was no life [*sic*] for the fans, how can we ask the fans and players to go to this country when it is 50 or 60° in July? [...] The best time to play is winter. [...] What is the problem for the Premier League to finish at the end of May instead of the beginning, and recuperate this time in December? We have to put the World Cup and the fans first."

Breathtaking stuff, all the more so since Platini had sung a rather different tune immediately after Qatar had been chosen to host the 2022 tournament, suggesting a switch to a cooler time of the year in the Middle-East, that's true, but also reminding us that, "the temperature in Dallas [at the 1994 World Cup] was over 40° in 1994, if I'm not mistaken, and nobody criticised the US at the time." He didn't mind the idea of air-conditioned stadiums and fan-zones then, it seems. He also thought it might be a good idea to have the 2022 World Cup games played outside as well as in Qatar, so that it became a Gulf-wide competition — not such a stupid notion, come to think of it, but one it might have been more suitable to put forward before the vote had taken place and after having informed the Qataris themselves. That other bidding countries — Australia, the USA, South Korea and Japan — might be aggrieved didn't seem to have crossed Platini's mind. The provisos and specifications around which they'd built their dossiers, spending fortunes in the process, could apparently be jettisoned on a whim of the Fifa vice-president, but the apostle of fair-play wasn't perturbed in the least. The fact is that only one of the twenty-two members left in the Fifa executive committee after the ban imposed on Amos Adamu and Reynald Temarii had requested a copy of the technical report compiled by the organisation's own inspectors, a report in which Qatar 2022 was the only bid given a 'high risk' rating. It's true that these gentlemen are known for their very relaxed attitude to 'detail' and that, in that respect if not all others, Michel Platini is no different from his fellow Exco members. After all, this is the man who said that, "in Spain, the owners are the fans, the *socios*," when only four of La Liga clubs are run on these lines, and who had to be reminded that Uefa's

Financial Fair-Play (FFP) regulations would have to be approved by the European Commission before they could be implemented. A micro-manager Platini is not.

Still, tearing up the rule-book which had guided everyone — Qatar included — during the bidding process was surely unthinkable. Wouldn't the losers have every right to pursue the matter in the courts? When asked these questions, Platini responded with the insouciance of an 18th century *roué*. "Who will remember the words in 12 years?" he shrugged. "In 12 years, everybody will be happy to have a very well-organised World Cup and not remember what's happened before. When I organised the World Cup in France, we did [things] differently from what we proposed in the bid." That's what Platini is so good at: to proffer enormities which are so, well, enormous, that whoever hears them is momentarily lost for words, by which time he's trampling daisies in another field, singing a little air of his confection.

"When *I* organised the World Cup..." True, Platini was one of the chief coordinators of France's World Cup Committee. But poor Fernand Sastre, the French Football Federation administrator for whom bringing the tournament to France had been the ambition of a lifetime and who died on 13 June 1998, three days after its opening ceremony. This is Platini's way.

Platini's glowing endorsement of the "magnificent" Qatari bid has landed him in some awkward spots since the December 2010 vote, however. When the emirate's ruling family bought Paris St-Germain FC in June 2011 through Qatar Sports Investments (QSI) and immediately started pumping millions into the ailing club (€42m on purchasing Javier Pastore from Palermo alone), it could have been expected that the crusader for FFP would step forward and issue a stern warning to the new owners. And he did — after a fashion. "We don't know their budget yet," he said in March of this year. "They'll come to present it [to Uefa]. We have to observe, adapt, that's not easy. We must stay true to a philosophy which has been endorsed by Uefa — and we will and the PSG owners will as well, otherwise they won't play in our competitions, or they'll have other problems, but I don't know anything at all [about that]." The Al Thani family must have been trembling when they heard that. Speaking to one of Platini's closest aides, the Uefa general secretary Gianni Infantino, at a recent football forum, it became clear to me that "I don't know anything at all" would be the default response to most if not all questions about the actual implementation of the rules which are supposed to represent Platini's legacy to the football world. Real Madrid's project of building a fantasy island in the Gulf to raise gazillions of dollars: fair or unfair? "We'll see." Manchester City's sale of naming rights to Etihad: fair or unfair? "We'll see." The decision by Uefa to centralise the negotiation of TV rights on behalf of everyone else, anything to do with (Qatar-based, and Qatari-owned) Al Jazeera's transparent plans to become the exclusive broadcaster of football's major events? "..."

Vagueness, of course, makes it easier to disguise (and live with) contradictions, with which Platini's speech and "philosophy", the word he uses himself, are replete. "I know I'm defending something which is not defensible anymore," he sighs, portraying himself for a second as the slightly old-fashioned but engaging uncle whose views are tolerated by the family because of his advancing years. "I'm not a great fan of foreign owners, but the laws are the laws, and I can't do anything about it." Sulejman Karimov's spending at Anzhi Makhachkala? "At least the man who is putting all this money into Anzhi comes from there, so he has a local connection, and that's fine. It's a new world." Eh? What about the Glazers at Manchester United then? You'd expect him to tear into the Yanks, but no, not really. "I'm not bothered by their debt, since they're able to pay it back." You must have heard how Uefa and the European Clubs Association (ECA) have agreed to tick off one friendly from the international calendar; it was less widely reported that ECA, which had made veiled threats of going it alone and creating their own European tournament, got something more from Platini's organisation: clubs will share €100m from profits generated during Euro 2012 and "an estimated €150m from the 2016 edition". ECA's been very quiet since then. Where does bribery start? And corruption?

It becomes maddening, after a while. Another example: what constitutes the 'identity' of a club for Platini would baffle anyone steeped in a British football culture and, dare I say, quite a few of the *juventini* who adopted him as one of their own when, having run down his contract at Saint-Étienne, he joined the Old Lady in 1982, the French club receiving only a nominal fee. For him, identity has to do with the owners, the players, the coaches, who now "come and go" and, down the list, the fans. His opinion became clear in his address to a group of supporters' organisations in April 2012 when he admitted fans were the "only identity" left, but then let slip that these fans to whom "football belongs *as well*" [my italics], would have their views taken into consideration "when we would be able to do so." Why, thanks a lot! His weird obsession with the faults of English football, which he jokingly puts down to "the legendary rivalry between England and France, that's all" leads him to statements which, were they directed at a different target, would not go down at all well, coming as they do from the head of a pan-European organisation. "When you have some English players on the field, they are playing not so bad," he quipped in January of this year. We're still waiting for observations of that kind about Serie A, which provides three of the top five "clubs that fielded the fewest association-trained players" in the 2010-11 season, according to a recent International Centre for Sports Studies (CIES) study[2].

But I realise that I'm falling in the trap that Platini sets for whoever follows his meandering track with a critical eye: it is I who get lost. His own progress has been mapped ever since he retired as a player, 25 years ago, and probably before that. In 2015, regardless of his denials, he will be anointed Sepp Blatter's successor by Fifa. Blatter, whom he says "is no angel... a typical politician" but "not corrupt, honest, 200%"; Blatter whom he'll try "to help finish his mandate well, because it

---

[2] Namely Internazionale, AS Roma — the top two — and Udinese.

is for the good of the game." He says, he doesn't know "what I will do in four years." Can we have a guess, Michel?

One thing he will not be too concerned about until then is the well-being of his 33-year-old son Laurent who, in January of this year, became legal advisor for the European operations department of a rather large and wealthy corporation: Qatar Sports Investments. **B**

47

Interview

"No boss likes to have anyone
intelligent underneath them."

Socrates

The former Brazil captain talks about why footballers have a political responsibility

By David Tryhorn

"Do you want a beer? They have the coldest draught beer in Brazil here."

Those were the first words the Brazil legend Sócrates said as I met him in his favourite bar, Pinguím, in his hometown of Ribeirão Preto in São Paulo state. He had greeted me with a bear hug and spoke openly about his career and his political and footballing beliefs and convictions. He must have talked for over four hours.

Sócrates passed away in December 2011 and it was the drink that caught up with him in the end. By his own admission he drank heavily. I had interviewed him twice previously for two documentaries I had made — the first time, he was two hours late (sleeping off a hangover) and the second time, he was already under the influence. But he never became a George Best-like figure. He was not a shambolic drunk. He was a *bon vivant*, a larger than life figure with a lifetime of tales to tell. Forthright in his views, passionate, opinionated and humorous. Always humorous.

Sócrates will of course be best remembered as the captain and figurehead of Brazil's 1982 World Cup team. With his beard, mop of curly hair, smoking habit and languidly graceful presence on the ball, he became an instant cult hero. A doctor who played better backwards than most players did going forwards according to Pelé, there was no better embodiment of Brazil's beautiful game.

But it was at his São Paulo based club, Corinthians, where he made his biggest impact. In 1981 and at a time of military dictatorship within Brazil he led a movement called *Democracia Corintiana* (Corinthian Democracy), a radical plan to democratise an entire football club and transform Brazilian society through football. In his beloved Brazil, Sócrates became a symbol of democracy when there was none. In short, he was a revolutionary. This was my final interview with him — we were back in the bar and he was back to talking about what he loved most: a combination of football, philosophy and politics.

🔵 *Have you always been such a free thinker?*

I'll tell you a bit about my old man. My father. My father didn't study — he couldn't, up there in the north-east of Brazil — but he learnt everything he knew there. His study was free. He ate books up. So when I was born it was as if I was born into a library, among so many complex social theories that exist in this country. It's a country with huge potential in every way but a country that doesn't properly educate its people. I think I was born with this spirit — the spirit of reflection and of questioning things, especially in regard to social issues.

◉ *When you were a player you used to remove the sports supplement in the newspaper when you offered it to a teammate to read. Did you not believe in your profession?*

No, that wasn't the case at all. I did that to encourage those around me to read. Brazilian footballers tend just to read the sports section. I'd buy the paper, take out the sports pages and leave the rest for one of my colleagues to read. I was trying to highlight the fact that the most important news wasn't to be found in the sports supplement — it was important to read about politics, the economy and other related affairs. So I did it to try and get people to read about other things.

◉ *So you had nothing against sports news?*

No, although I would never read it anyway. When I played I never once read the sports news.

◉ *And now?*

Now I read it. When I played I would never read it because I think it can only interfere with the job you're paid to do. Positive or negative criticism will affect you one way or another so I preferred not to pay any attention to it. If someone speaks highly of you then you might start

to believe them! I preferred not to know! [laughs]

◉ *You have often said a footballer has great power but lacks the education to use it properly. Could you expand on this? What power do you actually think a player has?*

A footballer has a lot of power. It's the only job in which the employee has more power than the boss. He has the masses in his hand and the capability to mobilise them. But he has to realise that he has this power and use it wisely when there is a social cause to fight for.

One of man's main objectives since the dawn of time has been to acquire political power so that he can have an effect upon the community in which he lives. There are various ways of gaining political power but all of them lead to the same result — political power generates popularity and popularity generates political power. Footballers *have* this popularity and so they have incredible political power because the media hangs on their every word. How far-reaching their message is then depends on their status as a player and how popular their team is. But it's an incredible thing to possess, not to mention the fact that they have great economic power — at least the better players do.

◉ Do you think Brazilian footballers have much economic power?

Certainly in relation to my era. The riches on offer here are far greater than they were 20 or 30 years ago. The change might not have been so dramatic in Europe as it has been in Brazil and players still don't earn as much as they should due to a lack of organisation and administration, but at least it is better than it was. The chances of becoming rich by playing football are far greater these days. And wealth gives you independence, political power and the freedom to manage your own life. The only thing they lack is education. Education, knowledge and information.

⚽ *What can a player do with all that power?*

Transform society. During my time as a player I was able to transform society. I was an active participant in the democratisation process of my country because I was famous and popular. And so I used my political power to change society. All you need is a social conscience, a political understanding and a desire to fight. The only problem is that most players don't have that level of education and so they don't live their lives in that way despite all the power that they have.

⚽ *But surely most players prefer to look out for themselves?*

It depends on how actively they want to get involved. People can be apathetic.

⚽ *Do you think players have a responsibility to look beyond themselves?*

I think they have a social responsibility, especially in a country like ours that is lacking in so much. Footballers can be the spokespeople of their communities — you can be like an MP without a seat. They just have to realise that they can change the society in which they live. That's my vision.

⚽ *But there is often a 'code of silence' among Brazilian players. They rarely*

speak out for fear of punishment...
We have a society that is politically unaware. That's one of our biggest problems alongside this lack of education. And that's due to a couple of the regimes we have had over the past century. We have had two dictatorships that have taken up nearly 50 years of that time and so you're eventually left with a generation who lack the same sense of political awareness. In truth, that relates to all of society and sport is a part of that — possibly the most visible part of society.

⚽ *Can you tell me a little about your plans to ensure players can only turn professional on finishing their secondary education?*

That's one of my hopes and I'm fighting for it in Congress. The way I see it, a footballer is a national figure — he's someone who is incredibly well known and listened to even more than the president of Brazil. He's the ultimate symbol of status and success. And especially for those less well off, he's a life objective — he is where thousands want to be. So if this guy has got to where he is with the bare minimum in terms of education and knowledge then he's encouraging future generations to aspire to the very same thing. And then what happens? Well, we're creating generations of kids who are more and more uneducated and uncultured. They're already poor, they're fucked, so why would they worry about studying? Their idols never studied so why will they do any different?

So I'm trying to use football as a means to get the next generations properly educated. If you want to become a footballer then you'll have to study. And even if they don't turn professional — and only a minority ever do — everyone will still at least have the basics of an education behind them. We can't escape the fact that football is the only hope for a lot of kids. And so they need educating. This way you're encouraging kids to study.

What's your part in that process? What are you doing to promote the change?

It's the government's job really. I just want to just convince politicians that it's important. I want to get an argument out there that I think very few people — if anyone — have really considered. It's crucial that we don't just look at football as an entity in itself but as a part of society. And a footballer must be treated as part of society so they need a better education.

What's the probability of anything happening?

It's about getting it talked about among the right people. And that's not easy.

How did Corinthian Democracy begin?

I'm in love with democracy. I don't think there is any man-made regime that is more coherent or makes more sense. For example, in your family most issues concern each and every person. Then you can discuss those issues — everyone participates — and you then choose the best course of action as a majority decision. That's what democracy is all about. I was always in love with that and always fought for that. But for that to happen in any society or any community then someone somewhere has to

relinquish some power. No one can have more power than anyone else and so everyone has to have a certain degree of humility. That's my vision, the fight I've undertaken all my life and somehow it became ingrained in me. It was a personal battle. I fought for things that were relevant to my daily life and my job.

I wanted an active participation and not simply to suffer the consequences of my job because in reality I was just a worker who enjoyed an interesting opportunity completely to alter the structure of an entire football club. There was a crisis at the club, we'd had a poor season and a new president came in. But the players began to enjoy more open and progressive talks with those who ran the club. So as captain, I came up with this solution to take the club forward — "let's put together a democratic regime within the club where we all decide what is good for everyone." And then what do you create with that? Responsibility. Everything that involved the group was decided by vote. Simple things such as what time we trained, what time we travelled to away games, where we would stay... everything was voted for. It was a bit like Mr Chips, the school teacher. Even new signings were put to the vote. We chose those who we thought most suited to the new Corinthians way of life. And it was the majority vote that always won so everyone's vote had the same weight. A club director had the same input as the reserve goalkeeper. The kitman or masseur were just as much a part of the structure of the club as me, captain of Brazil. And that gave an incredible level of participation for everyone, independent of their status within the team.

There is an incredible amount of competition within a football team. Your first priority is to play and then your next priority is to stand out from your team-mates. That makes for a very competitive environment. But by getting everyone to participate in a collective process we reduced that level of competition and results improved because we had an incredible group spirit without any individualism. And that's when Corinthian Democracy was born.

⚽ *Did everyone accept the new regime or was there any resistance?*

At the beginning a lot of people worried about having their say and offering their opinion for fear of reprisals. In that era, the government had always come down heavily on anyone who spoke out against it. Football wasn't any different and so that's what people were used to. But over time, the players gradually became more outspoken and courageous with their opinions. There were some people who were against the whole thing but I suppose that's only natural for those who had never been involved in or seen anything like it. They had never voted after all or seen a society where the majority had the say. But if someone didn't want to participate then that was his problem. It's like anyone who doesn't vote — fair enough, but from now on you can't complain if things don't go your way because you didn't participate in the whole process when you had the chance and so didn't have your say.

⚽ *Are you proud of what you achieved with Corinthian Democracy?*

I look back on it with enormous pride and pleasure. I've never lived through anything so beautiful and so fantastic. It was the realisation of a specific moment in time we all lived through — when Brazil had

a military dictatorship. Through popular culture — in this case football — we were carrying out a perfect democracy in a country that was being ruled by an unbelievably right-wing military dictatorship. We were, without any shadow of a doubt, bringing the issue of democracy into the collective conscience because we were popular figures at a popular club — Corinthians. Conservative forces within society tried to destroy the movement but at the same time more progressive elements in society came to help defend the movement and even improve it. It was a social process using football as its base and it was way ahead of its time. I can't even imagine when something similar will occur again like that. It's impossible just to imagine it, as football is a very conservative, reactionary sport. But for all those who lived it, it was something incredible.

⚽ *Were there a lot of people who wanted to disrupt the movement?*

Of course. The conservative forces within football were obviously benefitting from the status quo that the dictatorship allowed. So they didn't want us there. We were a 'bad example'. But that micro-society we formed at Corinthians wanted to do something different and we did it. That's what interested us. To be honest we survived a long time. As it was an ideological fight there was a lot of pressure against us. We lived in a very different country to the one we live in today. The conservative powers had a lot more power than they do today and we hung on in there despite the immense pressure being difficult to bear at times. But the institutions that wanted to transform society supported us. In fact, we grew alongside [the future president]

Lula's Workers' Party. We generated their first financial resources. We put on a concert at the club, a game of football, a barbecue all to raise funds for Lula's very first campaign.

⊕ *Corinthian Democracy worked because you had a successful team. But does an average professional have the same power as a top-class player?*

That's an important point. Some people acquire enough political power to transform society. But the majority don't. But that's the same in any community — some people stand out at what they do and others don't. The ones who don't have no power. How could they?

⊕ *So it all depends on talent?*

Yes. It depends on talent but also the *will* to fight for something. If they have the power but don't want to use it then it's all pointless, really.

⊕ *Do you think it's possible for someone to play professionally and study at university?*

It's all a question of priorities. Brazilian football is extremely conservative — it does everything to prevent the individual from a decent education because if that's the case then you're only going to be a nuisance once you're successful. No boss likes to have anyone intelligent underneath them — someone who knows their rights. So the system is there to try to keep everyone in their place. But if the player really prioritises his education then he can manage both. That's ultimately his right as a citizen. But the powers that be try to leave a player without an education — to make sure

that the guy has no awareness of the power that he actually has.

The movement became more and more political in attempting to overthrow the dictatorship and re-establish democracy in Brazil. It ultimately failed following the non-approval of a vote guaranteeing presidential elections.

⊕ *Did you not feel that when you left to play in Italy in 1984 that you were abandoning something that you had started?*

I was devastated. Absolutely devastated. Because fighting for something is part of life. You have various fights in life of varying importance. You start one and then you want to win another. We had fought for two years for democratic elections to take place in choosing the president of our republic. Just by taking the argument to the streets we were able to mobilise over a million citizens to attend a rally at Anhangabau in São Paulo. There were maybe 1.5 million people there. It was madness.

But the act went to Congress and it wasn't approved. They castrated the movement and it destroyed me. I said during those last polls that if they passed the amendment I wouldn't leave the country. As it wasn't passed I thought I should stick to my word and leave.

⊕ *Did you truly believe that Congress would pass it?*

I cried when I heard the result. I believed in popular movements. But ultimately it was the government who would decide one way or another. But I guess everything was just delayed for a few more years — the dictatorship fell not long afterwards. A transitional power took over but at least it wasn't a military regime anymore.

Why did Corinthian Democracy end?

I think my exit was the main factor as I was the most articulate of the group. I fought the hardest and I was the one who communicated our ideas to the public and to the press. When I went to Italy there was a lack of leadership at Corinthians. Another thing — they brought in 10 new players when I left so the atmosphere within the club changed. The group of people changed. So the movement had a different perspective and different aims.

So was it a football club trying to change a country?

It wasn't just a club trying to change things. I think we reflected society's needs at the time. The club was more like a catalyst to get certain issues and arguments out in the open. So that's what we did. But we weren't an isolated group of people trying to make a change. There were lots of us trying to transform Brazil. What we had that other groups didn't have was the ability to get the message heard. We had far more strength and power than an isolated individual because Corinthians was a popular club playing the most popular sport in the country. And so we became representatives or spokespeople for the masses.

Do you think football remains extremely conservative today?

Absolutely. Nothing has changed. Football has a tumour that has devoured everything.

Do you think Corinthian Democracy could happen again?

It would depend on our society and how far people wanted to go. That sort of thing can't happen anywhere or at any time. You have to have a series of factors determinant to a place and a period of time. Democracy in Ancient Greece only happened in that one particular place at that one particular time. It all depends on a variety of factors. A revolutionary process always starts with the capacity of an individual or group of people who say, "Let's do something different here, even if everything seems fine." You have to wait for or create the suitable conditions for that process to occur.

Is there any class prejudice in Brazilian football?

No. Brazilian society is certainly prejudiced, especially from an economic viewpoint — it's not by chance that poor people in Brazil tend to be black — but you have a lot less economic and racial prejudice in sport. In fact, playing sport offers you a far more profound and well-rounded view of the realities facing our country because people of every class and race rub shoulders together and in that aspect sport is a very democratic pastime. When I was a kid playing for Botafogo-SP, I played alongside this other boy who couldn't even afford to eat. So there I was doing my little courses and studying medicine and this kid couldn't even eat. I went to his house and I understood the reality in which he lived.

This is what happens here: up to about 30 or 40 years ago Brazilian footballers learnt their trade in the streets. It was something for those who lived on the margins of society. And because it wasn't for the elite then the middle classes never really concerned themselves with it — certainly not playing scouting young talent. So the less well-off did well and it was a chance to have some sort of professional success in life. When the sport began to grow and became more commercial and so generated more money, the middle classes who ran the clubs became interested in the playing side of things. They saw football as a legitimate profession and joined the competition for places. But the middle class is a very easy class to read. As far as I'm concerned, they have less footballing ability but all the economic power. They run the clubs and always have done.

Their political power then made it more difficult for poor people to get the same chances they used to have. They had the talent and of course that talent was still well valued — just a few more doors became closed to them. It's a lot harder today to get into a club than it was 40 years ago because people of other classes are now competing for places and they often have more opportunities or recourses to obtain those places.

● *What do you think of institutions set up by ex-footballers to help their communities and educate through football?*

They're great but ultimately that's the role of the government. Those institutions only exist because the government hasn't taken on its responsibilities. I dream of the day no one has to do that. That's the ideal.

● *Is it true that you ran as an 'anti-candidate' in the Brazilian Football Federation elections in 2001?*

Yes. I only ran as an 'anti-candidate' to get people talking really... to open up debate. What is this federation like? It's like a dictatorship. No one gets to join in — just them. They are the only ones who can have their say and they do what they want. No one can mess with them. So I just wanted to get a debate going and to try and change things at the top and get more people involved. No footballers are involved in the federation and yet theoretically they are the ones who should have most interest.

● *Did you never think of working for a federation like Michel Platini at Uefa?*

My views are exactly the opposite. I want to change things. I don't value power. Being in power is easy. Transforming a society is something else. But I don't really see much hope of me working in football in Brazil. It's what I know best and it's my passion and there's no way I can work outside of sport with my CV. But then how can an ex-international footballer who is also a doctor and administrator be left out of the party?

● *You allegedly received an offer from Colonel Gaddafi to sponsor your candidature towards the presidency of Brazil...*

I saw that as a joke by Gaddafi. Maybe that's something I would consider one day but it's not something I'd like to do. I've been a political secretary here [in Riberão Preto] but I've never run for anything properly. It's never even entered my mind to be honest. It's a lot of hard work to sort out the little things! I like the bigger picture — national politics. But to get there you have to jump through a series of hoops and do a lot of different things that I don't particularly like.

What do you make of the Brazil's progress towards hosting the 2014 World Cup?

They'll pay a big price — a very big price. A lot of people will get rich. Not Brazilian football, not the clubs, not the players and definitely not the fans. But there will be people getting rich. They're building new stadiums — when we already have a lot — but they're building them anyway and they will never be used again. One of the host cities, Cuiabá, has got a project to build a stadium for about 60,000 people. If you took all the fans who attend games from all the clubs in the state (not just the city) you could fill the stadium just one-and-a-half times in a year. So they're building a stadium that no one will ever go to! The same thing will happen in Manaus and in Natal too, and even in São Paulo. They don't want to use the Morumbi [São Paulo's stadium]. They want to build a new stadium because someone's going to earn a lot of money out of that. As if that was the most important thing. Football's just a game on grass — who cares about the rest? Who cares about it? Who wants to build a stadium for 60,000 people that most people will watch on TV? And Brazilians won't be at the grounds — they won't have the money to afford tickets.

You won't have 60,000 people watching Nigeria, Cameroon, the US or Italy even. Only the Brazilian national team will attract that amount of people.

Can Brazil win?

Brazil only play to win. They can always win it but who knows if they will or not? But a World Cup isn't something the best team wins. It's more of a circus. You play seven games in a month! It's not a league championship. It doesn't mean anything winning it — what's important is being the best on the right day at the right time. I'd like to see an international league championship. That would be great. A tournament over four years — home and away. It would be great. Brazil v Italy in the Maracanã and then three months later Italy v Brazil in the San Siro or the Olimpico. If it was like that, Argentina would have won in '94, Brazil in '82, Holland in '74, Hungary in '54... and it values good football. You shouldn't be world champions because of one game. Look at France in 2002 — they lost in the first round because they lost Zidane through injury. Once they lost Zidane they didn't have a team. Two or three months before the World Cup though, they were the best team in the world. Make it a league championship and in a month Zidane would recover and France could win the title. It values the product and the spectacle — which is all that's good about football. Otherwise one player gets injured and it's all over. There's no fun in that. It's good for business that way. World Cups are good at making money for a few people. Ⓑ

EFFIELD FC
E BIRTHPLACE OF THE BEAUTIFUL GAME

SHEFFIELD FC
ORIGINAL RULES & INNOVATIONS

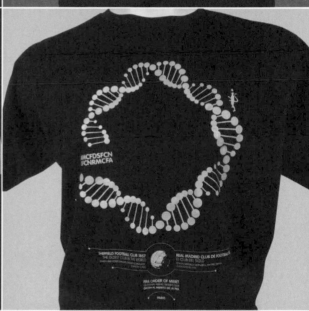

EFFIELD FC & REAL MADRID CF
E TREE OF MERIT

SHEFFIELD FC & REAL MADRID CF
DOUBLE HELIX

HEFFIELD FC 1857
HE WORLD'S FIRST FOOTBALL CLUB
Y GOALSOUL

Established on 24 October 1857, Sheffield FC pioneered what became the world's favourite game. The club introduced many of the innovations that we now take for granted. From the first throw-in, to the first free kick and corner, they invented and documented many of the modern game's original rules and regulations.

They are also one of only two clubs, the other being Real Madrid, to be honoured by FIFA with an Order of Merit. Both clubs received the prestigious award as part of FIFA's Centennial Celebrations in Paris 2004.

In association with Sheffield FC, and in recognition of the immense importance and value of the club's heritage and influence - goalsoul are proud to bring you this stunning, highly original collection.

goalsoul
KEEPING THE GAME BEAUTIFUL

See these and the rest of goalsoul's unique range at www.goalsoul.net

58

Theory

"People who start a coaching career
are frightened to leave their country
for fear of being forgotten."

Roy the Rover

Roy Hodgson explains how his travels have shaped his coaching philosophy

By Philippe Auclair

Roy Hodgson is very good company. He, unusually in English football, is a man with a hinterland, having worked in Sweden, Switzerland, Italy, Denmark, the United Arab Emirates, Norway and Finland as well as England. He speaks five languages and will discuss modern American literature as happily as he will football. On May 1 this year, he was named England manager. This interview — which dates from before then — offers an insight into Hodgson's methods and core beliefs about the game.

⊕ *Do you feel you're underappreciated in England, having worked abroad for so long?*

There aren't many English managers, I suppose, who've had the sort of career that I've had, outside the country. With the amount of money that is going around in the Premier League, not many people are tempted to move abroad. But I'm quite happy with my reputation in England. I don't feel in any way underprivileged. I've now been a manager for 36 years, and only eight of those – not even that, actually, more like six and a half – have been spent in England. So I can't really expect to be as well-known as people who've done nothing but coach in England. It doesn't concern me. And I'm quite pleased that, outside of the country, I managed to forge a reputation which still lives on.

⊕ *Do you think more coaches should coach abroad?*

People who start a coaching career are frightened to leave their country for fear of being forgotten. Secondly, of course, the type of money they can earn in Scandinavian clubs, for example, or Cyprus, that type of country that could provide a market, is going to be a major disadvantage. But the main disadvantage is that, if they don't succeed abroad, they'll miss out completely and come back to nothing. And thirdly, it takes a bit of an effort to move abroad with your family, to perhaps learn a foreign language so that you can coach in that language and come to terms with a different culture... all of these place an extra burden on a young coach.

⊕ *Languages don't seem to have been a problem for you?*

I speak five languages: English, Swedish, French, Italian and German. I learnt French at school — and even taught it at a minor level, when we played in South Africa, back in 1973. We had a morning job and in the afternoon, I'd coach for the Northern Transvaal

Football Association. When a teaching vacancy came up in that academy, the headmaster came to me and asked me to fill it. I'd just qualified as a Physical Education teacher, but he needed someone to teach French and I got thrown in at the deep end! [laughs] Having said that, when I went to Neuchâtel, in January 1990, it was quite a shock to have to speak French again... but it was French or nothing!

To be honest, I learnt Swedish mainly out of courtesy. It wasn't a *sine qua non* of coaching, as the players were so good at English. In fact, they somewhat preferred the coaching and team talk to be in English – it was a bonus for them. When I spoke in Swedish, it helped one person: myself. When I spoke in English: 25 or 30! What you've got to do in any coaching job, whether it is moving to Sweden as a young man, where being English gave you a slight advantage, or something else, you've got to win the players' respect. They might be prepared to give you an extra chance because you happen to be English. But if you can't convince them that what you're going to do with them is going to be worthwhile, then the advantage of Englishness will soon pass over; just like the advantage of being a former fantastic international player. It might give you the benefit of the doubt for a while longer. But nothing more.

How different was Swedish football from English football when you arrived at Halmstad in 1976?

People have got preconceived ideas about 'English football is this', 'German football is that'. Our idea of German football, for example, is based on what we remember from the very successful German sides of the 1970s — the national team and Bayern Munich. To me, these are cock-eyed ideas. What Bobby [Houghton, who was working at Malmö] and myself introduced to Sweden was not so much 'English football', the long ball game and so on, than a different style of defending. Instead of playing with a team that was very spread out from one end of the field to the other, with a libero who stays in his penalty area and a centre-forward who never tracks back, we set up a system of zonal defence, a back four, people pushing up and, of course, getting the ball forward into the final area much more quickly. Interestingly, in my first year at Halmstad, we not only won the League, but scored 57 goals in 26 games. I don't think this has been achieved since. And the Swedes didn't like the idea that their game was dominated by two English guys. Bobby had won it in 1974 and 1975, I won it in 1976, he won it in 1977, I won it in 1979! It was obviously not with a 'Swedish style' and it's only when Eriksson appeared in the 1980s with Gothenburg that, all of a sudden, it was possible to talk of a 'Swedish style'. In actual fact, I don't know what Eriksson did to 'swedify' the game, except copying everything we'd done.

Have your ideas on the game changed much since then?

If someone showed a video of myself coaching in 1976, I would be horrified, as I hope that, in 36 years, there has been some kind of progression. But in terms of the larger vision of the game, there hasn't been much change in my philosophy, wherever I've done my job: putting the players first, making sure the team is organised, making certain all the players in the team know their roles, supporting them every which way you can, making sure that every training session was thoroughly organised and that everything you want to happen on the Saturday has been rehearsed and practised — all of those things remained the same in Sweden, Switzerland, Finland, Italy, Denmark or England. Of course, to a certain extent, styles of play do depend on the players you have at your disposal. If you take Inter, the main challenge was to change a team that had been playing mostly man-for-man and turn it into a zonal team. That we did in the first season I was there, and quite successfully. What's more, with players who were not huge stars: Bergomi, Paganin, Festa, Fontalan, Carboni, Ganz, Zanetti... we're not talking about the type of players people associate with stardom. In the second year, bigger names joined in: Zamorano, Djorkaeff, Winter... And when the 'bigger names' came in, they forced us to change our style, because a player like Djorkaeff is a difficult player to fit into a system. He didn't want to do some of the things we wanted him to do, because it wasn't his game and he didn't want to do some of the things Sacchi wanted him to do, because that wasn't his game either! My point is: you might have your philosophy, your ideas, your concepts, but there's always going to be players in that team who're going to be too good to leave out and whom you'll have to organise your team around. You can't afford to be too inflexible. In an ideal team, you've got 11 players who are up to the job, each of them suited to his role, each balancing the other. In an even more ideal situation — if you're Manchester United or Milan — you'll have 22, not 11. And you have to keep them happy, which is not easy.

Does the weather affect styles of play? How much of a problem was that in Sweden?

The influence of the climate is particularly felt in the pre-season, in the actual season less so. In Sweden, the pre-season is inordinately long. You finish in November. In December, the players are given free time. But then you've got January, February, March and half of April before you start playing football. That's a long time to occupy. In England, it's five to six weeks; in Italy, eight weeks. But I must stress that things don't change as much as you'd think. Of course, it's nicer to train on beautiful pitches in England or at the Appiano Gentile than on a gravel pitch in the middle of January in Sweden. Of course, there's no comparison in those terms. But when it comes down to what you're trying to do as a coach, how you plan your sessions, and so on, I don't think that changes a great deal. Coming from Sweden first, then Sweden to Switzerland, then Inter, I don't think there was great deal of change in my ideas of what should happen on the field; but of course, the atmospheric conditions, the quality of the training fields, the help you get and finally, and most importantly, the quality of the players you're working with, that's what changes — not the underlying principles of your vision of the game.

And how different was Sweden culturally?

When I went to Halmstad, the players were part-timers; they earned money, but had jobs on the side too. I was on my own, in a little office, where I used to sit for a couple of hours because it was in my contract and I would be there from 10 to 12 every day, preparing the training session, of course, then staring at the wall with nothing else to do. But if you go there now, there's probably a staff of 25. And at Premier League clubs far, far more. At Halmstad, I fulfilled all the functions — and don't forget that in 1976, foreign players were not allowed to play in Sweden, otherwise I would've been player-coach. That rule was only changed in the late 1970s. But going there wasn't a difficult decision. I was so active on the training field that I still had my 'playing time' as it were...

Was it a big leap to move into international football with Switzerland?

What impressed me with the Swiss managerial job was how I was chosen. I'd had a difficult time at Neuchâtel, working there after Gilbert Gress, who turned a lot of people against me — I'd been told to come because he wanted to leave, which wasn't true, and you can imagine his reaction... I got on very well with the players, but my reputation wasn't that high outside of the club. Then we were in the European Cup, when we beat Celtic 5-1 and went on to beat Real Madrid. So all of a sudden, from being virtually not spoken about, my name became flavour of the month. I got a phone call. "Do you want to become the manager of the national team?" I thought, here we go, it's just like in England, you win two games, and you're a fantastic coach. But I went to see them, and said, "I have a question to ask you: why are you interviewing me? I'm not Swiss!" "That's a good question," he answered, talking two pieces of paper. "Here are the names, of which you're one," he said. "And there, on the other piece of paper, are the qualities we're looking for. I'm interviewing three or four

people, and the job will go to the one who scores the highest, is that ok?" It was.

How do you think your qualities fit with a checklist the English game might draw up?

The media use terms like 'sexy' in relation to football and that doesn't fit my description too well...[laughs]. When I was at Blackburn, the German national team contacted me with a view of my becoming their manager. But Franz Beckenbauer, who had a huge influence in the German game, to his great credit, put a block on me, saying it'd be a terrible admission of incompetence if it weren't possible to find a coach who was German. And I find myself on coaching seminars having to defend the opinion that English coaches are not intrinsically better or worse than their foreign counterparts. We see France, Italy and Spain as glamorous and exotic, because we know what we've got here.

You seem in some ways quite cautious, particularly as regards the finances of the clubs you work for...

It's important to run a club on sound business lines. I don't understand how clubs can consistently claim that they're working properly when they're working at such an enormous loss. How can it be a success to be in hundreds of millions in debt every year? The only year Inter made a profit since Massimo Moratti took over was my second season there. I'm proud of that.

Wenger works that way. In some ways, it's a naive way to work. We're in a league where two successive defeats mean someone's knocking on the door. The sensible way for a manager to work is to have no sort of recognition whatsoever of the business side of things. 'I want this player, I'll get him and I don't care if we're going to pay him twice what he should be getting, because it's going to get me two more points...' knowing full well that the team will win a couple more games, and he'll move on, and someone else will be left with the mess. That's not my philosophy. Everywhere I've managed, I've left a platform for my successor to build on and this is a great satisfaction for me, even if I don't necessarily get the recognition for it. **B**

Matchday Hospitality

Up close & personal

That's Matchday Hospitality at Fulham

The beautiful game has never looked better than it does from the stands of Craven Cottage, our intimate 19th Century stadium on the banks of the River Thames. Yet as well as getting you closer to the action on the pitch, we take pride in offering truly personal service.

Matchday Hospitality at Craven Cottage really is the best way to get up close and personal to the beautiful game.

For 2012/2013 Seasonal Hospitality options, call our hospitality team on (+44) 020 8336 7555, **email us at** hospitality@fulhamfc.com **or go to** www.fulhamfc.com

Like a Shooting Star

How Ternana soared and then crashed with Corrado Viciani's high-tempo style

By Luca Ferrato

It began, and then it was over. For two seasons, 1971-72 and 1972-73, Ternana, under their coach Corrado Viciani, as they said at the time, walked on the moon. They moved the ball rapidly across the pitch, played an extreme passing game for 90 minutes, did everything at great pace, operated with a philosophy so well defined that it was almost obsession and played in a way that seems a precursor to the Barcelona of Pep Guardiola or the AC Milan of Arrigo Sacchi. Viciani's *gioco corto* seemed so unreal, so otherworldly, that in his book, *Il gioco è bello quando è corto* [*The Game is Beautiful when it's Short*], Gianluca Diamanti could scarcely believe it had happened at all. "Did Ternana really walk on the moon?" he asked "Or was it a mutual but unrealised dream? Did we actually play in Serie A for a single season?"

Terni, in Umbria, is famous mostly for its steel factories — certainly not for football. Viciani arrived there in 1967 and led Ternana to promotion to Serie B in his first season. He left to manage Atalanta and Taranto, but returned in the summer of 1971 to begin the miracle. In 1972, Ternana won a first-ever promotion to Serie A, an achievement made all the more satisfying by the fact that Perugia, their hated local rivals, had at that stage never played in the top flight. The most important games that season, not merely

in terms of points but also self-esteem, were the fixtures against Lazio, which brought a 1-0 win and a 1-1 draw. People from the capital have commonly considered the Ternani to be *burini* — 'peasants'— and gave the impression of regarding matches in Terni as holidays in the countryside.

Viciani's training focused on physical preparation, something unusual in the Italy of the early seventies. Their players ran faster and harder than their opponents, combining their intensity with an intricate passing game. Promotion was secured with a 3-1 win over Novara on 18 June. Giorgio Mastropasqua, who would go on to play for Juventus, Atalanta, Bologna, Lazio and Catania, was 21 in 1972. "That was an incredible team, with an amazing manager," he said.

"I was very young at time, and I played as a *libero*, with Fernando Benatti and Mauro Agretti as right and left-back respectively. Angelino Rosa played at the centre of the defensive line, just in front of me, but sometimes I played in front of him, because I was a *libero* in the 'Dutch style'. Giancarlo Alessandrelli, my teammate also at Juventus, was in goal, but our secret was probably in midfield, where we had players like Romano Marinai, Antonio Cardillo and

Bruno Beatrice who ran up and down the pitch. Salvatore Jacolino was the centre-forward and sometimes Franco Selvaggi and Nicola Traini helped him. As you see, there were no famous players, no one who left Ternana and had an important career elsewhere. So, the key was Viciani: I never had a manager like him for the rest of my career. He was more a philosopher than a coach. Sometimes he cited Camus or Pericles, but with his players he operated like a dictator."

As one of the other players put it at the time, "It's not true that he does not let us do what we want, but the important thing is that what we want is what he wants…"

What he wanted was a close passing game. "Kick-and-rush play is dull," he said. "Somebody invented the sweeper and he plays in that position just to collect all the long balls." Viciani was fundamentalist in his belief. On the night of the European Cup final between Ajax and Internazionale in 1972, he announced on television that he was supporting the Dutch. "It's necessary for Inter to lose by three or four goals," he said. "It will be very important for the Italian football movement. The Dutch are playing real football, but in Italy managers are interested in playing defensively, in playing horrible and unaesthetic football." As it was, Ajax won 2-0, and Italian football declined the lesson.

Viciani, though, was obsessed with the Dutch model and, as such, he was the precursor of managers such as Nils Liedholm and Arrigo Sacchi. "The most important experiment in collective football in Italy was introduced by Corrado Viciani," Luigi Cavallara, the author of *Interismo-Leninismo*, explained.

"He had a lot of average players, and he forced them to play with short passes to move together on the pitch."

"Italians need to learn the verb 'to run' in football," Viciani said. "For now they only know the infinitive form… When you play you get tired both physically and psychologically. If you play 'automatically' you can reduce the stress. Everybody should know how to find their teammate, everything should automatically scroll. Look at what happened with the German and Dutch national teams. It seems that the players run a lot, but first of all, they are well-organised."

Ternana made their Serie A debut on 24 September 1972 against Napoli at the San Paolo. As they had so often in Serie B, Ternana dominated the game, but this time they lost by a single goal, undone by their naivety at that level. The following Sunday, October 1, the Stadio Libero Liberati hosted its first top-flight match, against the AC Milan of Gianni Rivera, Karl-Heinz Schnellinger, Albertino Bigon and Pierino Prati. Ternana controlled the game. Cardillo, Beatrice and Marinai ran from start to finish, crossing the ball again and again into the box. Milan struggled to stem the flow, but the game ended goalless.

Until December, it seemed that Ternana would survive, but their form suddenly collapsed. Viciani's style of play was simply too exhausting to be sustained at that level and Ternana failed to win a single game in the second half of the season. They totaled just 16 points and, naturally, were relegated.

Viciani departed for Palermo in Serie B and again imposed his *gioco corto*.

Although they failed to win promotion the following season, they did reach the Coppa Italia final, in which they faced Bologna. The *rosanero* took the lead through Sergio Magistrelli, but in injury-time the referee Sergio Gonella gave the *rossoblù* a disputed penalty. Beppe Savoldi converted, Bologna won on penalties and the fairy tale of Corrado Viciani came to an end.

Viciani managed until 1990, making a return to Terni in 1988, but his *gioco corto* never had the same impact again. Thanks to Sacchi and his success at Milan in the late eighties, Italian football gradually accepted the usefulness of collective play and zonal marking, and so adopted a model similar to that Viciani had advocated. Forty years on, nobody in Terni has forgotten the man who walked so briefly on the moon. Ⓑ

The Skilling Fields

Manchester United are just one of the clubs influenced by the coaching model of Wiel Coerver

By Steve Bartram

God-given gifts. Innate ability. Natural talent. Myths one and all in the eyes of Wiel Coerver, the man who broke down the greats and put their secrets in a toolbox for every footballer to use. What nature seemingly gave only the select few, Coerver handed out to the masses through a pioneering coaching method designed to arm players for any individual battle that awaited them in the war of football.

The Dutchman's mantra was thus: take the best attributes of the best players, drum them into youngsters with situational, repetitive learning and watch them prosper. Master the ball, master the opponent, master the game: a well-founded concept which, a year after his death, can be judged a resounding success. Coerver Coaching now has bases in 28 countries and claims to have taught 1.5 million players and coaches.

His influence goes far beyond grassroots. Coerver's theory is manifested in some of the modern game's outstanding players who were exposed to his methods to varying degrees during their formative years. Robin van Persie studied Coerver daily in his youth, as did Ruud van Nistelrooy. Arjen Robben was a devotee and Wesley Sneijder dabbled, while youngsters like Danny Welbeck and Tom Cleverley have risen through a

Manchester United youth system infused with fundamental Coerver concepts.

This legacy, however, has come at a cost. A belligerent character, Coerver spent his whole coaching career fighting for his beliefs and unleashing fierce attacks on any coach who failed to grasp his instructions. His dogmatic approach led to an enmity with Rinus Michels, a sacrosanct figure in Dutch football and an adversary with whom battle was futile. Accordingly, Coerver developed a reputation as a controversial coach and, in his homeland at least, was never fully accepted.

From his birth in Kerkrade, on the German border, in 1924, Coerver swam against the mainstream. In Kerkrade, the most common career path led down the town's coal mines, but a subterranean life held no allure for him. He doggedly pursued a career in football and represented VV Bleijerheide and Rapid JC — now Roda JC. A tall, graceful centre-back, Coerver oozed elegance and liked to carry the ball out from defence.

As a player, Coerver's greatest achievement was winning the Eredivisie in 1956 with Rapid. Three years later, at 35, he turned his hand to management and took on his first role with the amateur club SVN, before moving into the professional game with Sparta Rotterdam. That would be his most settled role — he took on six more positions over the following 12 years — but his managerial zenith came in 1974 at Feyenoord, where he masterminded an Eredivisie and Uefa Cup double, winning the latter by beating Bill Nicholson's Tottenham in the final. Although the two-legged affair, won 4-2 on aggregate by the Dutch, gained greater notoriety as the tie which introduced English hooliganism to the continent, Coerver's side halted a run of six successive triumphs for English sides.

However, vexed by the ongoing success of Ajax and Bayern Munich — both of whom won three successive European Cups in the seventies — as well as the apparent domestic monopolies of the likes of Real Madrid, Club Brugge and Liverpool, Coerver embarked on a continent-wide tour of training grounds, forensically trying to uncover what kept these clubs at the forefront. Starved of a definitive answer for their collective success, he began to look at the individuals within the teams, focusing especially on Johan Cruyff's exploits at Ajax.

What was Cruyff doing differently to everyone else? He had a change of pace and a superior intelligence, clearly, but his pre-eminence was born of his armoury of skills: something other players didn't have. Whenever Cruyff found himself caged by an opponent, his chicanery would pick the lock. Coerver studied him, analysing each move and writing down its execution and situational usage, even down to the angle of the opponent's approach. Once satisfied that he had catalogued Cruyff's entire arsenal, he set about learning them

himself. Coerver mastered them all. If he could do it in his fifties, he reasoned, surely the players he was coaching — by then he had settled briefly at NEC Nijmegen — could learn them at their physical peak.

His management career continued apace, with fleeting spells in charge of the Indonesia national team and the Dutch side Go Ahead Eagles, before a heart attack in 1977 altered his career path. Warned against the rigours and stresses of management, and also told to work in a warmer climate for the good of his health, he concentrated on pinning down his coaching method. He widened his approach and studied all the game's greats. Di Stéfano, Puskás, Charlton, Best, Beckenbauer and Pelé: all equipped with different skills suited to their individual games and positions, yet Coerver could take each man and create a blueprint. Moreover, his focus shifted depending on whom he was teaching. No longer required to improve peak athletes, he realised that if he could teach children — primarily in the eight-to-twelve-year-old band — then he could prompt the evolution of a new footballing animal for whom comfort on the ball was total and instinctive.

Coerver toured the world and gave lectures, pioneering the use of video analysis to pinpoint the secrets of the greats. His gospel was also spread by those who had worked with him. The Dutch midfielder Frans Thijssen, one of Coerver's star pupils at NEC Nijmegen, had been crowned England's Footballer of the Year with Ipswich Town. Their manager Bobby Robson, hearing Thijssen's glowing recommendation of Coerver's methods, invited the Dutchman to meet him and the pair struck up a lasting relationship of mutual respect. Robson would later endorse Coerver's coaching manuals.

Coerver's big break, however, came in 1983 through a chance encounter with the former Wimbledon youth player Alfred Galustian and the former Scotland winger Charlie Cooke, who were coaching together in America. The pair attended a presentation Coerver was giving at a soccer expo in Philadelphia, in which the Dutchman illustrated his points with a small group of youngsters who demonstrated tricks and moves on command. Galustian and Cooke were captivated and approached Coerver immediately after the presentation. Thereafter, the trio worked together sporadically for two years, before, amid a disagreement over the direction of the project, Coerver agreed to sell the naming rights of his programme to Galustian and Cooke.

Parting with the naming rights to allow his programme's development under the stewardship of others didn't, however, stop Coerver from continuing his coaching. In the mid-1980s he approached the Dutch football federation (KNVB) and pitched his method as a means of giving the nation's footballers a head-start over the rest of the world, a programme that would develop young players versed in the arts of possession and movement but fundamentally comfortable as individuals within a team.

The problem, however, lay in the pitch. No patter, no charm, just orders. Coerver told the KNVB in that it was their responsibility to develop good, technical coaches before the programme could be implemented and made clear that their current staff's standards fell well short of his requirements. Talks were off to a bad start. The presence of Rinus Michels, back in charge of the national team for the second time, proved an equally imposing obstacle. The man who had given the world Total Football and had led Holland to the 1974 World Cup final was a national hero but remained an awkward figure.

Inevitably, there were disagreements. Michels quickly introduced his proposal for four-v-four training programmes to encourage contact with the ball, citing heuristic learning as the way for the players to develop in the natural environment. Coerver agreed, but stressed that the small-sided games needed to be stripped back further still, to three-v-three, two-v-two, one-v-one, one-v-two, two-v-three and three-v-four, to submerge the players in every conceivable situation they could experience in real games.

If they couldn't dominate an opponent in four-v-four, he argued, they would have no chance of doing so in seven-v-seven or full-sided games, and therefore it was imperative to arm each boy with the tools to dominate one-v-one situations first. Michels, however, didn't believe in teaching and learning techniques in isolation, within repetitive environments. With the two men at an impasse, there could only be one winner in the eyes of the KNVB, who distanced themselves from the Coerver method.

Having parted ways, neither party looked back. The Dutch swaggered to victory at Euro 88, with Gullit, Rijkaard, Koeman and Van Basten thriving under Michels' management, while Coerver continued to plough his lone furrow as a renegade coach. By this point, he had earned a doting disciple: René Meulensteen, then a youth coach at NEC Nijmegen. Meulensteen had happened upon a copy of Coerver's book *Blueprint for the Perfect Footballer* and had imparted its contents to NEC's Under-14s. Their spectacular results convinced him that Coerver's path was the right one to follow.

It was while watching a youth match with NEC that Meulensteen fell into conversation with the prominent Dutch journalist Johan Derksen, who had written the preface to Coerver's book. Derksen acted as a conduit, passing on a videotape which Meulensteen had had professionally produced, showcasing Coerver's methods and messages. As it became clear that the two coaches shared a vision, they met in a pub in Valkenburg, South Holland, in a summit which would have profound consequences.

"It was similar to when I had my first meeting with Sir Alex Ferguson," says Meulensteen, now the first-team coach at Manchester United. "When you first meet somebody you've always heard a lot about and you've always seen on TV, then suddenly you're eye-to-eye with them, it's strange. Wiel was looking right through me. He had a look that said, 'What do you want from me?' We nearly had our first fight there and then, because I told him I was heading over to do a coaching course in England. He said, 'What are you doing these courses for? What are they going to teach you?' I pointed out that if, in the future, I wanted to defend our shared philosophy and I'd never been on any other course, people

could always say that I'd never tried any other methods."

Meulensteen attended the courses in England in the summer of 1993, but soon set off for the Middle East as he received an invitation to become Coerver's assistant in his latest expedition: coaching the national youth teams in Qatar, under the regime of Mohammed Bin Hammam, then the president of the Qatari Football Association. From day one, Meulensteen recognised that working with Coerver would provide a broad education.

"I landed in Qatar, and then the next morning, at 7am, we were walking up to one of the local stadiums with two balls and going to do some moves and turns," he says. "He just wanted to see what I could do. By 8am it was 30 degrees and he had me showing him all my moves, and he was just shouting '*as-raa*' [Arabic for 'faster'] and that was the first thing he drummed into me.

"He was 69 at that time and thin as a door but he was there waiting for me outside his apartment at 7am every morning. In terms of working he was always busy, obsessive in many ways. Because of his heart trouble he had a very strict diet and everything that had fat in he would wrap in napkins and squeeze the fat out of it. He ate a lot of watermelons and he made training exercises with the pips. He would act them with the pips and then write them down. He'd use matchsticks for goals. Wherever he was, he was always thinking about football. He couldn't switch off. But he enjoyed it because he had his own little apartment in Qatar, he loved the hot weather and everything was good for him."

Coerver returned to Holland every three or four months to visit his wife and deposit his earnings. He insisted on being paid cash by the QFA, never used banks, and his borderline paranoia in financial matters made for unusual situations. "I remember one time, just before he went home for Christmas," recalls Meulensteen. "We went along to the FA and he got his wages — $40,000 for four months — all wrapped up in elastic bands, and he took it back to his hotel. When I picked him up the next morning, he was wearing a really tight, old school tracksuit. He put his feet up on the dashboard and he said, 'René, this is the most expensive tracksuit you've ever seen,' and he pulled his trouser leg up, and there were all these blocks of money wrapped around his legs!

"So that day he let me take the training session with the kids and he just wandered around the outside of the pitch with his shirt off, just tapping the ball, taking little touches. At one point I glanced at him and had to do a double-take. I just started laughing. All these 100-dollar notes were dropping off his legs and blowing around. So I walked behind him and picked up all up and said, 'Wiel, you've got to stop, your tracksuit is devaluing with every step!'

"He was funny, without even realising it. At the same time, though, he was still always fighting with everyone, even at his age. With that money he wanted to take an Iranian carpet home to Holland, so he spent ages haggling for one, then we both crammed into a taxi with this carpet poking out of the windows and he ends up rowing with the driver over the fare. He got out and he whacked the guy in the side of the head with the carpet and just walked off."

Coerver's insatiable drive to try and implement his ideals in footballing outposts meant that, after four years in Qatar, he sought further challenges. He went on to take youth coaching roles in Abu Dhabi and Egypt, while Meulensteen embarked on a successful club management career in Qatar. In 2001, he came to the attention of the then-director of Manchester United's Academy, Les Kershaw. By now renowned as one of the world's leading youth coaches, Meulensteen presented his methods, still firmly steeped in Coerver tradition, to a club which had just won its third straight Premier League title. It soon transpired that the Dutchman was preaching to the converted.

"One reason we hired René was because of his knowledge and experience in the Coerver programme," Sir Alex Ferguson revealed in 2006. "The intention was to improve the technical ability of all the young kids, and of course Wiel Coerver had a tremendous influence on René and I was quite aware of that. That was fine by me. I also used it all the time when I was manager and coach at Aberdeen 20-odd years ago. I thought it was very important then and I think it's even more important now. It is a great way to improve skills and is necessary for all players, not only youth players."

Soon after Meulensteen's arrival at United, Ferguson noted the results of the Dutchman's changes to the youth training programme and gave him the extra duty of working with senior players who were coming back to fitness or needed a booster in technical skills. When those sessions began to reap noticeable rewards, they were prescribed at all levels of the club.

"I always took them through a specific skills programme related to their position," says René. "You're not changing anything; you're tacking things on. I worked with Ryan Giggs not long after I arrived in 2001 and just chatted things through with him. He just had to reinvent himself a little bit and use his skills to change angles quicker and manipulate play further infield, rather than running along the line. Now he links play, finds the pass, disguises everything beautifully.

"With every player, you're looking to add little things. Diego Forlán, Ruud van Nistelrooy, Cristiano Ronaldo, Patrice Evra, Darren Fletcher, Michael Carrick... even Paul Scholes. Anyone. Top midfield players make you believe you're going one way, then it's a quick spin and turn and create a completely different picture. The amount of times you see Scholesy now do a little Cruyff, or a little stop-turn, and get out of tight situations is incredible. They have always responded really well to anything I've tried to teach them. I always told Wiel all the time that any influence I was having at United was directly because of him and his work." As Meulensteen's career took off, Coerver's slowed. He settled into a role as the face of the Coerver Coaching programme and, even when bedbound a fortnight before his death, scribbled down new drills for Cooke and Galustian to work into their curriculum. When he passed away at the age of 86, on 22 April 2011, the news barely rippled across football; yet when Michels had died six years earlier, there was a general outpouring of sorrow.

"Michels was a people's man," explains Meulensteen. "Coerver could never be a people's man. Everyone knew him as an innovator and a very determined man who had a strong passion about skill development and technical players, people who could make a difference. They also knew he was a very difficult man who upset a lot of people, but there's still a great respect for what he achieved and believed in."

Mawkishness could never pass as a fitting tribute to Wiel Coerver. As an argumentative figure who devoted his working life to interpreting the minutiae for the masses and providing players with an arsenal of trickery, a more apt legacy is that his work will forevermore be a tool for players who wish to equip themselves for battle.

LIONEL MESSI:
GENUINELY SIGNED BY THE WORLD'S BEST

ICONS FIRST DID A SIGNING WITH LEO IN 2006 WHEN HE WAS ONLY 18 AND HAD JUST BROKEN INTO THE BARCELONA SIDE.

TODAY HE IS THE BEST PLAYER IN THE WORLD AND HE STILL ONLY SIGNS FOR US.

VIEW THE FULL MESSI RANGE ONLY AT WWW.ICONS.COM

Thanks for seeing us through our 1st Year

Year One - Digital and hard copies available at www.theblizzard.co.uk

Issue One
June 2011

Issue Two
September 2011

Issue Three
December 2011

Issue Four
March 2012

Year Two

Issue Five
June 2012

Issue Six
September 2012

Issue Seven
December 2012

Issue Eight
March 2013

76

The Asian Market

"...that paying spectators in Japan
should feel obliged to salute the
performance, regardless of its quality,
appeared genuinely to grate with the
one-time pasta waiter..."

The *Gaijin* of Gamba

*Fan culture has begun to challenge Japanese hierarchies.
The only European Gamba ultra explains how*

By Ben Mabley

The culture of Japan is famously hierarchical. Alongside the universally familiar scenarios of manager-employee and *sensei*-pupil, the natural order of *jōge kankei* — literally 'relationships of above and below' — even extends to individuals within the same social group, in which the clearly defined statuses of *sempai* and *kōhai* refer respectively to the more- and (usually younger) less-experienced members. While a 19-year-old university student, say, may defy certain conventions with her choice of loud clothing or orange hair dye, she will still feel obliged to show deferential behaviour towards her 20-year-old friend in the year above. But even then, it is still not quite that simple. Fundamental to a deeper understanding of Japanese social customs are the intrinsically — though not exclusively — associated concepts of *uchi* and *soto*.

Essentially meaning 'inside' and 'outside', these terms distinguish between the social groups relative to a given subject. The statuses of *uchi* and *soto* are not necessarily static, however; they can vary according to the social setting or context, and it is important to maintain an awareness of all of this in order both to act and speak in the appropriate fashion. For instance, within a business environment, the customer obviously represents an 'out-group' that needs to be deferred to and treated politely (at least, if you want to keep their custom), while everything to do with your own company then automatically becomes your 'in-group'. Although it may normally be your duty to remain humble and respectful when dealing with your boss in the second person, he is relegated to the status of mere mortal once again when you refer to him in communications with your customer, as you both represent the same 'group' in the context of dealing with another.

Roles can even be switched entirely in external settings if, for example, the guy from the office who gets to sit in a fancier chair happens to be a member of the same sports or martial arts club, where you then happen to be the more experienced *sempai*. So engrained is the requirement for correct behaviour with respect to groups and statuses, that companies will often require employees to sit through refreshers on things like the correct deployment of 15°/30°/45° bows and on who goes where at the table, in a car or even in a lift, depending on who else is present. Even to the Japanese, the fluidity of the groups can become confusing — a classic sociolinguistics problem places you in a friendly game of golf with your boss and his best mate, who is managing director at one of your major clients. If this customer remarks that your boss is playing a blinder, should you react with humility or shared deference?

The reason that this is a sociolinguistic issue is also the most immediate factor behind why all of this is so important. In an excellent illustration of how language and culture can develop in an interrelated manner, with one often having certain parameters defined by the bounds of the other, Japanese has clearly distinct manners of speech which represent perhaps the most constantly obvious signs of social context and which directly affect all sentence predicates. Even a verb as simple as *taberu* (eat), which may be used 'as is' in informal settings within the 'in-group', should be extended to *tabemasu* in polite conversation, replaced by *itadakimasu* for humility, or by *meshiagarimasu* to elevate the status of the eater.

To give a quite extreme example, one might casually say, "*mite ne*" when telling a friend to "look at this", but the perfectly standard, "*go-ran tamawarimasu yō o-negai mōshiagemasu*" carries essentially the same lexical meaning — only with some brilliant extra nuances which, to translate the untranslatable, might read, "I humbly and politely express my humble request for you in your nigh-on imperial majesty to do me the honour of taking a most honourable look." This is still just the tip of the iceberg, but to cut to the point, there is a clearly inherent requirement for Japanese mentally to establish their relations with every other participant in the conversation before they even open their mouths.

While rule-breakers will stand out like a sore thumb, the need to keep up correct appearances can inevitably get stressful, and in a few rare cases it *is* rejected. As a teenager breaking through with the J. League side Bellmare Hiratsuka in the mid-1990s, the future Roma and Bolton Wanderers midfielder Hidetoshi Nakata caused a stir by refusing to use respectful language when addressing older club-mates. His reasoning was that if Japan was serious about adopting the world's game, then be they captain or new boy, every member of the eleven should be considered and therefore act as an equal. 'Hide' probably only got away with this attitude because of his precocious footballing talent, though he did rub a few senior journalists up the wrong way when he applied it to them as well. Even today, it is still considered maverick for teammates not at least to get their *taberu* and *tabemasu* right. Fortunately, though, Japanese football has found a happy medium beyond the days where some university and even Japan Soccer League players might select a recipient for their passes based on age and thus seniority.

The obvious exceptional case in such a racially homogenous nation is the foreigner who, unless of East Asian origin, will always remain *soto* to the stranger because of the way they look. Indeed, the written character for *soto* is also the first in the Japanese word for 'foreigner' — *gaikokujin*, correctly or *gaijin*, casually and sometimes pejoratively. But a more valid distinction arises the moment you open your mouth. If you make the effort to learn a bit of the language, you will often enjoy significant favour. The fact that the honorifics are generally the hardest thing to master, meanwhile, means foreigners are not really expected to know how to use them anyway. In my experience, this then brings the wonderful positive that getting away with using less formal language serves in turn to make the situation more relaxed; breaking down barriers and allowing a greater degree of intimacy to be achieved more quickly. Paradoxically, being more *soto* can actually help you become more *uchi*.

I first encountered the Black and Blue ultras at Gamba Osaka back in autumn 2003, as a recently-arrived exchange student at the Osaka University of Foreign Studies. Even more so than the rest of Japan, the western Kansai region is definitively baseball country, with the fanatically-supported (albeit surprisingly unsuccessful) Hanshin Tigers and their legendary Kōshien ballpark evoking greater spiritual resonance as symbols of local pride than perhaps any other sporting entities across the archipelago. In its attempts to introduce professional football into a modern society with plenty of other, pre-existing distractions, the J. League had established a 'hometown' rule that emphasised local roots and social contribution instead of American-style franchise models and, even in its first decade, this had been a great success in places like Urawa (Reds), Kashima (Antlers) and (Albirex) Niigata. But for Kansai, it was impossible to escape from the ubiquitous, yellow-and-black shadow of RBIs and strikeouts.

Of course, the local footballing authorities probably didn't make it easy for themselves when Gamba — sensibly the sole Kansai representatives in the J. League's original 10 — were joined in rapid succession by another Osaka club, Cerezo, as well as Kyoto Purple Sanga and finally Vissel Kobe just up the road. Coinciding as it did with a bursting of the early-1990s Zico/Gary Lineker/ Kazuyoshi Miura bubble, this expansion saw attendances at Gamba's Banpaku stadium drop by nearly two-thirds between 1994 and 1996. Baseball had an intriguing influence on the makeup of those who remained, too. While the suited 'salarymen' kept loyal to Kōshien, a nationwide trend for younger people and women to start favouring football was particularly pronounced out west. Official J. League surveys have suggested the overall gender ratio is 60:40 for male and female supporters; in Kansai, and at Gamba in particular, it is virtually an even split.

I did, in any case, require a football fix and with Kyoto a little too far to visit regularly, my first Saturday in the country was spent at the magnificent Kobe Wing Stadium, which hosted three matches in the previous year's World Cup. Positioning myself just to the left of the central gathering of fans behind the goal, I watched as two conductors stood at the front with their backs to the pitch and encouraged their followers to belt out enthusiastically — if not entirely convincingly — a repertoire containing a fair amount of bastardised English and Portuguese. But even the presence of the one-time Genoa forward Miura, then 36 (he is now 45 and, incredibly, still active with Yokohama FC in J2), could not prevent a 3-1 defeat to Júbilo Iwata, while the fans' defiance was literally stretched with their version of Vindaloo by Fat Les; three whole syllables lost to replace the familiar lyrics with "We will fight with you... Vissel!"

The experience was rather like a first date that had only gone OK — I might have accepted a second but only if they made the move and given that nobody had spoken to me all afternoon, that seemed unlikely. Cerezo, meanwhile, had me craving an escape through the toilet window. Even if most people had purchased the team's bright pink shirts, the ambience was inescapably pantomime-like, with barely any hardcore to speak of and many 'supporters' preoccupied with their *bentō* lunch boxes. It may have been homemade rather than hospitality, prawn sushi rather than prawn sandwiches, but the overwhelming majority of the small attendance seemed to be there on a day out and not because of any inherent, emotional need to support the team. The only real noise came from the few hundred travelling Oita Trinita fans at the opposite end, carried over by the Nagai Stadium's terrific acoustics.

With Gamba, however, it was different. There was an instant spark — even if that did come in the form of a 21-year-old bloke whose aged, crimson complexion suggested that the paper cup of beer in his hand was not quite the first he had purchased that lunchtime, let alone that season. Arriving at Banpaku with my Dutch coursemate Alex, our first instinct' had been to marvel at the quaint surroundings of a facility that hadn't quite made it onto the Fifa shortlist; its 23,000 capacity being slightly variable depending on how many were willing to squeeze themselves onto the grass banks behind either goal. In truth, this wasn't really an issue as we enjoyed plenty of space to stretch our legs, until our slurring new friend Shinsuke spotted the unlikely opportunity to practice his English. "Let's go," he beckoned; leading us to join his friends, front and centre.

There were no salarymen in sight. Instead, I was now surrounded by a group of perhaps two dozen imposingly-built, shaven-headed gentlemen in black clothing depicting images of skulls with daggers thrust through them, a prominent '*vaffanculo*', and various other Italian words whose meaning I neither understood nor imagined to be especially friendly. Fortunately for our immediate safety, the men themselves actually were — and very much so, once Alex and I had acclimatised to their harsh Osaka dialects and demonstrated our own, fledgling knowledge thereof. We shared a *kampai* ('cheers') with our paper pint cups — which never do make as satisfying a clinking sound as the real thing — before the designated 'call leader' made his way through to take his place atop an upturned beer crate and set the crowd in thunderous motion: "Are we going to make some noise today? Are we here to get behind the lads today? Are we ready to go? Gamba, Gamba, Osaka Gamba!"

Even after three years of full-time study of this country and its ways, the whole environment was distinctly removed from any image of Japan that I had previously held. Goals — of which the first arrived after just eight minutes — were celebrated rambunctiously in a mosh pit-like melee at the front of the grass with little care for spillage, beer or emotional. Singing was constant, mandatory and largely based upon familiar melodies from Serie A and the rest of Europe — enabling me to make an immediate go of joining in with the appropriate smattering of *forza*, *olé*, and *alé*. The use of *vaffanculo* — being all about context and status, Japanese doesn't really do its own swear words — was liberal, though Gamba's eventual 3-1 victory over Nagoya Grampus Eight meant that it was only required to abuse the home team's unpopular manager before kick-off and then on one other occasion in displeasure at the referee for a cheaply conceded free kick.

Numbers were admittedly low, both in the Black and Blue section and in the ground as a whole, where a crowd figure of just over 10,000 left huge spaces in the two main concrete stands. Over to my left, there was another, slightly larger gathering that seemed to consist primarily of the more reserved young males and schoolgirls I had expected to encounter, with their own leader who started few chants unilaterally and mainly just mimicked what ours did. But it was quickly apparent that I had just lucked my way inside the most — only? — intoxicatingly unrepressed group of football fans in western Japan, and that both they and their sister organisation, the Brigate Neroazzurre stood to our right, were quite serious about their adopted Italian theme. Appropriately, it was with the demeanour of a wannabe mafioso that 'Michel', eyes hidden behind dark glasses, stepped down from his beer crate pedestal and coolly shook my hand as he departed for whatever important duty awaited him behind the stand.

Shinsuke and his companions were generously enthusiastic to further our acquaintances at the next home game against FC Tokyo — a minor grudge match against representatives of a "cold, unemotional" capital with which these Osakans were quick to contrast and disassociate themselves. Emphatically won over by their joyous release of tension at the narrow 1-0 victory, I joined them again in the pouring late November rain for a 5-1 final-day drubbing of

relegation-bound Kyoto — a sorry fate for a side whose Park Ji-Sung-inspired Emperor's Cup success back on New Year's Day 2003 had represented a first ever trophy for any of the miserably underachieving Kansai quartet. This latter fixture brought my first real opportunity to chat to the Black and Blue leader, with whom I exchanged contact details on the pretext of conducting an interview for dissertation research during the winter break. Instead, Michel was the one to e-mail me — with an invitation to join the group on their road trip to Kashima for the opening weekend of the 2004 campaign.

Late one Friday night the following March, I sat with the naughty boys at the back of the bus for an 11-hour journey whose gruelling nature, they assured me, would be eased both by the beer cooler and by the promise of freshly barbecued *horumon* — beef offal or, literally, 'discarded stuff' — for breakfast. Michel, whose real name had fallen into virtual disuse since he had declared his pre-J. League love for Juventus and their French number 10, introduced me to his friend who simply went by 'Inter' — Alessandro Altobelli presumably having failed the test for an effective, easy-to-pronounce nickname in Japanese. Alongside him on the rearmost row were 'G', as in "G for Gamba"; 'Massimo', whose handle dates back to an old part-time job at an Italian restaurant; and the joint leader 'Dai-chan', a tough-looking, godfatherly presence further back in the stand and such a master of the Osaka dialect's rolling R's and sentences that a foreign name just wouldn't have suited.

Dealing out the six-pack of Kirin which I had contributed, Michel reminisced about the football fever that had fleetingly gripped Japan — including Kansai, when it was just Gamba — a decade previously. At first, everyone would just sit or stand wherever they could get tickets, but over time, friendships were developed among fans that regularly populated the same sections. Soon enough, a number of 'leader types' emerged in different parts of the stadium who, whether previously enamoured with European football or simply caught up in the freedom of expression that Banpaku permitted, took it upon themselves to get the crowd singing. Once they got really clever, these leaders then started communicating via walkie-talkies — literally to ensure that everyone was singing from the same song sheet. When the J. League's early novelty wore off and attendances began their sharp decline, it was generally the ones who sung that stuck around.

One by one, the chanting groups relocated to the predictably christened *Curva Nord* behind the north goal, to form one big super-group called Gambino in 1994. However, as numbers fell, so did the level of consensus as to how best to support the team. The characteristically Japanese, regimented style sat uncomfortably with Michel and his faction, who instead wanted to develop an Osakan interpretation of the rather more emotive following manifested across Italy and the rest of Europe. After five years, they broke away, leaving the 'boring, normal ones' in official Gamba merchandise to their own devices on the left-hand side of the *curva*. Surprisingly, given the intimidating imagery they had chosen for their own, original designs, none of the guys seemed aware that their English name 'Black and Blue' could carry

connotations of bruising — it was simply chosen, explained G, after the team's colours and to leave the Italian *neroblu* free for use in songs.

"We all came from similar backgrounds around Osaka and the rest of Kansai," he continued, "and we all felt the same about demonstrating our local pride through football. So the decision to do things the Italian way was definitely a conscious one. Quite a few of us were into Serie A before Japan even had a professional league and the fact that 'Gamba' itself is Italian for 'leg' [as well as being the stem of the Japanese word for 'come on!'] made it easy for everyone else to get on board too. Since we were essentially starting from zero, the passion we saw in Italy was a great model for us to base ourselves on; especially once the initial buzz and era of packed stadiums was over.

"In fact, a handful of us still try to spend a long weekend in Italy during the Japanese close season to see what we can learn. We sit with the fans of Inter or Atalanta, and we actually bring tape recorders to capture their songs. After the games, we get the Italian ultras who recognise us to write down their new chants, and then on the plane back, we ask one of the air hostesses to tell us what the lyrics mean in Japanese. We then write our own versions, mixing Japanese or Osaka dialect with a bit of Japanised Italian as well, and these have since evolved into the songs we use today."

Massimo shed further light on the Osakan ultras' ethos. "Everyone in Black and Blue knows their stuff. That's why we want to see good football. We'll always get behind the team and we'll rightly applaud them when they win, but why should we be clapping if they lose? The baseball fans might do that for Hanshin Tigers, but that's not the kind of standard we want to follow. It really annoys me that certain people still think this is normal. I believe our way works, though. Gamba did have an advantage in that people could come to Banpaku before the other local football teams existed, but it's more than that — people tend to go for the atmospheres they prefer. Everyone likes us, and that's why Michel and the rest of us have been able to lead proceedings on the *curva*. That's why you're here as well, right?"

The idea, in particular, that paying spectators in Japan should feel obliged to salute the performance, regardless of its quality, appeared genuinely to grate with the one-time pasta waiter and hinted at a deeper-lying issue. Somewhere south of Nagoya, about four hours into the journey but still almost 300 miles from our destination, the atmosphere on the coach had grown hazier and contemplative. Bloodshot eyes and skin alike beginning to clash with his red Hawaiian shirt, Massimo swivelled around on the seat in front of me and seized the opportunity to get a desperate — if slightly slurred — admission off his chest.

"I *hate* Japan," he said in determined English, before switching gradually back to his native tongue. "The so-called country of *wa*. What do you call *wa*?"

"Harmony."

"Harmony! Right. Well, I hate my boss too. He's a fucking idiot. We don't have any freedom. We work hard all week, and then we suddenly get told to come

in at the weekend. They expect us to do overtime or extra shifts, and they don't even let us know our shifts until the last minute. I really want to travel, but we get hardly any paid holiday and then they get funny if you want to use it in successive days — even just a couple. It's just so frustrating here. They never cut us any slack. And, of course, you're supposed to respect seniority in Japan so you can't ever get angry with your boss when he's refused you one of your entitled days off, either. Even if he's stupid or unreasonable, I can't shout at him when I'm upset, because I'd be the rude one and I'd get fired.

"This stress gets to you, you know? So Gamba is the one outlet I have. Here, I can let myself go. I can have a few drinks and a laugh. I can shout for 90 minutes, tell the players what I think if they're rubbish, or call the referee a wanker if I want to. Japanese society is *tatemae* — saying and doing things for appearances' sake — but this is the one place I can be open with my *honne* — what I really want to say — instead."

Perhaps 'unrepressed' was not the right word after all, then — or, at least, the circumstances beneath the ultra surface were rather more complex. The Black and Blue guys, quietly nodding at Massimo's diatribe, may have considered their fire and freedom as symbolic of Osakan identity, but it had undoubtedly been fuelled by the oppression they felt within Japanese society. The ability of this small group of people to express themselves on the terraces set them apart from the more regimented or family-oriented majority, but the difference was also a similarity: their Saturday football was becoming the same social opiate as has been the case for working-class, hardcore fans in Europe and Latin America. How, I sleepily wondered to nobody in particular, could the inevitable perpetuity of similar stresses be affecting the rest of the nation?

Evidently reluctant to leave things on such a serious tone, meanwhile, Massimo decided to wish all of his friends a good night in person by stripping to his leopard skin-print thong and clambering through the bus with feet balanced on the headrests either side of the aisle.

I had gone into that longest of Saturdays in Kashima — the return journey was another all-nighter starting a few hours after the final whistle — feeling like an invited outsider but was quickly led to snap out of it. Michel gently mocked my wariness of intruding upon their breakfast ritual of surprisingly tasty offal washed down with a rather-too-early can of Asahi Super Dry and made sure I was on hand thereafter to help decorate the away end with flags and banners before the general public were admitted three hours before kickoff — a process that needs to be repeated even for home matches since J. League clubs tend not to own their stadiums. Given their lack of time off work, I could only admire the commitment of those who did this every week, even if I did fear somewhat for their wives and children.

Having shared their pain at having an unlikely victory snatched away by a last-gasp leveller from Toru Araiba — the Kashima right-back who had left Gamba over the winter because he "wanted to win things" and earned his

own big *vaffanculo* banner for doing so — I proudly donned my new Black and Blue scarf for further road trips to Okayama, Nagoya and Kobe as well as every home match before the end of my university placement in September. An away derby with Cerezo in mid-June was a memorable celebration of victory and *Schadenfreude*; though really, any team that insists on playing in pink and accepts sponsorship from a major brand of processed pork products thoroughly deserves to be greeted with a drift of cut-out pigs impaled on pitchforks anyway. And I'll confess my guilty pleasure, having spent secondary school as more of a football geek than someone who was actually good at playing football, at finally being one of the cool gang.

One night, in a bar near my dormitory — from which I could see the Banpaku floodlights if I peered around the window a little — Michel suddenly dared me to join him on the beer crates as 'call leader' for my final fixture before returning to complete my studies in the UK. The main man ended up serving a two-match ban for getting a little too lippy with a security guard at Vissel Kobe, but remained true to his word by ensuring that I would stand alongside his regular partner, Aki, instead. To face and instigate the songs of two thousand people on the grass bank was a terrific buzz, fuelled further by a ceaseless stream of alcoholic farewell gifts that made preparing for my flight the following morning somewhat arduous, but in hindsight I had underestimated the challenge. Choosing from a repertoire of maybe 40 chants was like trying to remember all 92 English league teams in 10 minutes — you might know them all, but the same four or five keep popping into your head. I felt an uncomfortable sense of responsibility for Gamba's dismal 3-1 defeat to Tokyo Verdy.

Nevertheless, the unique experience — and real honour— cemented my intention to return to this warm-hearted and vibrant metropolis after graduation. Throughout the development of our friendships, there had naturally been a constant desire to learn on my part, while for Michel and the others, the rare opportunity to engage with a foreigner from a traditional football country undoubtedly worked in my favour too — even if most of my frontline experience in England had been at Taunton Town. Perhaps, then, this was a perfect example of how a *soto* status can actually prove to be a source of interest and a paradoxical benefit on the road to becoming *uchi*. Alternatively, in terms of football being the global language that the cliché might have us believe, I had already been more *uchi* than I had realised all along.

For a while, I entertained the thought that *uchi-soto* was less relevant in Osaka, or at least among the Black and Blue ultras, because of their rejection of Japan in favour of local identity. But the thought process that later led me to conclude otherwise stemmed back to an initially unremarkable 4-0 victory over Shimizu S-Pulse in April 2004. Despite an attendance of only just over 8,000, the queue for the monorail platform at full-time stretched back more than half an hour because of the crowds of people who had been enjoying the *sakura* cherry blossoms in the Expo '70 memorial park next door. These pink flowers are among the most classic examples of Japanese cultural iconography and 'full bloom' predictions dominate the weather forecasts as they make their way northwards from Okinawa to Hokkaido. Glorified picnics or piss-ups they may be, but everyone from elderly couples to skin-headed football supporters will eagerly partake of prolonged sessions of *hanami* — literally, 'viewing the flowers'.

This enjoyment of the cherry blossoms forms part of Japan's deeply-rooted fascination with nature and, in a broad sense, with the seasons. The flowers provide a focal point for celebrating the colours of the dawning spring, which is then mirrored by a similar appreciation of deep autumnal tones in the leaves, or *kōyō*, come November. But while such seasonal awareness lends itself to stirring themes of beauty and impermanence in art or literature, as well as a host of cultural festivals and other annual traditions that retain their significance today, it can sometimes reach the point of overemphasis. As a Westerner, I have been asked by countless Japanese football fans, students, and even the chancellor of a university how I got on adapting to their 'unique' collection of four, wholly distinct seasons. A hint, in reply, that it may not actually be all that different to the UK is frequently met with bamboozlement; soon evolving into the assumption that British humour is odd indeed.

The 'distinct' part of the myth, however, is promulgated to the point where, in effect, it may as well be a reality. Public transport, schools, and other communal spaces are artificially (and powerfully) cooled or heated according to a calendar, which is rigidly enforced regardless of what it may actually say on the thermometer. Similar trends apply to clothing, whether by prescription — such as the widespread 'cool biz' office style for the hot summers — or free will. One lunchtime on campus, I was the subject of exasperated laughter from two Japanese friends in winter coats for wearing short sleeves in late February; it was an unseasonable 22°C outside.

Wide-scale generalisation, and the unquestioning acceptance thereof, are by nature terrifically effective tools for the perpetuation of half-truths and stereotypes. In Japan, such tendencies often appear particularly pronounced — even enjoyed — and while acknowledging the risk of hypocrisy in such a statement, this is a phenomenon to which many expats soon develop a sensitivity since the distinct identity of Japan is commonly the central theme. Comparisons with the rest of the world can suddenly become most sweeping. Having grown up in rural Somerset, I am especially partial to an unfathomably oft-repeated myth that states that Japanese roads are narrow, but roads in other countries are wide. Even when the contrasting example is not quite stretched to cover the entire planet, I was once privy to a simple lovers' tiff that was amusingly extrapolated to hypothesise fundamental incompatibility with the entire nation of Norway.

The basic pretext here, of course, was that both parties were representatives of their respective national identities and that Japan in particular should be so clearly distinct as to render everything else 'foreign' – a standpoint prominently supported by the school of *Nihonjinron*. Literally meaning 'theories/discussions about the Japanese', *Nihonjinron* basically asserts that the uniqueness of the Japanese culture and mindset stems from the characteristics of a distinct,

homogenous race with its own separate history. This isolation, it professes, therefore accounts for everything from thought patterns being shaped by the native grammar and vocabulary, to behavioural influences that stem from that most classic peculiarity, the four seasons. Critics both overseas and domestically, however, reject the more extreme elements of *Nihonjinron* theory as nationalistic nonsense.

It is, of course, often hard to determine the point at which nature stops and nurture takes over. Gøran Vaage, a post-doctorate fellow of sociolinguistics at Osaka University, explains how Japan's apparent desire for categorised generalisation operates on a popular level. "Here, we will often get light-hearted programmes on television that label each of the nation's prefectures according to certain human character traits," he said. "You can discover the blood type of your favourite celebrity or footballer just by looking them up on Wikipedia, such is the obsession with its significance. Of course, this may be similar to a more worldwide fascination with zodiac signs, but the situation in Japan is exacerbated by a lesser preoccupation with cold logics and absolute truth."

Inevitably, Vaage's latter point is closely related to a desire for harmony and if the givens with which we are presented — especially by our superiors — are less likely to be questioned, it is easy to see how their significance within cultural conditioning will grow, even excessively, over time. The end result, perhaps, is a Chinese whispers effect that alters the angle from which many Japanese may approach 'differences' and characteristics that may indeed be distinct and beautiful — which is clearly far removed from (and quite preferable to) lazy jingoism.

Either way, this idea of harmony promoting such mass conscience takes us back to the hierarchical nature of Japanese culture and to the 'groups' that tend to come with it. Harmony, loyalty, and *jōge kankei* ('relationships of above and below') come in all manner of groups, from sports clubs to society in general, but while such qualities may lead people to the notion of groups, one might just as easily claim that the idea of grouping results in the development of these qualities. Do the Japanese like to group, or is it just that they like to be grouped? Does the implication of group culture by the whole idea of homogeneity within *Nihonjinron* itself, for that matter, confirm that this is all nothing more than cyclical abstraction and thus everyone else can actually have four seasons too? Throw in the intrinsically coexistent concepts of *uchi* and *soto*, and it turns out that this whole group thing is actually very complicated indeed.

The vertically structured relationships and inherent suppression of individuality within the supposed ideals of groupism represent, essentially, the specific elements of Japanese society that my friends in Black and Blue detested. Their Saturdays at the football, however, allowed them to rebel against the Japanese norm — the anger and helplessness they felt at surrendering their freedom to the whim of their employers — through their own eccentricity and appreciation of a sport that was theirs before it was Japan's. It was only ironic that what had worked out as the most natural way to go about

doing this was to form a group of like-minded people with similar traits.

The Gamba ultras may not have been as regimented as the Kobe fans or as orderly as those at Cerezo, but they still acted together and, with Michel and other figureheads clearly present, there was still a semblance of hierarchy. While Black and Blue were indisputably correct in asserting their greater capability and suitability for the central role in whipping up the atmosphere behind the goal, the resultant pecking order embodies a perfect *uchi-soto* duality with the members of the less rowdy Gambino group and indeed the other, non-affiliated supporters. Put this way: it was a brilliantly Japanese way of being un-Japanese.

However complex the deeper reality may be, the underlying concept of an ultras-inspired hardcore grounded in social discontent and, more obviously, their superficially non-Japanese — even anti-Japanese — manifestation inevitably leaves us with an elephant in the room. Much like the streets and bars that surround them, J. League stadiums are extremely safe by global standards but the Gamba Osaka fans' alternative approach has earned them a certain notoriety both locally and nationwide. An unwaveringly 'Italian' philosophy dictated that the guys in Black and Blue cared little for their public perception but it has frequently brought them into conflict with the club itself. Back in 2004, Dai-chan saw this as the epitome of all that was wrong with the country.

"Most of the people working in the Gamba offices don't know

anything about football — they're just businessmen from Panasonic [of which Gamba is effectively still a subsidiary] moved sideways at the whim of the company," he said. "They look at us and we're obviously not like them, you know? They don't afford us much respect and they'll happily ban people if they can find an excuse. We might even have a positive impact on crowd numbers and on the team, but to the management, it's as if we're just a hassle."

In eight years and almost 200 matches since, I have never personally witnessed anything that could be classed under the 'hooliganism' label which, regrettably, many Japanese still associate with English football. However, it was not until some time afterwards that I learned that 25 October 2003 had represented a landmark occasion for the *Curva Nord*. The straw that broke the camel's back for Michel and his faction to resign en masse from Gambino four years previously was the unilateral expulsion of two members following a skirmish with some Shimizu S-Pulse supporters. But the split only made things worse and took a quite literal form in spring 2000 when a fight broke out between rival Gamba fans over the placement of banners for a home game with JEF United Ichihara. Thereafter, ropes and security guards were used to divide the *curva* into two — Gambino on the left, Black and Blue and Brigate Neroazzurre on the right — with each side singing different songs simultaneously. This patently self-defeating status quo persisted until an uneasy truce was announced about an hour before I stepped foot inside Banpaku for the first time.

That said, despite the reunification and the relative harmony that subsequently

ensued, a difficult process of evolution has been forced upon Osaka's hardcore supporters — and their sometimes controversial presence and status — as the second decade of Japanese football's professional era has progressed. Akira Nishino, the manager booed so mercilessly as Gamba limped to a sadly typical tenth place finish overall in 2003, suddenly instilled a successful version of Kevin Keegan-style attacking football that resulted in unlikely title glory in the final minute of the 2005 campaign. The grass banks were concreted over that winter with proper terracing, which has been sold out ever since as regular silverware followed. Both team and fans attracted a higher profile. Although our membership grew also, the prominently central Black and Blue now represented a smaller minority within the overall whole.

Success brought intensified rivalry both on and off the pitch — none more so than with the 2007 Asian champions Urawa Reds. In May 2008, a small group of teenagers affiliated to the main ultras under the subsidiary banner 'B.B. sez. Tokyo' had the bright idea of chucking water balloons at Reds fans adjacent to the away end at Saitama Stadium. With tensions further inflamed by a confrontation between the two sets of players at full-time, the Urawa hardcore made their way around the ground to charge the Gamba supporters. Several hundred others barricaded the exits to trap the travelling contingent inside for over three hours.

Watching on television — by chance, I had stayed in Osaka to catch the FA Cup final between Portsmouth and Cardiff City — I was disappointed to see several of my friends in Black and Blue shoving their counterparts back from the opposite side of a flimsy plastic 'segregation' fence. Mere handbags by European standards, perhaps, but the incident nevertheless went down as one of the ugliest and most infamous in Japanese football history. It also presented an unwelcome early problem for Kikuo Kanamori, the Gamba president who had been appointed less than two months earlier to take the newly trophy-laden club's off-pitch development to a higher level. In March 2012, he kindly invited me into his office to reflect upon the whole affair.

"[After the Urawa incident] I received a great many e-mails, letters, and telephone calls," he said. "People were telling me that their children were too frightened to come to the stadium anymore. One female supporter asked me, 'Why do you let them get away with behaviour like that?' I agreed with their views completely, and so we took rapid and severe measures. Those who had threatened the safety and security of the stadium environment were immediately handed life bans and stricter policing was implemented to ensure that these people would never be able to enter again. We were faster than the opposing club on this occasion to take such measures, and I actually got a number of messages from supporters of the other club praising us for our excellent work."

The B.B. sez. Tokyo group were barred completely, while after a hurried succession of emergency meetings both with and without the club, it was agreed that Black and Blue should voluntarily disband. For the rest of the league season, we took a more reserved position towards the back of the stand, leaving the leadership duties to a reluctant but cooperative Brigate Neroazzurre. Shamed into silence, several of our senior members were nonetheless unhappy with the club and Kanamori for their readiness to take credit and quickly produced interim *Non Mollare Mai* ('never give up') T-shirts with a covert, secondary message in Arabic that supposedly translated as, "The president wears a wig."

For the latter, victorious stages of the Asian Champions League and the subsequent Club World Cup, however, Michel was back at the front and the surviving Black and Blue members formed a 'new' group called 'Sledgehamor Bros' — Dai-chan insisted upon a somewhat anachronistic compound with the Old English *hamor* — in early 2009. I put it to Kanamori that his sanctions might as such be seen as a temporary means of letting the ultimately short-lived public outcry blow over.

"No, not at all," he insisted. "The very essence of that group was altered — they were only allowed to start taking part again once they changed their way of thinking. I told them that it was a matter of whether or not they could serve as leaders for the chants and songs in a manner that allowed everyone in the entire stadium to enjoy themselves. They had to understand that it was not just about them having fun; they had to understand they were leaders. We made those in charge of the group aware of their responsibility.

"In Japanese, we often use the word *hijōshiki* [literally 'something you don't see every day; something extraordinary'], and this is what they were looking for in their support for the team. I told them that wanting something different is fine, but we will not accept any behaviour that threatens the safety and security of others... These people think that it's them who have built this club. They don't believe it's actually a club for everyone."

Certainly, the homecoming of the rebranded Sledgehamor Bros to the front of the terraces was only really the beginning of a fractious period of rebuilding, behind the scenes, on the path to rediscovering their essence as ultras for Osaka. The aftermath of the Saitama incident fostered a siege mentality among the senior members in particular, whose default guideline — "What would the Italians do?" — only grew more embedded as a result. When Gamba suffered a club record run of six successive home defeats in summer 2009, Michel and Dai-chan instigated a *curva*-wide protest for two hours after the final whistle which culminated in further heated discussions with the president until well beyond midnight. Kanamori suggests that his corporate experience in dealing with labour unions helped him to diffuse the situation but the supporters' paranoia only intensified the following March when, five days before a long-awaited first visit to Cerezo since their 2006 relegation, we were banned from using our supposedly 'incendiary' derby songs and the word *buta* ('pigs') in particular.

A bit of self-policing was necessary in order to stave off the threat of future punishments but it has taken time to find the right balance. As recently as July 2011, I received a bollocking from Michel for not being seen to help tidy away the banners — a 10-man job performed by 40 — and then from Dai-chan for not having

followed 'due procedure' in inviting non-members (who were quickly expelled) to the empty back row of the Sledgehamor Bros section one weeknight. Previously, friends were welcomed; there never used to be a procedure to begin with.

I questioned whether this new-found expression of rules and authority didn't represent retrogression toward some of the negative aspects of Japan's culture that were formerly seen as targets for rebellion. Now that most original Gamba ultras were into their forties, perhaps it was inevitable that their non-conformist spirit be dulled by the infusion of assumed seniority. But was the hostility to outsiders really necessary? Without an equivalent political agenda, did we really know *why* we were still mimicking this idealised impression of what goes on in Italy? More worryingly, the older members now hold hierarchical influence over many more underlings who almost certainly do not — a root cause, surely, of those water balloons back at Saitama.

Happily, Dai-chan's olive branch soon reassured me that nothing, including his own authority, must be considered unchallengeable. "You shouldn't expect any special treatment, Ben, but that's because you're not a special guest," he said. "You're one of us and your opinions are as important as anyone else's. Thanks for speaking up — keep them coming."

Without doubt, the *curva* has steadily grown into a more united and uniformly atmospheric place to be over the past year or so, following a couple of false starts in the previous two seasons. A supporters' alliance has been formed between representatives of Sledgehamor Bros, Gambino and Brigate Neroazzurre calmly to discuss issues pertaining to the support as a whole and to determine a general, overall direction which can then be presented in constructive talks and negotiations with the club. Shortly before kickoff at home matches, Michel now makes a point of encouraging the main and back stands to get involved too by pitting them, and their respective halves of the *curva*, against each other for a light-hearted volume contest. Even the use of Italian is being gradually phased out, with sweeping changes unveiled at the start of both 2011 and 2012 to replace lyrics like *forza* and *facci un gol* with properly pride-inducing Osaka dialect. (In fact, Dai-chan even hired a recording studio to put his surprisingly impressive voice to the updated words for a new supporters' website, which is open to anyone.)

Even Kanamori is delighted that the positive dialogue eventually established between management and supporters has brought them to an understanding. "I think they [Sledgehamor Bros] have already become a positive influence," he said. "Thanks to the fans behind the goal, around 60% or 70% of the entire stadium are now clapping together, singing together and excited about supporting the team. I think that the support as a whole has become very impressive indeed. In my work, I meet with fans all over the place. And I have met several people who have told me, 'I stopped going to support Gamba behind the goal because I didn't like the atmosphere, but I have started going again now.'"

The only remaining source of real contention, as both parties are quick to acknowledge, is that we are still not allowed to refer to Cerezo as 'pigs', be it verbally or pictorially. Kanamori rejects my suggestion that it's only a bit of banter — and actually pretty tame at that — saying, "The British have a keen sense of humour. People get the joke. But Japan is a nation of samurai and jokes like that aren't acceptable here. As a people, the Japanese are highly reserved and, essentially, we are not taught things like jokes and humour. It is not part of our culture."

My friends are unanimous in their response — this is, and always has been, the whole point. Japan may be one thing, but Osaka is another. Jokes and humour are so much a part of the *local* culture that, even if you must bracket this city with the rest of the country, the Osaka accent and dialect that were routinely mocked by those from the capital a generation or so ago are now seen as funny in a highly desirable sense because all the good comedians on television are from round here. It is only sad, say Dai-chan and company, if the rest of Japan is unable to join in; and, as nobody is slow to point out, the Gamba president does not actually hail from Osaka. At our annual meeting ahead of the 2012 season, the consensus is that we should be ourselves but pick our battles and for the first time, the previously tacit 'Sledgehamor Bros philosophy' was actually formalised in writing:

- Sledgehamor Bros emphasises camaraderie, and acts together as a united team no matter what;

- Members shall always keep Sledgehamor Bros in mind and

maintain a constant awareness of its activity, which should be considered as part of all members' lifestyles;

- The basis for Sledgehamor Bros activity is 'Osakan identity';

- 'Osakan identity' refers to freedom and humour, great vibrancy and bustle, flamboyance and passion, a tough bad-boy image, etc;

- Sledgehamor Bros rejects stubbornly Japanese values and ways of thinking that are only accepted in Japan. The model for Sledgehamor Bros activity is our own interpretation of world football culture, and Italian ultra culture in particular;

- In the stadium, Sledgehamor Bros members are released from the self-restraint of our normal daily lives; to assert our own individuality and freely express our raw human emotions.

The rest of the A3 sheet typed up by Michel and Dai-chan outlines details of a new membership system — which is semi-inclusive, but only to those who first demonstrate their worth and are then willing to pay the nominal annual fees — as well as various rules, stances, and concepts defined by the core philosophy. These range from the belief that Gamba Osaka itself should be considered as no more than a mere operating company for a team that it has failed to establish as a local icon, to a rule that no women be allowed within the central Sledgehamor Bros area bar the two recognised female members, Chika and Mako (whose roles, *plus ça change*, are largely administrative). Eight years older but proudly little the wiser, and still rather fond of public nudity, Massimo is keen that the ultras' traditional values be correctly passed on to the latest batch of teenagers and twenty-somethings: "I do stuff that makes people think I'm a right *aho* (idiot), and I'm going to keep on doing that. I want to show the younger lot that it's actually OK to do what you want."

As we prepared to leave the municipal hall that served as venue for the meeting, I expressed my appreciation to Dai-chan for at least having stressed that we should not be looking to copy the Serie A fans directly. He gazed over the recent intake, then down at his sheet of paper, before laughing awkwardly. "Yeah…" he said, "but unfortunately this *is* still Japan. You've got to have guidelines. You've got to have models. And you've got to have rules. Otherwise they just won't get it." Ⓑ

Sing when you're Winning

How the need to appear successful turns fans in Singapore from the S.League to the Premier League

By Ian Griffiths

To the casual observer, with average attendances just about up on last season, a new television deal in the bag and plenty of noteworthy action on the pitch, all would appear to be going swimmingly for Singapore's S.League. Indeed, add all that to the Football Association of Singapore's (FAS) grand S.League Version 2.0 plan, designed, primarily, to increase the league's wow factor, and you could be forgiven for thinking that those behind the S.League were, free from concern, ready to push on and scale even greater heights. Everything, so it would seem, is rosy in the FAS's garden.

It would be an easy mistake to make.

While the current situation is — on the surface at least — brighter than usual and the valiant effort to improve en route to a better future both admirable and necessary, strip away the corporate hyperbole and the S.League's long-term future still appears to be dominated by questions rather than answers.

When the S.League (or to give it its full name, the Great Eastern-YEO's S.League) first appeared in 1996 — thanks to a dispute between the FAS and their Malaysian counterparts which had seen the league and cup double-winning Singapore team withdraw from the Malaysia Cup two years earlier — optimism abounded.

Amid razzmatazz galore, Geylang United snaffled the first league title, leading to a general consensus that the country's new S.League — modelled on Japan's J.League and heavily financed by the Singapore government — was set to be a rip-roaring success. That initial feel-good factor was not to last.

Instead of the steady upward trend planned by the FAS, there followed a wearisome succession of peaks and troughs. Initiatives designed to stimulate football in Singapore began to appear on a regular basis as officials thought they could solve the country's footballing woes by, for the most part, making grandiose announcements on which they couldn't deliver.

At a national level, the 'Goal 2010' project aimed at ensuring Singapore's place at the Fifa World Cup finals in South Africa came and went without success, while the decision to hand Singaporean passports to players born oversees brought short-term success, yet seemed to ignore the fact that the imported professionals were forcing young local talent to the periphery.

Domestically, the introduction of laughably poor non-Singaporean teams such as Sinchi FC from China and Sporting Afrique, based in Singapore but made up solely of players of African descent, saw the S.League lurch from one public relations disaster to another. In an instant, mediocrity ruled the day as the S.League floundered, seemingly incapable of attracting the masses it needed to survive.

Granted, there have been some triumphs along the way. Three regional titles for the national team, the founding of a national football academy as well as the current participation of Singapore's Under-23 side, the Young Lions, in the S.League are signs that at times the right moves were being made, that there is some hope.

Nevertheless, for that modicum of hope to be turned into something that can endure, the FAS needs to understand that the problems blighting its key product cannot be solved merely with the announcement of a Version 2.0 which, on the whole, flattered to deceive.

This shiny vision — shepherded in last January by the S.League's new CEO, Lim Chin, a former colonel in the armed forces — promised, among other things, the arrival of quality foreign talent with box office appeal who would then operate outside the current S$10,000 per month salary cap. Despite names such as Robbie Fowler and Laurent Robert being bandied about, fading stars who would nevertheless still have appealed to the Singapore audience, the first big name is yet to arrive at Changi Airport.

Lim's attempts to take the S.League and its current 13 teams onwards and upwards may yet become a reality but it

is difficult not to think that both he and the FAS have failed to recognise (or chosen to ignore) the biggest issue damaging the S.League — Singapore's cultural reluctance to support its elite division.

Since gaining independence from Malaysia in 1965, Singapore has expanded, enjoying rapid economic growth and becoming a model for similarly small countries succeeding against the odds. Primarily due to the government's insistence that hard work and an individual's determination to rise to the top will always bring results, the stellar transformation has given the overwhelming majority of the nation's citizens jobs and housing. There is a general sense of well-being and shameless self-promotion that many are reluctant to forego, and most want more of.

In the Chinese dialect of Hokkien this need to be the best, this need to impress and not only keep up with the Joneses but beat them, is known as *kiasu* — literally "the fear of losing". It now manifests itself on a daily basis.

From outrageously selfish driving and people being barged out of the way in the mad rush for seats on a train to the '5 Cs of Singapore' concept (where heaps of cash, credit cards, condominiums, cars and memberships at some expensive country club are deemed as must-haves to impress others), the dread of coming last and the overriding need to get on in life no matter what have become omnipresent through huge swathes of the island republic's population.

Of course, a desire to become better and have more in life is not a uniquely Singaporean notion. However, what makes its case so noteworthy is the extent to which the *kiasu* approach now impacts on life here; a relentless tide which has seen the self become far more important than the community and, consequently, left the S.League reeling.

Among those non-S.League believers I have spoken to, the general consensus is that the league is starved of quality and lacks the pulling power of either the Premier League or Spain's Primera Division. Of course it does, but that is of particular concern in a land obsessed with striving to be associated with the best.

Despite the FAS trying to convince Singapore that the opposite is true, S.League fixtures on non-Premier League nights are routinely ignored, while at the weekend the chance to watch Home United take on Geylang United is passed up in favour of watching the action from Old Trafford or the Camp Nou, perhaps even at the Manchester United café at Boat Quay, one of Singapore's most popular watering holes.

After all, to be in the company of Europe's elite is a far more desirable state of affairs for someone who has, in their own mind at least, the highest of standards to maintain both at home and among friends. It is in effect, a badge of honour, an indication that the S.League naysayer backs a team synonymous with winning and is therefore something of a hot shot himself.

Pledging allegiance to one of football's giants obviously happens elsewhere in the world, but what is striking is the general ease with which Singaporeans align themselves to a side several thousands of miles away and yet blatantly ignore one

that may be just up the road. There are millions of Premier League supporters in Malaysia and yet attendances for local league games are high.

Then again, when you consider that from an early age Malaysians learn to love the state they live in with a passion, it is only natural that tribalism rules. These well-defined boundaries give rise to the rivalries we see as a matter of routine in Europe or South America, partisan leanings which are virtually non-existent in Singapore where, given the country's size, it is almost impossible to generate intense inter-community rivalry.

Coupled with the Malaysian passion for live football — something Singaporeans tend to look down on, wrongly comparing it to the rarefied Premier League atmospheres — it makes sense that the Malaysia Super League champions Kelantan regularly jostle for newspaper column inches alongside Liverpool.

As well as the attraction of the Premier League, the S.League has also suffered on a purely practical level, thanks to the infamously long hours Singaporeans work and the reluctance of parents to let their children become professional footballers.

The first of those issues is no particular secret. Regular surveys confirm that Singapore's citizens work more than most (46.2 hours per week according to 2010 statistics), driven as they are to go above and beyond to achieve what they want in life. With the average working day being a minimum nine-hour slog and S.League games kicking off at 7.45pm, many people have neither the time nor the inclination to eat — and eating is an important part of Singaporean culture —

and then watch the S.League at the end of a busy day.

On top of that, and with an already ridiculously small talent pool, the S.League is robbed of potential new recruits because of parental beliefs that more is to be gained through study, which in turn leads to better jobs and a better salary, than training on a football pitch. In a country which has no state pension and therefore an obligation for children to look after elderly parents, this is particularly salient.

As if that weren't bad enough for the S.League, Singapore once again has a side playing in the Malaysia Super League, LionsXII, 28 years after the last team played there. Cue taxi drivers talking about the good old days, times of yore when Singapore, driven on by legends such as Fandi Ahmad, Lim Tong Hai and David Lee battled with Malaysian states, stirring up national fervour on the way.

With jingoism coursing through their veins again, the average Singapore football fan is now far more likely to watch the likes of Shahril Ishak strut his stuff against Malaysian powerhouses Selangor or Terengganu, than scream in delight as Singapore Armed Forces ace Fazrul Nawaz bedazzles the Tanjong Pagar United defence. LionsXII has been a body blow to the S.League.

But amid the gloom, there are rays of light. Among the Premier League throngs, there are sets of fans such as the Hougang United Ultras — known to friends and family as the Hougang Hools — who proudly proclaim at every game that, "You can stick the Premier League up your arse." It's welcome pride for an area in a country where security guards often ask rowdy fans at international matches to cheer more quietly and communal identity has all but disappeared.

Then there is the recently launched 'Support Our S.League' campaign and the hundreds of people who live, eat, sleep and drink the S.League. They are a committed band of believers, from fans and school kids to press officers and kit men, who do their best to stir passions and arouse interest amid widespread disinterest.

Without these few, the S.League's battle would have been lost long ago. If those hardy souls are to see the S.League treated with the respect it deserves by the rest of the nation, the FAS must realise that its attempts to solve the issues it faces are more complicated than they appear. Changing policies is one thing; changing mindsets is another. Ⓑ

97

Photo Essay

"Devotion is the key"

The Hard Core

Images of the fans who followed Zenit St Petersburg as they won the Russian championship in 2010

By Misha Domozhilov

In 2010, Zenit St Petersburg became Russian champions for the second time, their Ultra group celebrated its 30th anniversary and Russia was named as host of the 2018 World Cup. A momentous year ended with Ultras taking to the streets to protest against the government of Vladimir Putin.

In total, around 5000 Zenit fans consider themselves Ultras. Some are individuals, some are part of organised groups, some make banners, some concern themselves with singing, some are devoted to arranging choreography, some travel by train, some travel by bus, some drink heavily, some espouse far-right ideology. For all, devotion is the key: those who travel to the most away games are the most respected.

Ultras often graffiti walls, marking their territory and challenging or taunting rivals. Tattoos are common, a way for fans to prove their identification with the cause. On the terrace, the rule is that the team must be supported constantly, whatever is happening on the pitch. Drunkenness during the game is discouraged, chatting or whistling outlawed as chant-leaders orchestrate the songs and displays of flares and banners. The banners have a special status: rival groups will try to steal banners, bringing themselves glory and their opponents disgrace.

The title was won on 14 November. With Zenit 1-0 up at home to Rostov, news came through that CSKA had only drawn at Spartak Nalchik, meaning a win would secure the title. As Zenit scored a further four goals in the second half, fans, many of them topless despite the cold, began breaking down barriers for a triumphant pitch invasion in which the 'lucky' goal nets were stolen as souvenirs. Luciano Spalletti, Zenit's Italian coach, joined the Ultras celebrating on the pitch.

THE FOOTBALL RAMBLE

Football's most entertaining show—since 2007

Available every week on iTunes and thefootballramble.com

@footballramble

109

Fall

"...the police, the ambulance people,
I threatened them with a huge
kitchen knife."

The Centre-back and the Kitchen Knife

Claus Lundekvam opens up on his battle against the addiction that overwhelmed him after retirement

By Lars Sivertsen

On the face of it, the former Southampton captain Claus Lundekvam is a typical ex-footballer. Having been forced to retire because of injury in 2008, he lives in a house near the sea in his native Norway with his wife Nina, their two children and a dog named Lucky. He works as a regular pundit for TV2, the largest commercial broadcaster in Norway. All is well with Lundekvam. Except the story is slightly more complicated than that. A few years ago, shortly after his retirement, things went very badly wrong. "I would drink two litres of hard liquor and do between five and ten grams of cocaine every day," he recalls. "At that point I'd given up. I accepted that as a human being I was finished." Lundekvam, known to English football fans as a solid if unspectacular defender, became an alcoholic and a drug addict. And now he hopes to serve as a cautionary tale to others.

During the 1990s, Scandinavian players became increasingly popular with English clubs. They had a reputation for being dependable on the pitch and unfussy off it. They adapted well, both to English football and to English culture. Few players personify this stereotype more thoroughly than Lundekvam. Having

moved to England in the autumn of 1996 as an unknown, slightly gangly 23-year-old centre-back, he quickly established himself as a regular in Southampton's defence. Matt Le Tissier described him as being "like Alan Hansen: very comfortable in front of his own goal, less comfortable in front of the opposition's." Gordon Strachan, who managed Lundekvam between 2001 and 2004, went even further in deriding the Norwegian's attacking prowess, suggesting at one point that referees should book Lundekvam for time-wasting when he goes up for corners and that if a corpse were to lie in the penalty area it would get its head to more crosses than Lundekvam did. A career total of three goals at club level would seem to indicate that the Scot had a point. Still, while he was unlikely ever to do anything particularly productive in the opposing box, he was equally unlikely to let you down at the back. And because of that, he ended up making more than 400 appearances for Southampton over the course of 12 seasons, captaining the club for several years and earning himself a testimonial at the end of it all.

"I was extremely determined to perform well," he explains. Leaning back on a sofa at TV2's studio complex in Bergen, Lundekvam speaks with a calmness that constantly threatens to slide into detachment. Listening to him, you instantly understand what Strachan meant when he said, "He was carried off at Leicester and someone asked me if he was unconscious. I didn't have a clue. That's what he's always like." And although his face doesn't give away much, it's impossible not to spot the nostalgia tinged with pride when he talks about his career at Southampton. "The thing I'm most proud of is when I signed a new contract," he says. "Not becoming a professional footballer in the first place, but having proved to myself that I could hold my own in one of the best leagues in Europe, that was the most important thing." And after settling down on the south coast, signing for anyone other than Southampton was never on the cards. "I loved it there," he says. "I didn't know anything about Southampton before I went there, but I grew up by the coast and I loved the sea, so for me it was perfect."

Playing for Southampton between 1996 and 2008, Lundekvam experienced first-hand the revolution English football went through, both on and off the pitch. "There was an enormous change in every way: the way we trained, how everything was set up, the facilities, how everything was sorted out for us," he says. Today there are sports scientists, Prozone analysts, nutritionists and experts of every conceivable kind. In 1996, there weren't. "It was chaotic," he remembers. "I was brought over by Graeme Souness and he used to join in during training. He thought he still had it as a player and he would join in for five-a-sides and it always ended in a punch-up. Every

bloody week." And after five-a-sides and a punch-up with Souness, it's perhaps understandable that Lundekvam and his teammates needed a drink. "It was pretty much every day, after training we would meet up at the local pub," he says. "It was part of the culture, part of being social. I think I benefited from being out with the guys; I was accepted in the group very quickly, quicker than other foreigners. I was part of the gang." Harry Redknapp once bemoaned the difficulties of integrating foreign players into a squad because "they don't even drink." There were no such problems with Lundekvam. "In terms of alcohol, there was a free flow of it," he says. "But I never felt that the alcohol affected my performances. I knew what I had to do to perform." The suggestion that he might have played drunk, as Tony Adams famously did, is instantly brushed off. "I don't really understand how he managed to do that. It shouldn't be possible. I can admit that I came to training with a hangover some times; maybe I still had alcohol in my blood and I was always dreadful."

In spite of the odd hangover in training, Lundekvam was enjoying his football. "The first four seasons we didn't have the best of squads, but we had Le Tissier and we had a fantastic spirit, and that kept us up. There were two or three seasons when we had great escapes. I remember one season we had nine points at Christmas, we were second from bottom and we managed to stay up. It was a fantastic feeling. We then managed to establish ourselves in mid-table for a few seasons and that was a big accomplishment for Southampton as a club. One highlight has to be the FA Cup final against Arsenal; that was a big day. It was incredible. When you've been in

England for a while and you really get the English footballing culture under your skin, when you see how much it matters to the fans, then you understand what the FA Cup really means. So to get to be a part of that, it was huge." As a person, Lundekvam seems every bit as steady and unassuming as he was as a player.

As time went by and English football hurtled into the new millennium, there were notable changes — not just on the training ground and in how everything was set up, but in the culture. "Players increasingly became prima donnas," Lundekvam says. "Especially with the foreigners, less so with the British players as far as I could tell. At least not with the ones who came from the old school, the ones who had been taught that they had to work hard and clean their own boots. I think there's something to that, but it all started to change. I was basically an adopted Englishman towards the end and I would spend a lot of time with James Beattie and Wayne Bridge and guys like that. We went to London to hang out with the Chelsea players and the Arsenal players and that sort of thing. And you could tell with the foreigners, especially the French guys, that they thought they were bigger and better than everyone else. When you're a Premier League player now, you live in a kind of bubble where everything is taken care of for you. You hang out with all kinds of celebrities, movie stars and pop stars and whatever, that's the kind of circles you socialise in as a Premier League player — at least these days it is."

According to Lundekvam, there is a potential problem with the fact that top footballers have now become almost fully integrated into the celebrity and showbiz-scene. "The drinking culture in football has always been there and will always be there," he explains. "You have parties when you can, after games and especially after wins, but that's completely normal and it'll always be like that — I have no problem with it. But in society today there are so many other drugs that are out there, drugs that are very easily available in that circle of people I was talking about. There is an almost free flow of other drugs, especially cocaine. It's available to a much greater extent than before."

For Lundekvam, the problems only really started after he retired. "I was injured for almost a year. I had three operations on my ankle before I realised that it was the end. But I was 35, so I wasn't bitter about it, really. I'd experienced a lot and I even got a testimonial at the end of it." But adapting to life outside of football and, more importantly, outside of the spotlight, proved difficult. "I think I was looking for something to replace the adrenaline rush, the buzz you get, that feeling of really being alive. You get used to performing in front of thousands every week and when that's gone then suddenly there's a huge mental void which becomes almost impossible to fill. At least for me. I just sat at home or did what I wanted to do, go on holiday, whatever. It became a vicious circle for me where there was more and more alcohol and I started trying this and that, and suddenly you're in trouble."

He remembers trying cocaine for the first time. "I was down in Marbella with some friends, that was the first time I tried it. It's a typical place to go for a party and there's even more of a drug culture down there. And when you've tried it once then you have an experience with it that sticks in your head. You can't just try it once and think that you can stop it there, because it sticks with you. A lot of people can handle it, but some of us can't and we develop an addiction."

Things then went very badly wrong very quickly for Lundekvam but he managed to keep up appearances for a while. He was still living in Southampton with his wife and two children and for a period of time he combined life as a family man with his newly developed addiction to drugs. "I would drink a lot of alcohol and do a lot of cocaine and then I'd take 10-15 sleeping pills in the morning to get right again. I kept doing that for a while. I was smart enough to hide myself, I never showed myself outside when I knew I was on a lot of drugs, but both my family and those closest to me could obviously tell." This went on for about six months before his wife took the children and moved back to Norway. "I lived by myself for four months; my partner decided our kids couldn't live with a father who was doing the kind of things I was doing. And at that point I had given up. I accepted that as a human being I was finished. I accepted and acknowledged that I was going to drink and do drugs until it killed me."

His family, his determination not to let his two young daughters see him on drugs, had been the only thing holding him back. With them gone, things really got out of hand. "I just sat at home, because I had contacts and I had the finances to get whatever I wanted, I just had everything delivered to me." Constantly high, drunk or both, Lundekvam took to roaming around in his garden with a huge knife, hunting paparazzi. "With the combination of alcohol and cocaine,

you get an angst and a paranoia that's like nothing else and you think the whole world is watching you. So I unscrewed all the light bulbs in my house and I climbed the trees in the garden and crawled around out there." The light bulbs he unscrewed because he thought they were cameras. One night he spent several hours hiding in a cupboard. "I threatened everyone who came near me, the police, the ambulance people, I threatened them with a huge kitchen knife." At one point Lundekvam was successfully hospitalised, almost had a heart attack at the hospital, slept for twelve hours and went straight back out to have a drink again. "I've always been like that, if I do something I do it 100%," he explains. Unfortunately this also extended to substance abuse. He was arrested twice, first on 26 March 2010 ("on suspicion of being in possession of a controlled drug" according to a spokesman for Hampshire Police) and then on 16 April ("charged with section 39 common assault"), and he was hospitalised twice. Lundekvam eventually decided to end it all. He bought a one-way ticket to Rio de Janeiro.

"I still have the ticket, just to remind me," he says. "That was the plan and it was going to be the end. I contacted the guy I used to organise my travels, told him I wanted a one-way ticket to Rio. I paid for it and everything, but I never made it to the airport. I guess they wouldn't have let me on board anyway, but that was the plan. Because I knew that in Rio I would find the things I wanted, a free flow of cocaine and lots of gorgeous women. That would have been fine by me. It wouldn't have taken long." He had booked his flight during a drug-induced fit of despair in the middle of the night.

By morning he was unconscious, which probably saved his life.

Lundekvam isn't entirely sure how and why things turned. "It just happened one night, I think, when my head and soul gave in completely," he says. "Something told me that I just couldn't do it anymore. I was just so tired, I was so completely empty. I just couldn't take any more of it. And that made me very humble and I became incredibly sad. So I held my hands up and I asked for help. Thankfully I ended up getting the help I needed, because a lot of people tried, I went to the best psychologists, but none of them could help me."

On 17 May 2010 — incidentally Norway's national day— Lundekvam checked into the Sporting Chance Clinic. "I needed help from people who had been in the same situation themselves," he says. "They know what it's like. It's like they speak the same language as you. That's the difference. And of course they're very good therapists, in terms of knowing what's going on inside your head as an addict. So through them I got my life back." While still at the clinic, Lundekvam admitted to his problems in an interview on Norwegian television. He emphasised that the thing that haunted him the most was what he'd put his family through. When he left the clinic they were there waiting for him. His wife briefly moved back to England with the children but Lundekvam didn't want to stay there. "At that point I had so many terrible memories from the last two years in Southampton that I felt I needed a fresh start. So it was either moving to Spain or moving back to Norway. And there were people here in Norway who wanted me to come here, they told TV2 and suggested I could use

my experience from playing in England as a pundit and that sounded interesting to me." Now, two years later, Lundekvam is a highly regarded pundit on TV2's Premier League broadcasts.

When Lundekvam retired from football, he had nothing in particular to do with his time, he had a huge adrenaline rush to replace, he had a lot of money, he was part of a social scene where drugs were rife and for years he had been part of a culture where you pretty much had a drink whenever you could. It's really not all that hard to understand why things turned out the way they did. What is more ominous is the fact that this is the case for a large number of newly retired footballers, every year. "I'm totally convinced that there is a large number of unrecorded cases of this problem — in fact, I know there is," Lundekvam warns. "When you retire, it's a trap that's easy to fall into, because you still want to live up to your reputation as a professional footballer, with the image that goes with it, and that means a lot of drinking and a lot of other things. Retired footballers are a group of people who are especially at risk, I'm convinced of that. Because there's a transition there that's mentally incredibly tough, it's very hard to handle. From being a star and living that kind of lifestyle and then suddenly it's gone."

The issue isn't helped by the hype that surrounds modern football. "It's gone completely beyond the pale, both the financial aspect and in terms of your status — you get everything handed to you on a plate and that does something to you. But when those days are over, there's nothing that's more quickly forgotten than an ex-footballer. So then you're faced with an extremely tough battle. The only advice I can give is that you should get involved with something right away, something that gets you out of bed in the morning."

Following the deaths of Robert Enke and Gary Speed, it should be obvious that footballers are far from the invulnerable demigods they are often treated as and expected to be. "It's incredibly sad, but it's part of reality. And I can see that very clearly because I've been there myself," Lundekvam says. Still, depression and substance abuse remain issues that footballers, past or present, are reluctant to admit to or seek help for. "Especially here in Norway it's a taboo subject and we're very naive in thinking those problems don't exist here. So hopefully I can contribute to changing that by going public with my problems. It's such a big part of society, not just for footballers but for people in every walk of life, that if we have problems with alcohol and other things then we hide it. But of course that makes it very difficult to help anyone."

Lundekvam got the help he needed in time and is now living a more or less normal life. "It's a normal family life now. I feel very privileged, but at the same time life is challenging. Everyday life isn't always easy. You have to learn things all over again, as a sober person. It's an illness that you'll carry for the rest of your life, so you always have to be careful. But as long as I stay sober, I think things will fall into place."

"Isn't it terrible to know that you can't ever go for a pint again?" a co-worker recently asked Lundekvam. He thought for a minute before answering. "Yes, but thinking about what will happen if I do is worse." Ⓑ

My Name is Ally MacLeod and I am a Winner

How Scotland's humiliation at the 1978 World Cup knocked nationalism off course

By Dominic Sandbrook

One evening in May 1978, almost 30,000 people stood on the terraces of Hampden Park in a state of near-hysterical excitement. Festooned with flags, scarves and banners, they had come to wish good luck to their nation's World Cup squad before their flight to Argentina. They cheered as 10 massed pipe bands took to the field; they sang along with Andy Cameron, the comedian whose anthem "Ally's Tartan Army" had proved an unexpected hit. Finally, they roared their adulation as the 22 members of the Scotland squad stepped sheepishly out onto the red carpet, followed by their manager Ally MacLeod, the hero of the hour. Rarely had a British team departed with such high hopes; certainly none had ever had such a spectacular send-off, broadcast live on television. And as the squad's coach carried them south towards Prestwick Airport, thousands of people lined the road. One man, who had just jumped out of the bath, was dripping wet. Others held up children and babies to see the bus, housewives waved tea towels, bridges were draped with flags and banners. At Prestwick, hundreds of people gathered on the beach to wave as the plane lifted into the air, euphoric in the knowledge that they were watching the future world champions.

Whenever footage of the Hampden send-off appears on television today, it is always as the prelude to inevitable disaster. The fate of MacLeod's boys at the 1978 World Cup, where they lost disastrously to Peru, drew haplessly with Iran and crashed out with a pyrrhic 3-2 victory over Holland, has become an object lesson in the hubris of a small country that dared to dream. You have to force yourself to remember that, having knocked out the European champions, Czechoslovakia, in the qualifiers, the Scots were widely seen as dark horses to win the whole thing. Expectation was staggeringly high, yet tickets were in short supply. One fan told the press that he planned to hire a submarine to take him across the Atlantic, while an enterprising travel agent toyed with organising flights from a runway on the Shetlands. Some fans hoped to work their passage on a boat from Spain; "several dozen more", according to the *Times*, had flown to New York and were making their way down to Mexico, "after which their travel plans are, to say the least, vague."

Meanwhile, commercial sponsorship had reached levels unimaginable only 10 years before. To the amazement of the press, British firms paid £5 million to support the squad, with Chrysler at the head of the queue. The Trustee Savings Bank produced a special booklet, "The Flowers of Scotland", while the Valentine greeting-card company paid the squad £25,000 for the rights to sell their official team photograph in newsagents across the country. At Esso garages, drivers could pick up beer glasses engraved with the players' signatures for just 40p each, while other World Cup-themed products included T-shirts, shampoo, aftershave, talcum powder and, slightly bizarrely, a Scottish-themed soap on a rope.

World Cups never take place in a vacuum and Argentina 1978 was no exception. But while much of the international coverage focused on the host nation's military junta, British newspapers had rather more parochial concerns. The Scottish economy, fatally dependent on old-fashioned heavy industry, had been in deep decline for years. But now salvation seemed at hand; thanks to the discovery of North Sea oil, talk of Scottish economic and political independence no longer seemed far-fetched. By the end of 1975, polls put the Scottish National Party ahead of both Labour and the Conservatives for the first time, and in May 1977, a year before MacLeod's men left for Argentina, the SNP made record gains in Scotland's local elections, breaking Labour's control of Edinburgh, Aberdeen and Dundee. Little wonder, then, that many observers thought that success for MacLeod could have seismic political consequences. "With their lips Jim [Callaghan] and Maggie [Thatcher] may be shouting for Scotland," remarked the *Daily Mail*. "But in their political hearts they'll be rooting for those bonny outsiders from Peru and Iran." Indeed, if

the Scots actually won the tournament, thought the *Mail*, then Celtic pride "would be like distilled firewater. Hooched up on that, the nationalists could rampage to victory up there in any general election that followed."

A more experienced manager, conscious that no Scotland side had ever qualified for the later rounds of the World Cup, might have dampened the flames of excitement. Ally MacLeod was not that man. From his very first press conference, when he told reporters that he was "born to be a success", to his first words to his players — "My name is Ally MacLeod and I am a winner" — the former Ayr and Aberdeen boss seemed a Caledonian Brian Clough: cheeky, loquacious and endlessly enthusiastic. The fans loved him, largely because he played to their prejudices. Thus, on the eve of Scotland's warm-up games, he announced that he planned to use England ("a second-class nation") for "target practice".

Then he went even further: "You can mark down 25 June 1978 as the day Scottish football conquers the world. For on that Sunday I'm convinced the finest team this country has ever produced can play in the final of the World Cup in Buenos Aires and win. We have the talent. We have the temperament and the ambition and the courage. All that stands between us and the crown is the right kind of luck. I'm so sure we can do it that I give my permission here and now for the big celebration on the twenty-fifth of June to be made a national holiday: a national Ally-day."
Not even defeat to England could dampen MacLeod's confidence. His players had treated the game purely as a training exercise, he explained, and now

he was off for a few days' rest before the flight to Argentina. He would be using the break, he said, to do some last-minute DIY: "I'm putting in a new corner unit to hold the World Cup."

What followed has gone down in sporting legend, from the dilapidated Scottish team hotel in Alta Gracia, with no water in the swimming pool, no net on the tennis court and plaster peeling from the bedroom ceilings, to the two dead horses on the road to the team's Córdoba training ground. 14 minutes into their game against Peru, Scotland took the lead. But then everything fell apart, Teófilo Cubillas blasted home two superb goals and, before they knew it, the Scots had contrived to lose 3-1. Contrary to myth, the press reaction was initially forgiving. Even the English papers were relatively benign: the *Express*, for example, thought that the Scots had "lost honourably while trying very hard."

But then West Brom's Willie Johnston failed a routine drug test after taking the mild stimulant Reactivan and the boot went in. Now Scotland's march of destiny was beginning to look more like a night at the circus. "The match against Iran," said the *Times*, "clearly becomes the most testing in the history of Scottish international football. They are a team in disgrace and badly need to win to avoid further bad publicity."

Then came the most embarrassing 90 minutes in the history of Scottish sport. As against Peru, MacLeod refused to pick Liverpool's dynamic young midfielder Graeme Souness and, for all his rousing rhetoric, Scotland never got going. Jeered by a pitiful crowd of fewer than 8,000 spectators, MacLeod's players

toiled drearily until just before half-time, when the Iranians decided to help them out by scoring an own-goal of farcical proportions. Surely now the floodgates would open? Not a bit of it: 16 minutes into the second half, after Scotland had sunk back into their torpor, the Iranians scored a deserved equaliser. On the bench, MacLeod sat alone, his head buried in his hands, a picture of misery and helplessness. At the final whistle, he trudged off to a chorus of boos.

To Scottish fans who had spent hundreds of pounds travelling to Argentina, the shame of Córdoba was almost too much to bear. As the players trooped disconsolately towards the tunnel, they had to run a gauntlet of men in tartan tam o'shanters flicking V-signs at them. Later, while their bus was waiting to leave the stadium, they were surrounded by jeering supporters. "MacLeod ought to be ashamed of himself," one man, magnificently turned out in kilt, cape and tam o'shanter, his voice trembling with fury, told the television cameras. "It was an absolute shambles and a disgrace to Scottish football." The next day's papers agreed with him. Scotland might have drawn 1-1, wrote the veteran football correspondent Norman Fox, "but this was an even worse performance than against the Peruvians simply because Iran are such outsiders in the world of football."

"Never," he concluded sadly, "have they been so humiliated."

The next day, Chrysler pulled its adverts involving the Scotland World Cup squad. After all the hype, the headlines — "SCOTCHED!", "ALL THIS WAY FOR SFA", "DEAD END ALLY" — were predictably unforgiving. In Dundee, one record shop slashed the price of "Ally's Tartan Army" singles from 65p to just 1p, urging customers to buy as many records as they wanted and smash them to pieces on the counter with a hammer. Even the Tories got in on the act, with their Shadow Chancellor, Sir Geoffrey Howe, making a laboured comparison between the beleaguered Scottish manager and Britain's Labour Prime Minister: "the manager, Dead End Cally, who carries the can."

For many commentators, the implosion of Scotland's ambitions was a damning indictment of a national culture of self-deluding arrogance. MacLeod had arrived in Argentina "more as a cheerleader than as team manager," remarked the *Times*, yet "his attitude of 'let the opposition worry about us' was typical of a certain school of thinking that has too many followers in Britain." In the *Observer*, Hugh McIlvanney, himself a proud Scot, saw MacLeod's fall from grace as a lesson in the perils of Celtic chauvinism. "The seeds of the small disaster," he wrote, "are to be found in the natures of the people most devastated by it." For as McIlvanney pointed out, "most Scottish supporters gave every indication of being happy to be on the march with Ally's Army... They believed him because they wanted to believe him, because he talked like one of them, indeed could contrive, when utterly sober, to sound as the wildest of them might sound after a night on the liquid hyperbole. In the run-up to the tournament he behaved with no more caution, subtlety or concern for planning than a man getting ready to lead a bayonet charge. The fans echoed his war cries, never bothering to wonder if the other contenders for the world title would be willing to stand still and be stabbed."

And now, in the ruins of humiliation, the Scots were left with "the realisation that something they believed to be a metaphor for their pride has all along been a metaphor for their desperation."

There was, of course, a twist in the tale. On the day McIlvanney's piece was published, Scotland had one last chance to redeem themselves against Holland, who were many people's favourites for the trophy. The Scots needed an implausible three-goal victory to stay in the tournament and what followed is etched into the memories of every Scottish fan, from Archie Gemmill's splendid slalom to the bludgeoned goal by Johnny Rep that consigned MacLeod's men to oblivion. Eventually Scotland's 3-2 victory became famous as a magnificent failure, a kind of sporting Culloden. Yet as the next day's *Scotsman* remarked, their courageous performance only made what had gone before seem "all the more excruciating". Revealingly, the players flew home to a distinctly glacial reception. At Glasgow Airport, some were even jeered by the local baggage handlers. "Even the airport people were baying for blood," recalled the goalkeeper, Alan Rough. "It was like a hanging mob the way they were screaming at us. It was pretty much fever pitch; pretty bad."

After all the expectation, Scottish football's pretensions had been exposed before the world. Even the British chargé d'affaires in Buenos Aires sent a damning report to his Foreign Office superiors, remarking that the Scots had seemed "provincials out of their depth in international waters". As Scottish commentators pointed out when the document was released

30 years later, there was in this more than a little Anglo-Saxon satisfaction. "English sportswriters have sportlessly wallowed in the mud we've slung at the tattered Tartan Army. We've called them posers, big-heads, Ally's Follies, a 'sick joke of a team'. We've put in the boot, trodden on their bowed necks, danced on the graves of their hopes, and drunk their spilt blood like whisky," wrote the *Express*'s famously severe Jean Rook. She blamed the SNP, who had "alienated everybody south of the border she would have liked to put up between England and Scotland."

But the truth was that the SNP's bubble, like MacLeod's, had well and truly burst. Had Scotland contrived to bring home the World Cup, then perhaps the nationalist cause would have gathered even greater momentum. As it was, enthusiasm melted away like snow in the summer sunshine. When the government held a referendum on Scottish devolution the following March, only one in three people voted for it. The Scots had to wait another 17 years for their assembly — by which time their national game was in deep decline. And MacLeod? He had long since resigned, returning to his first love, Ayr United. But he never lost his sense of humour. "I am a very good manager," he said later, "who just happened to have a few disastrous days, once upon a time, in Argentina." Ⓑ

The Lions Sleep Tonight

Ten years after retaining the Cup of Nations, Cameroon failed to qualify. What went wrong?

By Jonathan Wilson

It hadn't been a great final, but then it hadn't been a great month in terms of the football played. Bumpy, small pitches had added to a generally defensive mindset to produce an attritional tournament that had yielded just 47 goals in 31 games. The 32nd game, the final, almost inevitably, finished 0-0.

Two years earlier, in Lagos, Cameroon had beaten Nigeria in the final in a shoot-out. Then, the decisive kick fell to the 19-year-old Pius Ikedia, a slight, short winger. His kick had struck the bar and bounced down, television replays later showed, over the line. He, though, turned instinctively away, believing he had missed. The referee, Mourad Daami of Tunisia, thought he had as well and, as Cameroon celebrated their third title, fans rioted.

The scenes at the semi-final in Mali, when they played the hosts, had hardly been less chaotic. Cameroon's German coach, Winfried Schäfer, yellow mullet gleaming, had wandered onto the pitch before the game with his assistant, Thomas Nkono, probably the greatest goalkeeper African football has ever produced. They stood for a few moments watching pictures of the first semi-final, between Senegal and Nigeria, on the big screen. Without

warning, riot-police grabbed them, slapped them in hand-cuffs and bundled them away down the tunnel. As Nkono struggled, his tracksuit bottoms slid down, bunching around his ankles. The police later claimed they hadn't been able to see the pair's accreditation badges and said they thought they'd been placing muti, black magic charms, on the pitch. It looked, though, like a deliberate attempt to unsettle Cameroon before the game. It didn't work and Cameroon won 3-0.

At the time, Senegal were the coming force in African football. They'd qualified for the World Cup and, with the likes of Pape Bouba Diop, Salif Diao, Khalilou Fadiga and El-Hadji Diouf, they had, as Cameroon did, a muscular side leavened by just enough flair. Physicality won out over technicality in the final, though, and it went to penalties.

Pierre Womé, in a troubling indication of problems to come, missed Cameroon's first kick, but as Amdy Faye and Diouf both failed to score, Rigobert Song was left with the chance to win it. He missed, but when Aliou Cisse missed Senegal's last kick, Cameroon became the first side since Ghana in 1965 to retain the title and joined Ghana and Egypt as the most successful sides in African history with four Cups of Nations.

Ten years on, Cameroon failed even to qualify for the Cup of Nations in Gabon and Equatorial Guinea.

We had, thank goodness, set off early from Takoradi to Kumasi. We'd just turned north at Cape Coast when my phone went. It was the sports editor of the *Sunday Herald*. "I was just wondering," he said after the usual pleasantries, "what you were up today? Are you at a game?"

I replied I'd be at Cameroon v Zambia.

"Aye, we'll take 800 words," he said.

"800?" I asked, a little stunned. Very few league games get more than 600, let alone an obscure Cup of Nations group stage match. "Errr, OK."

"And you haven't got a feature in the locker have you? Something you could maybe rattle out for us?"

"I could knock out something on how Berti Vogts is messing up Nigeria?" I suggested, knowing Berti-bashing was a popular Scottish pastime.

"Great. 1200. Thanks." Again, 1200 words seemed disproportionate, but freelances don't argue.

Two minutes later the phone went again. This time it was the sports editor of *Scotland on Sunday*.

"Which game will you be at today?" he asked.

"Cameroon v Zambia."

"Great. 800 words, thanks." I was recognising a pattern.

"You don't fancy a feature on Berti fucking up Nigeria, do you?"

He did. And commissioned 1200 words. I asked, as diplomatically as possible, what on earth was going on.

"Snow," he said. "There's snow everywhere. The whole fucking programme's cancelled. We've got nothing."

And so the mystery was explained.

Just as I was congratulating myself on four big commissions, though, there was a mighty thump. The engine of the van we were travelling in spluttered and wheezed. Our driver slowed and stopped by the side of the road. Cautiously he started the engine again. It sounded no better. He coaxed us to a garage a mile or two down the road and, as I paced about anxiously in the bright white sunlight, about a dozen local men pored over the open bonnet. At least one of them, thankfully, was a mechanic and we arrived at the stadium in Kumasi an hour or so before kick-off. I remember little of the 2400 words I bashed out before kick-off, but writing two match reports, thankfully, means the game is etched clearly on my mind.

There had been a lot of talk around the 2006 World Cup of the rise of a new Africa. Cameroon had missed out for the first time since 1986 and with Nigeria, after three straight finals appearances, also failing to qualify, four of the five African sides in Germany were debutants (admittedly one of those was Ghana, who had been the first great footballing power in Africa, but they hadn't won the Cup of Nations since 1982). Cameroon had been outplayed by a superb Egypt in their opening game, losing 4-2, while Zambia had been quietly impressive in beating Sudan 3-0. This seemed like a classic meeting of new and old, a gauge of how far the grandees had sunk.

Cameroon won 5-1. So much for the revolution.

Two years later, the sides met again in the group stage in Lubango. On that occasion — the only time Hervé Renard, the Zambia coach, has not worn a white shirt for a finals game and still his only defeat — Cameroon won 3-2. That is why Zambia's success in this year's tournament hurt Cameroon so much: in four years they went from hammering them, to beating them narrowly, to not even qualifying for the tournament in which they became champions. The difference in approach, the difference in philosophy, the difference in outcome is clear.

"In 2008," said Joseph-Antoine Bell, the great former Cameroon goalkeeper and now an eloquent and outspoken television pundit, "it was 5-1, but Zambia played well and gave four goals away and I said, 'Don't just look at the score: look at what happened.' They really did well but gave away four goals. If you'd played this game two or three times, it wouldn't be 5-1. Then, in 2010, Zambia were holding Cameroon really well, playing well, leading 1-0 and then Geremi kept a ball in play and that was how things changed. If we don't watch how games go, we don't see beyond the score. This is the way politicians see football. They just talk about the score and you don't look at what happens."

This, of course, is the argument Juanma Lillo made passionately in Issue One of *The Blizzard*, that the tendency is to look only at the outcome rather than the process, to become what he termed "prophets of the past" by taking the conclusion and working back through the game to find out why it was inevitable that the result fell that way.

And, looking at my match reports from that game in Kumasi, the evidence was there. "Cameroon had offered next to nothing as an attacking threat in the early stages," I wrote then, "and their only shot in the opening quarter was the result of a dreadful error from the Zambia goalkeeper, Kennedy Mweene, but when Geremi was presented with a free-kick opportunity 20 yards out on 28 minutes, he whipped his shot into the top corner with all the devil of old." Thanks to Zambia's rickety offside line, Joseph-Desiré Job and Achille Emana added further goals before half-time, at which Cameroon rather switched off. "Against a side with better finishers than Zambia," I wrote, "they might have sleepwalked into trouble. As it was, Zambia were poor enough defensively to gift Cameroon a further two goals." The fourth was the result of a penalty for a soft handball, the fifth came from a weak backheader. "They were lucky in that we created all the goals for them," said the Zambia coach Patrick Phiri. "All their goals were from mistakes or misunderstandings between the defence and the goalkeeper. I have never seen them play that way in 18 months of working with them. Maybe they were scared of the big names, I don't know."

Zambia were eliminated in the first round, while Cameroon, battling and scrapping, dragged themselves as far as the final, where they were beaten again by Egypt, this time 1-0. In the wider scheme of things, though, they *were* sleepwalking into trouble. Their preparations for the tournament had been appalling. In 2007, they'd played fewer matches than any other of the sides who qualified for the Cup of Nations finals in 2008. The German coach Otto Pfister, an irascible hard-drinking septuagenarian, had been imposed on the squad by the Sports Ministry. And Samuel Eto'o had been allowed to play one last league game for Barcelona so he joined up with his teammates a day before Cameroon's first match. It was chaos.

The man Pfister replaced was Jules Nyonga, who worked with the national team as either assistant coach or head coach from 1984 to 1996, returned as assistant in 2004 and then replaced Artur Jorge as head coach after the Cup of Nations in 2006. He led Cameroon through qualifying for the Cup of Nations in Ghana, but was ousted as the Cameroonian Football Federation (Fecafoot) turned — yet again — to a European coach.

Nyonga is a quietly-spoken bespectacled man in his mid-sixties. The courtyard of his house is dotted with pot-plants, the room where we spoke lined with objets d'art. In terms of temperament he seems more like an academic than a football coach but his anger about what is happening to Cameroonian football is clear enough. He led Cameroon through qualification for the 1994 World Cup but

was replaced by Henri Michel for the tournament itself. Having worked with Jorge, he was then asked to serve as deputy to Arie Haan. Nyonga had met him before, on the coaching course in Cologne from which he graduated in 1987; Haan never completed his diploma. The former Holland international lasted just three months — "embarrassed" by working with his former classmate, Nyonga believes —at which Nyonga took over and completed qualification only to be shoved aside for Pfister.

"There's a problem signing competent local coaches, a psychological issue," Nyonga said. It's a common enough problem in west Africa, the usual explanation being that players used to playing at a high level in Europe find it difficult to listen to a coach who has no experience of the Champions League. Nyonga refutes that, asking, quite reasonably, why any European player would respect the present coach, Denis Lavagne, a Frenchman who has no European experience at all but succeeded Javier Clemente last October. "There was no conflict when I was in charge," he said. "But there is stupidity. The current coach, who was drafted in from Coton Sport, doesn't even have the qualifications. He's qualified only to coach children. That kind of person would never get a job in, say, France. Maybe it's because he's white. Clemente was on CFA 52million (£65,000) a month. [Paul] Le Guen was on CFA 72m. The likelihood is that it's like a mafia arrangement. If you appoint a local coach you don't pay them as much so there's less for kick-backs."

When African countries first started turning to European coaches, there was a certain logic to it. They brought expertise, experience of tournament football and, to an extent, prestige. They could be trusted to overlook tribal distinctions between players. But even if Nyonga's suspicions about the money are inaccurate, European coaches have their drawbacks. "They definitely had a problem with the fact that very often they didn't understand local realities about how to prepare the team," Nyonga said.

For him, the classic example came in October 2005, when Cameroon went into their final World Cup qualifier, at home against an Egypt side that had already been eliminated, needing a win to finish above Côte d'Ivoire and secure their place at the 2006 World Cup. "We didn't qualify for the World Cup because Artur Jorge was in charge," Nyonga said. "I know the mentality of the players and I know the character of the public and the media. I told him not to prepare for this match in Cameroon, that we should go and prepare elsewhere and then come back two days before the game. But he wouldn't do it. The players kept being told it was a formality because Egypt were already out. They were getting phone calls all the time, from family and friends. Everybody thought it was a foregone conclusion, so the players weren't focused. The sports minister had put champagne on ice. We were just waiting for qualification."

It never arrived. Although Rodolphe Douala put Cameroon ahead after 20 minutes, Mohammed Shawkey levelled 11 minutes from time. But then, in injury-time, Cameroon were awarded a penalty. Eto'o was the designated penalty-taker but, depending whose account you believe, either he ducked the responsibility or Womé insisted he felt inspired. Womé's shot was hard and

low, but struck the post and the rebound eluded him. The full-back had to be smuggled to the airport the following day in an unmarked police car as gangs of youths sought retribution, attacking his family home, smashing his Mercedes and vandalising his girlfriend's hair salon.

After four successive qualifications, that should have been a warning, but it wasn't heeded. Fecafoot continued its policy of bringing in Europeans for major tournaments and that, inevitably, engendered a short-term outlook. As outsiders, their focus was rarely on anything other than the tournament that fell within the term of their contract (Nyonga names Claude Le Roy as an exception to this, pointing out the work he has done in developing African coaches; Alain Giresse's stint in Gabon, similarly, appears to have had long-term benefits). Perhaps more damagingly, they often thwarted the development of local coaches. The Catch-22 is obvious: European-based players don't respect a coach without European experience, but European clubs don't appoint African coaches because they so rarely see them working in an international environment.

While the urge to see white skin in the dugout doesn't seem to have gone away in Cameroon, steps have at least been taken to improve the basic structure of the game and, in 2010, after a dismal World Cup in which Cameroon, having lost to Japan and Denmark, were the first team eliminated, the position of technical director was created within Fecafoot.

Jean Manga-Onguene won the African Champions Cup in 1978 and 1980 with

Canon Yaoundé and in 1980 was named African Footballer of the Year. When he ruptured knee ligaments at a training camp in Germany shortly before the 1982 World Cup, the journalist Willie Niba said, there was "national mourning". Manga-Onguene is also Cameroonian football's first technical director. He is an elegant, slim man. When I met him in a restaurant in Yaoundé, he was wearing a dark suit and a purple-and-white striped tie; a diamond stud glistened in his left ear. His deputy, the former centre-back Jean-Paul Akono, another veteran of the great Canon and Cameroon sides of the late seventies and early eighties, could hardly be more different in appearance, a vast man with a high broad forehead sweeping up to a mass of tight grey curls. Manga-Onguene seemed the more thoughtful, speaking in short, precise bursts; Akono, swigging beer liberally, was quicker to laugh, anecdotes spilling from him. Both were good company, both, in different ways, blessed with an easy charisma.

"We had a very high position in Africa in the eighties and the nineties and we did not do what needed to be done to consolidate those achievements," Manga-Onguene explained. "We used to have academies across Cameroon where young budding talent could develop. In '91, '93 and '95 we went round the country prospecting for talent and at every stage we took the youth teams to join the sides preparing for continental competition. In 1995 we won the Under-17 Cup of Nations and a lot of those players progressed to the senior team. When you're doing well, the tendency is to stop investing, thinking things will always be the same. Now you have an Under-17 team where you see nobody coming from the Under-

15s — and that means something is fundamentally wrong.

"Too many players have been getting into the national team without having the appropriate training and that's problematic. If you have proper training, coaches can determine what their weaknesses are and try to improve them before they join the first team. Sometimes they are players knocking on the door of the first team who have not been drilled, who don't know what being part of a team is."

For Akono, the problems weren't just structural but to do with a change of attitude that has arguably been caused by Cameroon's success. As more and more players went to Europe and started to earn what by Cameroonian standards were enormous salaries, the mindset changed. "There was too much ego," he said, "each player trying to justify their roles in the team and make money. The issue of ego was not restricted to players at all, but also affected team officials, the federation. They have to take part of the blame for thinking the achievements of previous years were a natural phenomenon that would be hard to take away.

"For some time even when we were unable to win trophies, we were still performing. That was the time when we needed to be vigilant, when we should have been looking at the talent in the junior teams. The writing was on the wall from the bad run of results. We didn't look behind us to see others were making progress. Now they have caught up with us and we have only our eyes to cry with. It took a long time for people to realise the importance of having a technical manager at the head of the team."

A technical manager feels like a step in the right direction. It should at least encourage long-term planning and perhaps provide a thread of continuity beneath the knee-jerk populism of the sports ministry. And, as Zambia proved, continuity of selection can bring astonishing results. In a world of short-termism, the planner is king, even if only two of his squad play in Europe and one of those in the Russian second division. "There are now regional technical advisors at the level of regions and districts," said Nyonga. "They're starting to take care of looking after budding talent and trying to organise how young talent can come through. There are some players who have played for the first team for 10 years and only now they're fading are we looking for new players. That's the problem we're facing right now. The absence of a policy of continuity, of a permanent injection of young talent in the national team, so they can be heirs in waiting: now the whole team has to be reshuffled."

Théophile Abega was Cameroon's captain at the 1982 World Cup and a key part of the great Canon side. A sublimely gifted midfielder, he was nicknamed 'Doctor', and scored a magnificent goal in the final of the 1984 Cup of Nations when Cameroon beat Nigeria to claim the title for the first time. After initially responding positively to a request for an interview, he stopped taking phone calls but as he is now the mayor of the fourth arrondissement of Yaoundé — the largest district, with a population of 600,000 — he wasn't too hard to track down to the mayoral office, a low structure with a corrugated iron roof. After negotiating a busy ante-chamber in which women pushed paper assiduously, I was shown to a small, dark room at the back of the building.

A desk, stacked with mounds of paper, dominated the room, taking up at least half the available space. A lethargic ceiling fan did little to penetrate the stifling heat. Squeezed onto seats along one wall were three men, whether lackeys or petitioners I couldn't tell. And amid the paper, signing documents, was Abega, a cream-coloured stetson perched on his head. As I waited for him to finish, one of the three other men told me, as though imparting a great secret, "Abega wore the number 14 shirt at Italia 90, and it was the fourteenth World Cup. That's not coincidence." Maybe not, but neither was it true; Abega retired in 1987. Eventually Abega finished with his documents. He apologised for not returning my calls; he'd changed networks, he explained. And would I like to go to his place for dinner that evening.

Abega is now a full-time politician, a staunch supporter of Paul Biya, who has been president since 1982, but just because he is out of football doesn't mean he doesn't regret Cameroon's decline. "African football is on a downturn, because teams like Equatorial Guinea and Gabon are beating sides like Morocco and Senegal," he said. "Something is fundamentally wrong. In my day we went and beat these countries 7-0 or 9-0.

"Cameroon had great fighting spirit. That was our modus operandi in our heyday. Cameroonian players were once big and strong, but now they are like the Gabonese. We used to play a strong game with towering players, but now it doesn't look like Cameroon. I don't know why, but nowadays they are not physical any more. Sometimes we won games before they had started with our size. We intimidated the Italians in '82 [when Cameroon were a touch unfortunate to draw 0-0] even though they were notorious for the rugged game that they played. We could feel that they were scared to death. Now when we play Gabon or even Equatorial Guinea, they think they can win because they're capitalising on the sizes of the players. They realise that Cameroon don't have impressive footballers any more."

If Cameroon's players really have shrunk relative to other African sides, of course, there's not much they can do, but Abega sees other issues that go far deeper than football. "We have a federation which is not playing its role these days," he said. "They are playing politics, not football. There are some delegates who are trying just to bring players from the north because they control the federation. You have to pick the best players, wherever they come from. If they are all from the south, they are all from the south. You can't just pick people to keep each area happy."

Although Abega thinks the appointment of a technical director is a positive step, he is sceptical about the ability of his former teammates to do the job. "The coaches here have no professional experience," he said, by which he clearly meant "European". Côte d'Ivoire, despite their penalty shoot-out defeat in the Cup of Nations final in Libreville, Abega felt had got it right by appointing François Zahoui, an Ivorian who played for Ascoli, Nancy and Toulon. "We have nobody," he said. "Even Manga and Akono haven't played in Europe. Manga was a fantastic player but he didn't play professionally. He doesn't know what it is to be a professional. Professional is in your mentality, in your habits."

Even recent attempts to reform and professionalise the Cameroonian league Abega sees as doomed. "I doubt the professional league will help because the players are coached by managers who have never been professional," he said. "A lot of these teams don't have bank accounts, they don't have buses, they don't have the right structure." Certainly there was little in the game I saw, in which Canon beat Tiko United 2-1 in front of a few hundred people, to suggest any great quality waiting to emerge. Perhaps significantly, both sides were playing their first game under new coaches.

Abega is first and foremost a politician — even the question of whether he misses football seems to surprise him — and seems obsessed by concessions being made to the north. It is the ongoing wrangling between north and south that he sees as lying behind the most obvious issue Cameroonian football faces in the short term.

Nobody disputes Samuel Eto'o's talent. The Anzhi Makhachkala forward is clearly Cameroon's best player, but he is also Cameroon's biggest problem. Last year, he led protests over the non-payment of bonuses that resulted in a friendly against Algeria being cancelled. Fecafoot banned him for 15 matches but later commuted that to eight months. How keen Eto'o will be to return remains to be seen.

Although many acknowledge Eto'o was fighting a just cause, opinion is divided on whether his suspension is a good or bad thing for Cameroon. At the very least, there is a general acceptance that the gulf between his abilities and those of his teammates created tensions. "There is a tactical problem with the disparity of talent between Eto'o and the rest because every other player rushes to give the ball to Eto'o whether he's in a good position or not," Abega said, and that was readily apparent in Angola in 2010 when the forward would regularly pick up the ball 60 yards from goal with little support and a phalanx of opponents between him and the goal.

But that is just part of the issue. There were rumours of a power struggle between Eto'o and Paul Le Guen at the Cup of Nations which were given credibility by the exhaustion and disillusionment the former Lyon and Rangers manager displayed at the end of the tournament. Players too reacted badly to what was seen as the "condescension" shown by Eto'o to younger players. "There is a stark difference between the time when [Rigobert] Song was captain and now," said Nyonga. "He knew how to rally the team. He was less condescending. He considered himself as part of the team as opposed to Eto'o. He is a crushing personality, because of his wealth and international standing."

Given that Eto'o also paid bonuses for the rest of the team out of his own pocket, though, it's hard to deny that he genuinely cares about Cameroon. The problem may simply be that, with a lack of support, he feels he has to do everything himself and the result is that his efforts to improve Cameroonian football simply look egotistical. And, of course, even by

attempting to take responsibility, he opens himself to criticism.

"They don't like leaders," said Joseph-Antoine Bell, who himself clashed regularly with politicians and Fecafoot officials during his career as a player. That suggests merely a defensiveness or envy on the part of Cameroon's football hierarchy, but Abega hinted at a conspiracy that went far deeper. "Forces from the north", he insisted, had deliberately sought Eto'o's ban to try to bring fans out onto the street in protest, thus potentially destabilising Biya's government.

Cameroon's decline is part of a wider trend. World Cups should not be taken as the only way of judging such things, but the fact that no African side has improved on Cameroon's achievement of reaching the quarter-final in the two decades since is significant. There has been stagnation among the best African sides even as more and more African players have established themselves at major European clubs. Arguably, the exodus of African players to Europe has been counterproductive; the judgement is inevitably subjective, but the best side I've seen in a decade of covering the Cup of Nations was Egypt in 2008, the majority of whose players played in Egypt.

Thanks to the familiar problems of poor infrastructure, disorganisation and corruption, African national sides are no nearer winning a World Cup now than they were 20 years ago, but that is not to say African football has not improved. It's just that it has improved lower down the scale; there are fewer minnows and there are more sides, like Zambia, like Togo, like Angola, who can shock the traditional powers and win the Cup of Nations or qualify for a World Cup.

What that has done is to highlight the failure of the likes of Cameroon and Nigeria to progress and that might be the stimulus they need to start planning and investing seriously. Cameroon's creation of the post of technical director, perhaps, is the start of that process. Whether it is the right measure, whether Manga-Onguene and Akono are the right people, remains to be seen, but at least there is an acceptance of a problem and that is an essential first step. Ⓑ

Blind Veterans UK

St Dunstan's since 1915

"Basra, 2006. A sniper's bullet almost totally blinded me. But with help, I've rebuilt my life. And I'm always looking for the next challenge."

**Simon Brown,
Royal Electrical and Mechanical Engineers**

No one who's served our country should battle blindness alone. That's why we're here to help with a lifetime's practical and emotional support, regardless of when they served and how they lost their sight.

Please remember Blind Veterans UK with a gift in your Will.

Visit www.blindveterans.org.uk/legacies or call 020 7616 7953 today.

Blind Veterans UK
12-14 Harcourt Street, London W1H 4HD

132

Polemics

"...the real fan is a rhetorical device deployed to strengthen whatever argument the deployer wants to make."

The Real Problem

Is the 'real fan' being marginalised or is he just a rhetorical tool?

By Brian Phillips

"Real football, real fans." — Football League brand slogan

The 'real football fan' has had an interesting career lately. His extinction, at least from the top flight, is regularly lamented — "Are there any real fans left in the Premier League?'" the *Daily Mail* keened in 2008 — but an extensive media industry has sprung up to give him a voice: "real fans, real opinions" is the tagline of more than one football website. He's being bled pale by the greedy owners of his club ("Has the Premier League priced out all the real fans?" the *Guardian* wondered last year), which is hard, because one of the many things he doesn't like to do is watch football on television ("real football fans go and watch games", to quote one representative internet comment). Other things he doesn't do: criticise his own players ("Real Fans Don't Boo," as a recent blog post asserts); sit down, ever ("real fans STAND at the football, no excuses!" a Leeds-supporting forum poster writes); or support a top-four club (unless he happens to have been born within half a mile of the centre-circle at Old Trafford, in which case he has an excuse).

You can barely venture onto the internet these days without encountering the saga of the real fan and his struggles with the modern game. Of all the ways he's exploited, though, the worst may be simply as a straw man. It doesn't take a safecracker to work out that mostly, the real fan is a rhetorical device deployed to strengthen whatever argument the deployer wants to make. If you want to criticise Premier League ticket pricing, you could make the case that the league is pricing out lower-income fans — a legitimately important point. But if you tweak that to say that the league is pricing out *real* fans, you can recruit a whole other kind of authenticity into your argument. Start an online forum for *real* fans, and you flatter whoever joins it that their perspective on the game is not just more knowledgeable but also more genuine than that of the fakes and poseurs who populate other message boards. Call fans who've followed a club since before 1992 *real* fans, rather than traditional fans or old-school fans or any of the other terms you could use, and you suggest that everyone who's come along since then is a false fan. And why would anyone listen to a false fan's point of view?

The culture of sport is changing everywhere. But the culture of English football is changing at a really dizzying pace. In the past 20 years — you hardly need me to tell you this — football in England has undergone two major conceptual reconfigurations: the advent of the Premier League/Sky era in the 1990s, which transformed the commercial basis of the game and called into question settled notions of what a football club is for, and the very rapid technology-assisted expansion of the global fan base in the 2000s, which shook up old expectations about who the audience for a football league is supposed to be. In other words, both what the game was and who it was being played for seemed to acquire different answers, almost overnight. What had seemed (hindsight is admittedly a little rose-coloured in this description) a community endeavour suddenly appeared a capitalist kraken with tentacles unfurled to Taipei. It's no surprise that the nature of fandom would come into frequent question during this period, or that the 'real fan' figure — like his natural enemies, the 'gloryhunter' and the 'football hipster' — would be used to trace the anxieties and frustrations of an established English fan base trying to come to terms with whatever the hell was happening to their game.

Those last two words are a problem, though, because while the 'real fan' designation is by nature exclusionary — it defines a class of supporters who it says have the only legitimate claim on the sport, and too bad for everyone else — football doesn't actually belong to any one group of people. There are tens of millions of more or less non-traditional Premier League fans all over the world who, whether they discovered the league through commercial manipulation or not, now genuinely love their teams. (Besides, it's not as though the 'real fan' is a stranger to commercial manipulation: see the crypto-isolationist dog whistle of a Football League motto I quoted at the

start of this piece.) Arsenal fans in Africa often seem to take Arsenal more seriously than Arsenal fans at the Emirates. Which are the real fans? Some of the most fascinating football writing I've read in the last few years has come in separate pieces by Supriya Nair and Suhrith Parthasarathy on what it's like to follow a European club from India — climbing out of bed in the middle of the night, watching matches alone in the green glow of the television, biting down on shouts that would wake up the whole block. That's a form of passion no less real than the one that makes a Newcastle supporter drive to Swansea, even if it's a relatively new thing in the world.

More to the point: why should any of us accept that there's only one proper way to watch football? Where was the meeting that decided that anyone who doesn't fit the follows-one-team-loyally, sings-his-head-off, goes-to-the-pub style of fandom is worse than anyone who does? If there are a million varieties of love, I don't see why there shouldn't be a million varieties of love for football, which, after all, has no real importance beyond its ability to add some enjoyment to our lives. There's something spectacularly silly about fans policing other fans for their adherence to the laws of fandom, as if not having one favourite club, or preferring to watch from a seated position, is a VERY SERIOUS INFRACTION that should be SWIFTLY AND MERCILESSLY DEALT WITH. Because, you know, the economic recovery can't gather steam if Kyle in Ohio thinks it's fun to watch Chelsea on television.
Well, by 'real fan' standards, I'm about as fake as they come, so I'm biased. But at the risk of running against the indie-rock logic that prevails in these situations, I

think football culture has gone past the point at which any single notion of what a football fan is or ought to be can be viable. (Of course it's arguable whether football culture was ever not past that point, but there you have it.) Like it or not, the fandom of the foreseeable future is going to include people huddled over dodgy online streams, people watching on phones, people ready to snap shut their laptop lids if their bosses walk in, people sipping tea in the middle of the night — as well as people holding scarves up in stadiums. Some of these fans are going to have club loyalties handed down by their fathers and grandfathers; others are going to choose teams based on a player they like or a style of play, or not choose a team at all. All of this is okay.

Calling some of this activity 'real' and the rest of it 'fake' misses the point. 1975 is not rolling back around the block. We might as well acknowledge that we share the same goofy obsession and try to find some common ground in it, rather than frantically working to exclude one another from our narrow definitions of fandom. Really, this isn't so bad. People are fascinating everywhere, and the culture is where it is. That's not me talking; that's reality.

Where's Darth Vader Gone?

Is the age of football as a substitute for war coming to an end?

By Simon Kuper

If you had to choose a holy English year since the Second World War, it would be 1966. The year is almost as much a landmark as 1066, when William the Conqueror created the modern nation. For all the fuss about club football, the biggest football matches, the ones that fill living-rooms all along the street, have always been nation versus nation. When a national team plays, you sometimes get half a country's population or more watching on TV. In Germany, for instance, seven of the eight highest-rated TV programmes until 2008 involved the national football team playing in a big tournament. No club game can have that kind of impact. Nationalism is the strongest animating force in football support. You could even argue that since 1945 in Europe, football has replaced war as the main outlet for nationalist emotion.

However, in the last few years something significant has changed: emotional nationalism is fading from international football. It's being replaced by a gentler kind of "party nationalism" — people with flags painted on their faces drinking beer and flirting with fans of the other team— and also by post-nationalism. Just as old-style nationalism is becoming less important in politics, it's fading in football too.

Mihir Bose, in his recent history of modern sport, *The Spirit of the Game*, dates the start of sporting nationalism back to Baron de Coubertin's creation of the modern Olympics. Nationalism wasn't what De Coubertin wanted, of course: he thought that playing sport would turn gentlemen of different nations into brothers. That's why the five rings in the Olympic flag were interlaced: friendship between continents. But in fact, once the modern Olympics took off, and after international sporting fixtures became common in the 1930s, countries began to seek prestige by winning them. Mussolini was probably the pioneer, the first leader to take propaganda through sport seriously. But during the 1930s the practice became quite widespread among politicians. At the 1936 Olympics, Albert Foerster, the Nazi Gauleiter of Gdansk persuaded Hitler to come and watch Germany thrash little Norway at football. Goebbels, who watched the match with Hitler, wrote in his diary, "The Führer is very excited. I can barely contain myself. A real bath of nerves. The crowd rages. A battle like never before. The game as mass suggestion." But to Foerster's mortification, Germany lost 2-0. It seems to have been the only football match Hitler ever saw.

So football nationalism emerged in the 1930s, but there is one caveat: back then, "fair play" was as central to national prestige as winning. Watching a football international in the 1930s seems to have been almost an impartial experience, like going to the theatre. Even the infamous Germany v England friendly in Berlin in 1938, when the England team gave the Hitler salute just before kick-off, wasn't considered at the time to be just about winning. On the Monday after the game, *The News Chronicle* newspaper ran the front-page headline, "THE GAME AND NOT ONE FOUL". The *Times* said Len Goulden's cracking goal for England in the game "drew gasps of admiration from the crowd and is the talk of the town today." True, there was a new football nationalism, but games then weren't played in the same angry spirit they would be after the war.

From 1939 through 1945 a different sort of nationalism took over. But after 1945 something remarkable happened: war died out in Europe. The Harvard psychologist Steven Pinker, in his book *The Better Angels of Our Nature*, points out that there have been no interstate wars in western Europe since 1945, and, skirmishes in the Caucasus excepted, none in eastern Europe since Soviet tanks invaded Hungary in 1956. Pinker writes, "Keep in mind that up until that point European states had started around two new armed conflicts *a year* since 1400."

After 1945, Europeans no longer expressed nationalist emotions through war. Instead they began to express them through international football. This probably started in Germany in 1954 after the West Germans won the World Cup in the mud of Bern. The story of that day is one of the founding myths of the Federal Republic: crowds of people clustered around the only TV set in their neighbourhood, the train carrying the players home being mobbed at every station, people celebrating on the streets in both West and East Germany, and finally, at the official celebrations in West Berlin, when the national anthem was played, the West German president Theodor Heuss frantically trying to coach the crowd in the correct new lyrics so that they wouldn't sing the old, taboo line, "*Deutschland, Deutschland über Alles*". Of course most people sang it anyway. It was the national anthem they knew. The German phrase most associated with that day is, "*Wir sind wieder wer*", "We are somebody again." In other words, football had begun to create a proud new nation.

Over the next four decades, first World Cups and then European championships gained in importance, as more people bought TV sets and as interest in football began to spread through all classes of men — though not yet among many women. This is the era when World Cups became the most watched TV programmes on earth; a Philips executive once told me that sales of Philips TVs spike in even years, when there is a major football tournament. The most extreme TV viewing figure I know of is the 12.3 million Dutch people —three-quarters of the country's population — who watched at least some of the Holland-Uruguay semi-final of the last World Cup. (The Holland-Spain final actually drew slightly fewer Dutch viewers). Holland-Uruguay was the biggest shared postwar Dutch experience, just as France's victory in 1998 was the biggest shared French communal experience since the Liberation — with the difference being that in 1998, unlike in 1944, all the French were on the same side. In the decades after the war, national football teams had come to constitute the nation. Those 11 young men in synthetic shirts were the nation made flesh — more alive than the flag, more concrete than gross domestic product, less individual than the president or queen. In the Dutch popular mind, for instance, the Dutch football team now is the Netherlands in a way that nothing else quite is.

Nationalism always needs an enemy, and in this era from the 1950s through the 1990s the enemy for most European countries became Germany. English football's anthem, "Three Lions", is mostly about matches against Germany — which makes it particularly ironic that while the Germans were on their way to winning Euro 96 in England they liked to sing the song on their team bus. But it wasn't just the English. France's worst football moment — much more painful than Zinedine Zidane's sending-off in the 2006 World Cup final — was losing to West Germany in Seville in the World Cup semi-final in 1982. The Dutch, the Danes, perhaps half the countries in Europe date the best and worst moments in their football history to matches against Germans.

To some degree, we all know why. Here is Lou de Jong, a grey Dutch professor who spent about 50 years writing the official history of the Netherlands in the Second World War in umpteen volumes, talking to a newspaper after the best moment in Holland's football history, victory over West Germany at the European Championship of 1988: "When Holland scores I dance through the room. Of course it's got to do with the war." After that match millions of Dutch people celebrated on the street,

in the largest public gathering since the Liberation. The French TV commentator Georges de Caunes said that for French males of his generation, the flying kick inflicted by the German keeper Toni Schumacher on France's Patrick Battiston that night in Seville reawakened feelings from the war.

But the anti-German feelings weren't just to do with the war. The near-invincible post-war West German teams, from 1954 through 1990, were the might of the wealthy post-war Federal Republic incarnate. That peaceful might provoked resentment, even hatred. The German-British writer Philip Oltermann, in his new book *Keeping Up with the Germans*, writes, "I sometimes wonder if Germany in my lifetime has been hated with more passion than it ever was in the 1910s or 1940s." Holland-Germany matches have provoked clashes between fans on the countries' shared border, the closest the European Union gets to war; and after England-Germany at Euro 96, Germans — and people who were mistaken for Germans — and German cars, were beaten up in towns around England.

Yet in those post-war decades we all needed Germany, because the country gave meaning to international football. David Winner, the *Blizzard* contributor, says, "In terms of story the greatest nation in the history of football is Germany. A World Cup without Germany would be like *Star Wars* without Darth Vader." Germany was the perfect villain: the bad guy who killed the beautiful teams, like Hungary in 1954, Holland in 1974, France in 1982.

German dominance peaked in 1990: between July and October, Germany won the World Cup and achieved reunification. The team's coach, Franz Beckenbauer, the incarnation of post-war German superiority, said that with East German players about to join the team, Germany would be "invincible for years to come".

I happen to have been a witness to the zenith of post-war Germany. In September 1990 I arrived in Berlin to study for a year and on 3 October 1990, the day of German reunification, I wandered down Unter den Linden to witness the birth of the invincible Germany. The avenue was packed, but apart from a few East Germans scarfing champagne, most people were wandering around quietly too. Like me, they seemed to be just looking, not celebrating. Walking down the most pompous boulevard of an empire on the night of its greatest glory, you seldom realise that this is the moment that the empire starts to decline. But it was.

Germany's slide after 1990 — on the pitch and off it — helped hasten the end of hypernationalism in Europe. Contrary to what Beckenbauer expected, Germany has won just one football trophy in the 20 years since reunification. The economy also went through a long period of turmoil before recently emerging as Europe's prize pupil again. Interestingly, many German football fans seem to have welcomed their team's decline. Recently, Germans have coined the word *"Siegesscham"* — victory-shame — to describe their feelings in the post-war decades when their ugly teams kept winning prizes. A lot of Germans didn't want to be the old domineering

Germans anymore. In July 2006, early in the morning after Germany had won the World Cup's third-place play-off, I was on Unter den Linden again, and I was amazed to see thousands of people, dressed in German shirts, walking towards the Brandenburger Tor. I couldn't work out what they were doing, but it turned out that they were going to wait around in the baking sun for hours to cheer their team's arrival in Berlin later that afternoon. German fans were celebrating losers — and in many ways were happy to be losers. I've been to every World Cup since 1990, and it was in 2006 that I first noticed the shift from old-style nationalism to this kind of party nationalism. Oliver Bierhoff, the German team's general manager, remarked with surprise in 2006 that fans had become less interested in results.

This new, larger and yet reduced Germany has ceased to be Darth Vader. The team just doesn't provoke the same hatred anymore. At Euro 2004, when Holland and Germany met again in Porto, the fans of both teams sat together in the stands. Not only didn't they fight, but they didn't even seem to dislike each other. "A step forward in history," a security official at Uefa told me later. On the one hand it's nice that nobody hates Germany anymore, but on the other hand the loss of Darth Vader definitely makes European football less interesting. There may never again be a European football match as loaded as Seville 1982 or Hamburg 1988, and that is a loss. In part, what has happened is that since 1990 the war has faded from collective European memory. Finally, in Europe, the Second World War is over; not just the fighting itself, but the war in the head, too. You saw signs of the burying of the war in 2005, around the celebrations of the sixtieth anniversary of the liberation of Europe: French schoolchildren had a snowball fight at Auschwitz; a poll showed that many young Britons didn't know that "VE Day" stands for "Victory in Europe". World War Two was becoming like the American Civil War: remembered by history buffs but only vaguely by the general public, and no longer used as a terrible lesson for policymakers. Horst Köhler, Germany's president in 2005, recognised as much when he urged his country's parliament "to keep alive the memories of all the suffering". What he meant was that the memories were fading.

In fact, the World Cup in 2006 felt like a pan-European party to mark the true end of Second World War, which was why it had to end in Berlin. The tournament was a European-wide lovefest for the German hosts. A few days before the final, I attended a conference on football and history at the Haus der Wannsee-Konferenz in Berlin — the building where Nazi officials in 1942 had planned the Holocaust. The day I arrived the weather was beautiful and from the garden of this dreadful villa you could see people sunbathing all around the Wannsee. I went for a stroll with the official from the DFB, the German football association, whose job it was to deal with historical questions. If anyone had a question about the DFB and the war, they had to call him. I asked him if many journalists had called him about war-related issues during the World Cup. "No, nobody," he said.

True, there was a last flaring of the old passions at Euro 2008 before Germany-Poland, when Polish newspapers banged on about old wars. One paper even printed a montage of the Polish coach Leo Beenhakker (a Dutchman) holding aloft the heads of Michael Ballack and Germany's coach Joachim Löw. But Beenhakker and his players were furious with the story. The newspaper was humiliated. It presumably won't try that again this summer. True, you still get the odd football reference to Nazis and wars — English fans imitating RAF bomber planes at England-Germany games or Dutch fans in 2006 wearing orange *Stahlhelme*, modeled on old Germany army helmets — but it's almost always done tongue-in-cheek, as a silly joke. The war is being used to spice up what are now really just football rivalries.

International football is ceasing to be treated as a reenactment of Europe's horrible past. In fact, to some degree international football is ceasing to pit one country against another. More and more, fans watch tournaments with transnational loyalties instead of the old single-minded nationalism. I first noticed this at Euro 96, when Nike came up with a great poster for Eric Cantona, posing in front of an English flag: "'66 was a Great Year for English Football. Eric Was Born." Nike felt confident in mocking old-style 1966 nationalism and appealing to transnationalism instead.

In 1996, the Premier League was just becoming an international league for the first time and you were seeing some new transnational expressions of fandom. United fans had a song for Cantona based on the Marseillaise. Arsenal fans briefly sang *"Allez les rouges"* for their Frenchmen, and when the German striker Uwe Rösler became a cult hero at Manchester City, the club's fans wore T-shirts saying: "Uwe's Grandad bombed Old Trafford," in honour of the Luftwaffe's handiwork. In 1998, when France won the World Cup, the headline in the *Daily Mirror* was, "Arsenal Win the World Cup," above a photo of Patrick Vieira hugging Emmanuel Petit.

It was getting harder and harder to tell the different national teams apart. Before the 1990s, each country had had its own style, and that style was seen by most people as an expression of national character: the Germans were machine-like, the English played like warriors, the French were fragile artists and so on. But from the 1990s, as players increasingly moved between countries and played more international club football, they all started to become the same. Michael Owen told me that he'd grown up a European player, not an English one — and you saw it in his dives. Pre-Owen, the English had always considered dives as a marker of cowardly foreignness and to some extent they still do; but it's harder to see things that way now that English players also dive and also kiss teammates on the cheeks and sometimes also pass like continentals. Today's European footballers have joined the transnational wealthy class, which is more at home in first-class airport lounges than in the streets of their own countries. Members of this class live like their millionaire foreign peers, and so Cristiano Ronaldo, Wayne Rooney and Mesut Özil are now more like each other than they are like their 'normal' compatriots. Increasingly, when we watch international football, we know that we are watching cosmopolitans rather than our own countrymen. In the vicious Holland-Portugal game of

2006, when players kept getting sent off, two of them, Holland's Giovanni van Bronckhorst and Portugal's Deco, sat down next to each other on the bench and chatted while the match finished. They were teammates at Barcelona. In the next round, in the Portugal-England quarter-final, Cristiano Ronaldo helped get his Manchester United teammate Rooney sent off, but after the game Rooney sent him a friendly text. It's harder to feel blindly nationalistic about international football when the protagonists obviously don't.

Fans were even starting to choose which national team to support. I went to Brazil's first match at the 2006 World Cup, against Croatia in Berlin, and tens of thousands of people showed up in the famous canary shirts. But walking around the stadium before the game, I realised that very few of them were Brazilians. They were Germans, Japanese, Brits, people from everywhere who wanted a share in the Brazilian magic. Or there were the four guys in Argentina shirts I saw in the metro after one game in 2006 who suddenly started speaking German. I don't know how many people support national teams other than their own, but my sense is that it's a growing phenomenon.

It's no coincidence that in the last 15 years post-nationalism has invaded football, because in the same period post-nationalism has become the underlying ideology of the global economy. Marx said, "The ruling ideas of each age are the ideas of the ruling class." For more than 150 years, from the early nineteenth century until the late twentieth, the ruling idea was nationalism. As the historian Eric Hobsbawm has pointed out, nationalism suited the new means of technology that were then emerging: the train, the highway, and the radio and later TV that taught peasants the national language. These technologies helped create the nation.

But as technology improved, nationalism became redundant. The new technologies have created a supranational world: cheap flights, fast trains over long distances, international financial markets, the internet and cable TV channels that have helped teach the young generation the new global language of English. English, inevitably, has become the language that fans use to talk to each other at World Cups. In this new world, national governments just don't matter that much anymore. National governments in western Europe have forfeited their main tools of the past: wars, national currencies and national borders. The most important laws now tend to be made in Brussels. Belgium recently went a year without a national government — a caretaker administration kept an eye on things — and nobody noticed. National governments are becoming redundant. This is the backdrop to the decline of nationalism in international football.

The enmities that get people in Europe going these days tend to be supranational too. Except in Greece, you rarely see politicians campaigning on a hatred of Germans. Rather, the great popular motivating forces in Europe of the last 10 years have been anti-Americanism, during the Bush administration, and more significantly, hatred of Muslims. For many Europeans, Muslims have replaced Germans as the feared Other. The Euro-crisis has created a new, supranational reconfiguration

of enmities: now it's northern Europe against southern Europe. The Dutch don't hate the Germans anymore; they identify with their fellow northerners in the fight against supposedly feckless spendthrift southern Europeans.

Of course, most people today still support their national football teams, but this support is less serious, less of a life-and-death matter than it once was. This spring I visited Bilbao. Of course lots of people in the city identify primarily as Basques, not as Spaniards. And when Spain won the World Cup, I'm told that not many people risked running onto the streets drunk wearing red Spain shirts in the more Basque-nationalist medieval quarter of town. But in the newer commercial district, lots of fans did go out into the streets to celebrate Spain's world championship. In the past in Bilbao that sort of behaviour could have got you badly hurt, but not anymore. In Barcelona too, the capital of Catalonia, in 2008 and 2010, there were large public celebrations of Spain's victories. I suspect it's not that the celebrating hordes felt intensely Spanish and were out to make a political point. No: they were just enjoying the party. This is a kind of party nationalism, a holiday nationalism, where you paint your face with the national flag but wouldn't dream of dying for your country.

That leaves one last question: if people don't feel very nationalist anymore, what do they feel? Well, there's one thing they don't seem to feel: European. There's a longstanding idea in Brussels that what the EU really needs is a "Europe" football team. In 1982 the Adonnino committee, led by the Italian MEP Pietro Adonnino, proposed measures for creating European sentiment: a Eurolottery, the blue flag with the gold stars and European sports teams.

Today only one such team exists: every other year Europe plays the US in golf's Ryder Cup. Even that tends to be an essentially British-Irish team with a handful of continentals thrown in (a seven-five split in 2010). Nobody outside Brussels has shown any desire for EU teams in other sports. But 20 years after Adonnino another Italian tried again: in 2004 Romano Prodi, then president of the European Commission, proposed sending a united EU team to the next Olympics in Beijing. His spokesman pointed out that if such a team had competed at the Athens Games, it would have won nearly three times as many medals as the top country in the medals' table, the US. However, Prodi's suggestion was laughed out of the room.

In a Eurobarometer survey for the Commission in 2005, 63% of Europeans claimed to be "proud" of being European. But almost all of them were proud of their own countries too. Euro-patriotism doesn't replace nationalism; it accompanies it. The two feelings are complementary.

Euro-patriotism is widespread but rather weak. In that same Eurobarometer, only 12% said they were "very proud" of being European. The rest was only "fairly proud". Nobody ever ran drunk out of his house waving an EU flag. Football tournaments are still carnivals of nationalism. Nonetheless, Brussels can be "fairly proud" of what it has achieved these last 56 years: all those national flags and painted cheeks are the last, toothless manifestations of old European nationalism.

So what do people feel now? If they aren't so nationalist anymore, what is their identity? Look at Twitter and see how users identify themselves in their short public biographies. Surprisingly often, they describe themselves as supporters of giant football clubs. You might have a guy called Ahmed, who gives his location as "Bangladesh", and then describes himself not as a Bangladeshi or as a Muslim, but, usually in English, as, "FCB till I die", or "You'll Never Walk Alone – Liverpool FC". In a way these Twitter biographies are statements of identity: who you are, how you want to be seen by others. These people are using an international medium to identify as international people. When you spend some time on Twitter, you start to feel that the old nation versus nation set up of European championships and World Cups is a bit kitsch, outdated. Hobsbawm makes the point that nationalism is a comparatively recent invention, no more than 200 years old. In football and outside football, it now seems to be on the way out. Ⓑ

The Culture of Violence

The absence of leadership means there is little hope of Argentina's hooligan problem being solved

By Sergio Levinsky

In the past five years, anybody who has watched Argentinian football, whether official games or friendlies, will have seen that in the stands there is always an empty spacewhere fans cannot go. These are the "neutral zones" or "lungs", the means the football and state authorities have chosen to separate one group of fans from another, as though empty space can end hostilities. The lungs are an admission of defeat to those who seek to disrupt the spectacle.

They represent the surrender of the authorities and in that sense are not a solution to the problem of violence. The organisation *Salvemos al Fútbol* [Let's Save Football], presided over by Mónica Nizzardo, a director of the National B side Atlanta, numbers the dead from football violence at 261. Of those, 161 have been killed during the reign of Julio Grondona, the Fifa senior vice-president, as president of the Argentinian Football Association (AFA). Having taken control in 1979, he is in his ninth term of office thanks to the peculiarities of the voting system and his remarkable ability to cling to power.

The *barra bravas*, Argentina's ultra and hooligan groups, constitute a problem that is becoming increasingly serious not because there is no solution but because there is no will to impose a solution. Various governments, both the dictatorship and the democracy, have repeated their desire to eliminate the *barras*, but they have ended up being their accomplices in a mutually beneficial game. The authorities provide protection through money, free tickets, and subsidised buses while offering the opportunity to resell tickets and deal drugs in return for the *barras'* agreement to act as hired hoods to break up demonstrations, to vote the 'right' way in elections and to daub graffiti on the streets.

Every club in every division has a number of *barra bravas* who can count on the police not only to protect the areas they see as their own, but to stand back and turn a blind eye to what goes on in those areas, which has included murder and the infliction of grievous injuries.

Amílcar Romero, the foremost analyst of the violence in Argentinian football and the author of several books on the subject, points out that not only does the football system generate its own violence, but that it reflects wider societal trends. For years, huge numbers of Argentinian people have seen their purchasing power diminish while losing access to culture and jobs. That is reflected in the stadiums, where football and its attendant violence provide a stimulus to thousands of youths otherwise excluded from productive activity (a fact that offers one of the few coherent explanations as to why so many games are played during office hours). The ritual of 'defending the colours' — which offer an identity to lives otherwise largely devoid of purpose — is used to justify criminal activities.

Over the past few years a change has occurred and the tradition of fighting for the colours has often turned inward, so that fans of the same team but different *barras* end up fighting among themselves. That has been particularly true since 2009. That was the year when clubs saw their incomes increase through the *Fútbol para Todos* [Football for All] scheme by which the government took the rights to broadcast top-flight games from TyC, part of the powerful Clarín media group, insisting all games be shown live on public television. They paid 900 million pesos (£130m) per year, as opposed to the 180 million per year the clubs were getting under the previous deal, both ensuring that the clubs could pay their players (their failure to do so and the players' threat to strike having sparked the whole initiative) and conveniently hitting Clarín, which had consistently opposed both the government of the late Néstor Kirchner (2003-07) and his wife, Cristina Fernández de Kirchner (2007-11 and 2011-present).

That increase in revenue made the clubs and their business far more interesting to hooligan groups, who had been moving into other areas of criminality, opening the way for rival *barras*. As potential profits rose, so those original groups sought to reassume their positions of dominance and, as an investigation by *Salvemos al Fútbol* demonstrated, the inter-*barras* problem became one of intra-*barras*.

Squabbling for a share of the pot at home has left fans with less time and energy to battle with their supposed rivals. The result of the conflict becoming internecine has been a change in the nature of the violence. Not only has the death rate risen, but the violence is no longer confined to the stadium and match days, trespassing instead into the street during the normal working week. The violence that was once contained within the world of football has now passed into the daily life of Argentinians.

The extent to which that is the case is detailed by the reporter Carlos del Frade in his investigation into the city of Rosario, *Central, Ñuls, la ciudad goleada, fútbol y lavado de dinero* [*Central, Ñuls, the Hammered City, Football and Money-Laundering*]. He paints a picture of a sordid world in which a youth coach of Rosario Central, the former player Aurelio Pascutini, was forced to flee the city after his house was shot at because he refused to accept that the *barras* should take the profit from the transfer of promising players. Meanwhile, the other club in the city, Newell's Old Boys, which once produced such stars as Gabriel Batistuta, Abel Balbo, Juan Simón, Jorge Valdano and even Lionel Messi, fears for its future because frightened parents now take their children to other clubs.

In Buenos Aires in 2007, a gun battle broke out among two rival River Plate *barras*, terrifying fans who were peacefully sharing an *asado*. The incident became known as 'the Battle of the *Quinchos*' and was triggered by a dispute over the distribution of the €20million River had received from the sale of Gonzalo Higuaín to Real Madrid. The president of River at the time, José María Aguilar, was widely blamed for having let matters get out of hand. When, in 2011, River were relegated for the first time in their history and fans fought running battles with police after their defeat in a play-off, Aguilar, far from being reprimanded or ridiculed, was rewarded by Grondona with a position in Fifa that brought a high salary, a secretary and a driver.

Even ordinary fans have now started to turn against the *barras*. When Newell's and Independiente last year took the unprecedented step of banning singing on the terraces, fans condemned the *barras*, accusing them of being "mercenaries". Insisting on the 'lungs' to separate rival fans was pointless; now they are needed between different factions of the same team's fans.

It's a situation almost too complex to manage. At every game in the stadium of Atlético Cipolletti in the province of Río Negro in Patagonia, for instance, you can hear two competing chants, each urging on the home team to perform better. The rival *barras* work together to set traps for opposing fans but are then just as likely to turn on each other.

A similar scenario was played out in the final days of the 2011 Apertura when Boca Juniors faced Belgrano of Córdoba at the Bombonera. In the week leading up to the game, Rafael Di Zeo, the former leader of La 12, the biggest of Boca's *barras*, was released from a four-year prison term. He wanted to resume command while his successor, Mauro Martín, insisted he should retain control. The club directors, terrified of a major incident a few weeks before club elections, gave a separate terrace to each group from where they

hurled insults at each other and supported their team with competing chants.

But perhaps the most telling indication of the new reality came at the World Cup in 2010. There was widespread surprise and scepticism when Marcelo Mallo, the vice-president of Quilmes and a close associate of Aníbal Fernández, the chief of the cabinet of the Argentinian president, Cristina Kirchner, announced the creation of a government-supported body, the United Fans of Argentina (HUA), to travel, expenses-paid, to South Africa to support the Argentina national team. Many of the members of HUA were known hooligans, drawn from a wide range of first- and second-division clubs. Boca refused, because they had their own funding, but rivals fans from other clubs had no problems cooperating.

There were no major incidents in South Africa, but that venture shows the fundamental issue in Argentinian football. How can you fight against violence when the state funds hooligans' trips to the World Cup, when many of the hooligans are effectively employed by state officials? And then there is the supplementary question of how the struggle can be taken seriously when the club presidents who oversee the greatest chaos are rewarded with Fifa sinecures.

During a match between Vélez Sársfield and River in the 2010 Clausura, a young fan called Walter Paz was killed. The advocate of City of Buenos Aires, Graciela Muñiz, sought explanations. Vélez sent confused medical certificates, while AFA acted decisively — and sent a full team-list for both sides detailing substitutions, cards and goals. Such are the priorities of AFA. **B**

147

Fiction

"Now he could see misery with
eviscerating clarity."

The Glasses

A gift from a mysterious visitor changes life for a man on a Scottish estate...

By David Ashton

How Eck Livingstone came by the glasses was simple enough but the forces behind it were, and remain to this day, dark and mysterious.

He was walking disconsolately down one of the many scabby streets near to the housing scheme where he lived when... now here I must make clear that this street shall not be named, nor the scheme, nor the city that had swept it as far to the outskirts as was civically conceivable, because it is a condition Eck laid down that in telling this tale everything should be shrouded in anonymity other than himself, the boys and one other person who will surface later; if this does not appeal to you, find some other story. So, in the nameless scabby street, and Eck did disconsolate to a T being six feet five with stringy white hair, he was mooching along when a large car with shaded windows swept past with all its own wheels — which was not usual for the area. One of the windows wound electronically down and an object was thrown out of it to land at Eck's feet.

I am allowed to tell you one thing. The country in which this tale sets itself is Scotland.

The car revved up and disappeared in a puff of fumes, leaving Eck to stoop like a heron and pluck up the object.

It was a glasses case. Good quality, black, sturdy, not flashy. He opened it to disclose a pair of spectacles. They were rimless, almost square, the glass itself fairly thick. At the back of his consciousness, a bell rang.

Eck glanced around shiftily but the street was, even to his blurred sight, empty as last night's can of beans, so he carefully hooked the specs over his large ears.

His long sight was worse than that of an ostrich and abject financial circumstance meant that his only pair of specs, broken when he'd slipped on the remnants of a poke of chips, had never been replaced. The thrift shop where he'd got them was now closed. Such is life.

And so he lived in a dim dejected universe. But now — oh now!

Now he could see misery with eviscerating clarity. The boarded up shops, plastic bags blowing like tumbleweed and what resembled a trail of blood-smeared bandages wrapped round a defunct lamppost. He shuddered and put up a hand to remove the spectacles but stopped. Eck caught sight of himself in a broken piece of mirror that had been propped up against a wall. The glasses shone balefully in a stray shaft of pale light. Again that nagging feeling of visual remembrance. A police siren sounded in the distance so he quickly turned on his heels and quit the scene.

Eck lived a lonely life in his dead mother's council house. His diet was digestive biscuits, baked beans, fish fingers and twice frozen pizza. He had retreated as far from life as is possible without actually giving up the ghost.

This is as much as Eck would like you to know.

Over the next few days he noticed when he wore the glasses that his character was changing. Instead of meekly demurring when some old crone in the pound shop snatched at the last triple packet of digestives, he shoulder-charged her, body swerved a concerned social worker and made for the till. Aggression. Pure and simple.

But what really got him into trouble was football. He had never been that interested in the game — in fact any sport gave him migraines — but Eck found himself standing at the waste ground watching wee boys kick lumps out of each other: it was the school holidays so they had time as well as old tyres to burn.

One bunch in particular caught his attention. They had talent no doubt — yet how would he know what talent was? But he did. Or *thought* he did.

Suddenly the ball sailed through the air towards him. Eck grabbed it. Covered in muck and doggy detritus but... his ball.

"You need a system," he announced. "Without structure, it's a mug's game."

One of the boys picked up a half brick. "Gies oor ba' back," he said. "Or ah'll brain ye."

Eck did not move, the boy closed an eye the better to sight and then hesitated. Something about the way the glasses glinted bleakly in his direction stopped him in his tracks.

"You!" Eck pointed at a small Asian boy he'd noticed possessed a deal of skill but kept getting booted up into the air. "Name?"

"Bix," came the reply. "They ca' me Wheetie."

"And you?" Eck pointed to a fleet-footed but gormless specimen with fair hair flopping over the one eye.

"That's Daft Donal," said the half-brick boy. "Ahm Jazza." The missile was dropped and half-volleyed in the direction of Daft Donal who yelped and leapt aside.

Eck scrutinised Jazza. He was squat, with ferrety shoe-black eyes and a low centre of gravity. He looked born to destroy *galacticos* in the midfield.

"You can be captain," said Eck. "Wheetie and Donal on the wings — you win nothing without wingers." He threw the ball back to Jazza and waved a peremptory arm at the assembled motley crew. "Find your own level, like water. I'll soon shift you if you're not righteous."

They all looked to Jazza who blew the snot from his nose without benefit of hankie and squinted once more at this weird figure, white hair, white face, eyes magnified by the thick glass. The eyes did not blink.

"Okay," said Jazza. "Enough parlay. Let's play the fuckin' gemme."

Over the next three hours, Eck slowly moved the combatants from one team to another, changed back to forward, forward to back, found a centre-half who was crossed-eyed and therefore had uncanny anticipation of opponent's moves, and then a goalie called Rhino with the loudest voice known to man. "Maa ba'!!" he screamed as he flattened his own men along with anyone else in the way, punching the ball up into the dank air. A spine was being formed with Wheetie and Daft Donal the crafty deviants on the wing.

Darkness fell. Call it a day. Jazza headed off having spotted the social worker on the way to visit his family to check for bruises.

"Mister Goddard, haud on!" he bawled. "Ye have tae know the secret knock!"

The man turned and waved earnestly. He was middle-aged, sandy-haired, with a briefcase that he clutched protectively to his chest. Eck recognised him from the pound shop.

"Tomorrow. Ten sharp!" he shouted.

Jazza turned. The tall figure was almost obscured in the gloom but his glasses shone like a prison searchlight. The boy spat a gob of acknowledgement then ran after the social worker.

"Hey Mister Goddard, there's a paedo at the fitba'," he called. "Dead weird."

Eck smiled in a wintry fashion. "And the rest of you," he proclaimed in a voice that issued from somewhere he had never knowingly possessed. "Clean up your act. You look like a bunch of middens."

And so the weeks of the summer holidays passed. Some boys fell out, more joined, but the spine stayed firm, the wingers flourished, a centre-forward was unearthed — another Asian boy nicknamed Bendy-toy who could indeed contort his lanky frame to meet the inaccurate offerings coming in from Wheetie and Daft Donal. It is always the fate of a winger to combine the deftest of touch with an ability to fall over your own feet.

Jazza would become incensed. "Ah've seen better crosses on the Pope's backside!"

The team divided equally into Proddies and Papes with two Hindus thrown in, so religious insults were absorbed interdenominationally as it were — and there was always Eck.

Nothing mattered except the game. Rain, hail or shine he stood there like a lighthouse, obdurate, unflinching, glass surface reflecting the setting sun.

Occasionally there would be a flash of uncontrolled aggression, which seemed to surprise him as much as the team, but mostly it was patience, patience and more patience.

They played teams from the other schemes, lost a few early games then got on a run. Adults started turning up to bawl but the team only had ears for one voice. The adults gave up advice and started running the line. A strip was found off the back of supermarket trolley, luckily neither blue nor green — red in fact — and a name was found. Livingstone's Untouchables. LU For short. Lulu if you wanted to provoke their wrath.

For they were an entity now. A team. They could see their image in his glasses. A body with many legs and arms. Before every game Eck pronounced the mantra. "No-one can beat us. And if they do — it's an accident that will not be repeated."

Daft Donal was tricky on the right, but Wheetie on the left was a revelation. He left the intestinal tracts of defenders trailing like spaghetti as he twisted them like a corkscrew, then — and this is where the patience came in because Eck had him practise till he could land it on a bailiff's notice — speared the ball towards Bendy-Toy's angular head.

Then a wee man in a bonnet approached Eck and asked if they wanted to join the under-11 league. Seemed the local social worker had put a word in to some committee.

Livingstone's Untouchables were heading mainstream. All was set fair.

Eck has asked me to describe the following malignant events with dispassion.

He had now graduated from a harmless loony to a man of some substance in the community — but it did not save him. Eck came home one night to find two young men waiting in front of his council house. He recognised them as the attached drug dealers for the estate — brothers — dressed to kill.

"You are a financial threat," said one. "Tae our legitimate business."

They both had calm open faces, Paul Smith shirts, black knife-edge suits with, had Eck glanced down to observe, incongruous Doc Marten boots anchoring them to the cracked pavement. A pity he missed the Doc Martens.

"We need the boys for deliveries," said the other. "Your fitba' is distracting them from growing up in a proper fashion. So, stop it. Pronto."

A wise man would have nodded, made no eye contact, lived to fight another day, but Eck Livingstone had his glasses on. "Stick your demands," said he. "Where the monkey stuck his nuts. Pronto."

People heard the beating going on, but no-one came out to save him. Curtains closed, lights went out, shame-faced adults turned up the TV. Only Jazza made a move to the door but his equally squat father shoved him back.

"These boys are life-takers," he said. "They'll chib ye tae mince."

Mercifully the razors rested in the inside pocket but the boots went in. Eck might, in other times, have appreciated the accuracy as he huddled like a long foetus while the brothers kicked their fill. When they stopped he could feel his own blood, warm in the mouth.

"That's yer last warning," said one. "Next time, we'll act serious."

As they left Eck crawled towards the shattered glasses. His world in pieces.

Is that dispassionate enough for you?

The next day, the boys gathered at the wasteland which had now been marked out into a rough football pitch shape, lines drawn, rubbish cleared, ground flattened. Word had got round fast and all they could do was wait.

"Ah don't believe it," muttered Jazza. "Here he fuckin' comes."

Eck had glued the glasses back together but looked like the woman from the Odessa Steps, the surface like a spider's web behind which could be seen his eyes, bloodshot, the image splintered into so many versions of a once proud optic.

He walked stiffly, slowly, trying to hold in his mind a template of Clint Eastwood from a spaghetti Western — but Clint always had a horse at hand.

He finally reached the wasteland. Silence. The whole scheme held its breath.

"Let's play football," he said. "Time waits for no man."

One of the old biddies from the pound shop passed and shouted, "G'wan yersel' Big Man!" and the local social worker came round the corner as if he'd heard the call, briefcase tucked under his arm in an almost military fashion.

No-one moved from the boys. Rhino pawed at the ground scraping in frustration, Wheetie's feet twitched but he could not let them loose, Bendy-Toy inclined his body to the side as if trying to break free from chains, Jazza was stock still.

He blew the snot from one nostril and turned away. Eck watched him leave, an empty feeling in his aching guts, at least one rib was buggered, possibly two, but who cared anyway?

Jazza stopped at the centre circle and swivelled to walk deliberately to where his position in the midfield would be. Again silence. Rhino suddenly stamped his foot and charged towards the makeshift goalposts, Daft Donal scratched his head and ambled to the right, Wheetie darted to the left, the other boys and reserve team took up position.

Eck bent down awkwardly to pick up a ball that had somehow landed at his feet as the glasses case had so long ago. Finally he remembered. The picture that had been nagging at him for all this time. The glasses. They were a ringer for Alex Ferguson's.

He threw the ball towards Jazza who passed it neatly to Bendy-Toy at the centre spot.

Big Eck took a deep painful breath. "Let's play football," he said.

The story really ends there but, as is customary these days, there's always a coda, though I have been instructed by Eck to wrap it up quick. The drug brothers were waiting three nights later but, this time, one door after another slammed open in the scheme and a collection of men and women emerged with various implements of destruction, one a particularly evil looking garden scythe, in their hands. The brothers left. Pronto.

Livingstone Untouchables won the under-11 cup but were disqualified because Jazza was revealed to be a cut down fifteen years old. It ran in the family. Eck shrugged. Too bad.

Wheetie attracted scouts from all over and Manchester United even showed up. The boy's parents only trusted Eck who told the scouts, "I will deal with one man and one man solo."

And so it came to pass that one day a large car with shaded windows rolled up in front of Eck's council house and a stocky fellow emerged. He knocked at the door. Eck opened it and stood there with his ruined glasses. The stocky fellow entered.

What passed between is not known, although Wheetie became the first British Asian player to take the park for United. The important thing however is that, as the car sped away, the window rolled down and a glasses case flew out to land at Eck's feet. His agent's fee.

That's the tale. I have done the best I can. I will now pick up my briefcase and go on my round of hopeless healing. Each to his own. But just to end it?

Eck picked up the glasses case, opened it, and put on the tools of his trade. Jazza was appointed first-team coach.

Heading for glory.

154

Greatest Games

"A team that could be exhilarating
or exasperating, often within the
space of a few minutes"

Romania 4 Yugoslavia 6

World Cup qualifier, Ghencea Stadium, Bucharest, 13 November 1977

By Vladimir Novak

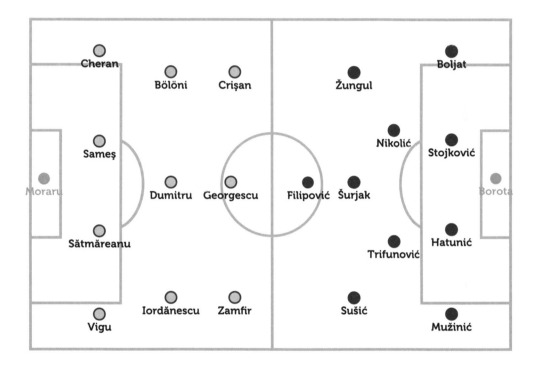

In his interview with Dragan Stojković in Issue Two of *The Blizzard*, Andrew McKirdy asked, "Serbian and Yugoslavian football has a history of drama and highs and lows. Do you think this reflects the Serbian psyche and do you think this is true of you?" Stojković is an intelligent man and a good talker, but his answer missed the point. He spoke about bad organisation, poor leadership, a refusal to take responsibility and the lack of a professional mindset, but he didn't touch the painful truth. The history of drama and highs and lows derives to a large extent from a confused national psyche that leads it simultaneously to overestimate itself and to have an inferiority complex.

The performances and results of Serbia and before it Yugoslavia are characterised by their erratic nature. Stojković perhaps didn't mention psychological factors because he was an exception. He didn't suffer that mixed-up psyche; he was always a great professional, a fighter, a winner and a genuine leader. Yugoslavian football has known few enough of those and the result was a team that could be exhilarating or exasperating, often within the space of a few minutes. No game, perhaps, has demonstrated that combination as well as the World Cup qualifier against Romania in November 1977.

If Yugoslavia were to qualify for Argentina 78, they had to beat Romania in Bucharest. Only the side that finished top of a three-team qualifying group made it to the finals and Yugoslavia had already lost twice, 1-0 away to Spain and 2-0 at home against Romania.

Four years earlier, they'd faced a similar situation. A win at home over Spain would have secured Yugoslavia qualification for the 1974 World Cup, but they drew 0-0 in Zagreb meaning they went to Greece needing to win by three clear goals to make it to West Germany. Greece had already been eliminated but they were perceived as awkward opponents. Yugoslavia swept into a 2-0 lead in the opening quarter of an hour, but Greece pulled one back on the half hour, Dušan Bajević was sent off after 37 minutes and then Josip Katalinski scored an own goal after a comical misunderstanding over a backpass with the goalkeeper Enver Marić: 2-2.

The coach, Miljan Miljanić, who died in January this year, gambled on youth, withdrawing Jurica Jerković and Dragan

Džajić for the 20-year-old Ivica Šurjak and the 18-year-old Vladimir Petrović. Yugoslavia took control again. Šurjak restored their lead after 63 minutes and then, in the final minute, Stanislav Karasi made it 4-2 to set up a play-off against Spain. They won a famous game 1-0 in Frankfurt to qualify for the World Cup.

In 1973, Yugoslavia's situation had been difficult; here it seemed all but impossible. Spain had four points from their three games and a goal difference of 3-1. Romania also had four points from three games and a goal difference of 3-2. With no points from two games and a goal-difference of 0-3, Yugoslavia needed not merely to win both games, but to effect a swing of four in their goal-difference. And, unlike in Athens four years earlier, this time they were playing against sides who themselves had something to play for.

Romania's focus was almost monastic and at one point it seemed that their coach, Stefan Kovacs, who led Ajax to the European Cup in 1972 and 1973, might not even turn up for the pre-match press-conference the day before the game. The squad was based at Snagov, about 20 miles from Bucharest and of great symbolic significance as the place where Vlad Ţepeş, Romania's great national hero Vlad the Impaler, is believed to be buried.

Romania had lost 2-0 in Spain a couple of weeks earlier and most of the local coverage was dominated by the question of how Kovacs might change the side, with particular attention paid to Mircea Lucescu, whose call up at the age of 32 had been a major surprise. In the end, he kept changes to a minimum. Dumitru Moraru replaced Cristian

Gheorghe in goal while Constantin Zamfir came in on the left for Ilie Balaci, but essentially it was the same 4-3-3 that had beaten Spain 1-0 at home and won 2-0 in Yugoslavia, as well as recording impressive performances in friendlies against Turkey (4-0), Czechoslovakia (3-1), Greece (6-1) and East Germany (1-1).

Emphasising their determination to win, the Romanian Football Federation (FRF) opted not to play at the 75,000-capacity 23 August Stadium, but at the newly built Ghencea, the home of Steaua. It housed only 30,000 but was renowned for the atmosphere it generated. Tickets sold out within two hours — even though Romanians knew their fate would ultimately be decided when Yugoslavia went to Spain a fortnight later.

Kovacs, of course, was already a legend as a coach and his squad was packed with experienced and highly respected names: Anghel Iordănescu, Dudu Georgescu, Alexandru Sătmăreanu, Ion Dumitru, Constantin Zamfir, László Bölöni... Yugoslavia, by contrast, were in all too familiar crisis. Ivan Toplak had been dismissed as coach after only nine months in charge following the home defeat to Romania in May and had been replaced by a three-man selection panel made up of Marko Valok, Stevan Vilotić and Gojko Zec.

Valok was 50 and had been a prolific striker for Partizan in the forties and fifties, scoring 411 goals in 470 games. His coaching CV, though, was rather less impressive: he'd won the league title with Partizan in 1964-65 and had taken the underdogs of Budućnost Podgorica to the Cup final — and a respectable mid-table finish —in 1976-77 but, that

aside, he had spent four years in Burma and had worked mainly at smaller clubs. Zec was probably the most deserving coach on the panel with consistent achievements at a number of top-flight clubs, culminating with the 1976-77 league title with Crvena Zvezda. Vilotić, meanwhile, was Yugoslavia's best-known and most respected youth coach. Valok was named head of the panel, but the fact it was felt necessary to appoint a panel at all suggested the federation (FSJ) didn't see him as a long term solution.

The home defeat to Romania also marked the end for a number of ageing greats: Branko Oblak, Katalinski, Bajević and Džajić never played for the national side again. 1977 had been a poor year in general for the *Plavi* [Blues].They also lost a series of friendlies: 5-1 in Mexico, 4-2 at home to the USSR, 2-1 at home against West Germany, 1-0 in Argentina and 4-3 in Hungary.

Valok reacted with a radical team selection: only two players who had featured in that defeat in May — Dražen Mužinić and Šurjak — were named in the starting line-up in Bucharest six months later. He picked two debutants — the right-back Mario Boljat from Hajduk Split and the defensive midfielder Aleksandar Trifunović from Partizan — and two players who had only one cap — the goalkeeper Petar Borota and the forward Safet Sušic. Much of the rest of the side lacked experience. The central defender Nenad Stojković was 21 and had played only three friendlies for his country. The other centre-back, Jusuf Hatunić, had only four caps. In total, Yugoslavia's starting line-up had won 90 caps, as opposed to the 269 won by

Romania. It also contained not a single player based abroad.

"Frankly speaking, nobody thought we could win," said the centre-forward Zoran Filipović. "And certainly not by the two or three goals we needed to. So we went into the game in a pretty relaxed mood."

That sense of relaxation was apparent the day before the game. After a light training session and the inevitable reception at the Yugoslav embassy, the players and the coaching staff spent the evening at the circus.

It was a mild and sunny autumn afternoon. The Ghencea was packed, far more than the capacity of 30,000 squeezing in. In the VIP section were the Argentina coach César Luis Menotti, the Brazil coach Claudio Coutinho and, of course, Spain's manager László Kubala, scouting his next opponent.

Conceding an early goal is never a good thing but some hurt more than others. For Yugoslavia, going 1-0 down in the first minute was a nightmare. From the kick-off, Romania attacked on the left, Zamfir beating two men before being fouled by Trifunović. The free-kick was more than 40 yards from goal, wide on the left, between the halfway line and the Romanian dugout. Everybody anticipated a cross, but Iosif Vigu's delivery came at a more acute angle than expected, catching Borota out and drifting under the crossbar. It was a dream start for the hosts and a dreadful error by Borota, who misjudged the flight of the ball and was then unable to react and correct

his mistake. Yugoslavia not only had to come from behind, but to do so with an inexperienced and traumatised goalkeeper.

Borota, who died in 2010 at the age of 57, became one of the great characters of the Yugoslav game. He joined Chelsea from Partizan in 1979 and made over 100 appearances for them but, gifted as he certainly was, he never quite shook off his reputation for eccentricity. He could be brilliant, but he also made some dreadful errors. The two biggest came in the year that followed the Bucharest game. In the first round of the European Cup in 1978, Partizan went to Dynamo Dresden with a 2-0 lead from the first leg. Nine minutes into the away leg, Borota caught a simple cross and then, inexplicably, put the ball down as though to take a goal-kick. Hans-Jürgen Dörner was lurking and calmly nudged the ball into the empty net as Borota lined up his clearance. Partizan lost 2-0 and went out on penalties. That same season, in the Belgrade derby, Borota conceded an almost identical goal. He caught a cross under pressure and, assuming a foul had been given, put the ball down for a free-kick, allowing Miloš Šestić a simple finish. Partizan lost 3-1.

With Yugoslavia rattled, Romania took control. Borota let a Bölöni cross sail over his head for Georgescu, who missed with a free header, and Bölöni and Zamfir also missed good chances in the first 10 minutes. The game could have been over almost before it had begun, but Yugoslavia, having survived, gradually began to claw their way back into it. Savisa Zungul hit the side-netting from a Šurjak free-kick and then in the 14th minute the *Plavi* equalised.

Šurjak initiated an attack in his own half, shepherding the ball to the halfway line where he found Zungul with a deep pass to the left. Zungul sent a firm, low cross into the box and Sušic met it six yards out. The 1000 or so Yugoslavia fans in the stadium came alive in a flurry of flags and banners.

Three minutes later they were celebrating again as Yugoslavia took the lead. Dušan Nikolić won the ball in the Yugoslavia half and played a quick pass into the centre-circle for Zungul. He deceived his marker by letting the ball run through his legs to Stojković, up from centre-back to join the attack. He played the ball forward to Sušić, who took the ball in his stride at full tilt and, from a position to the right of centre, lashed the ball goalwards from about 15 yards. His shot beat Moraru but slapped against the post, bouncing out to the edge of the six-yard box where Alexandru Sătmăreanu hacked it away. His clearance fell to the left-back Dragan Mužinić 25 yards out and he smacked a left-foot shot into the top corner for his first and — it would turn out — only goal in 32 appearances for his country. Mužinić as a goalscorer? With a goal like that? After Vigu's bizarre opener it was already clear this would be no normal game.

Sensing weakness, Yugoslavia poured forwards. Romania struggled to deal with their fluid 4-2-3-1 formation — and it was a genuine 4-2-3-1, over a decade before Juanma Lillo, who is usually credited as being its originator, developed a similar formation at Cutural Leonesa in Spain. Šurjak operated as the deep-lying forward, a central playmaker behind Filipović, with the wide players, Zungul (nominally on the right) and Sušić (left) constantly switching positions and Sušić regularly joining Filipović to become a second centre-forward. That they could play with such freedom was down to the platform provided them by the holding midfield duo of Trifunović and Nikolić (whose nickname was 'Staja', a corruption of 'Stiles' — as in Nobby) with Šurjak dropping deep to support when necessary. Yugoslavia were aggressive and fluent, an effective combination of the hard and combative and the creative and skilful.

The problem was the defence. Impressive as Yugoslavia were going forward, they always looked vulnerable at the back, in part because of Borota and in part because of Hatunić, who was dreadfully nervous at centre-back. At one point, a worried Mužinić ran to the bench and shouted at the coaching staff, "The midfield isn't helping us enough... nobody's covering space... we need more running and pressing."

Romania were always going to get chances and one arrived after 32 minutes. From Yugoslavia's point of view, it couldn't have fallen to a worse player. Georgescu had won the European Golden Boot the previous season, scoring 47 goals for Dinamo Bucharest. When the ball dropped to him, unmarked, in front of goal and with Borota inexplicably out of position, he only had to roll the ball goalwards to score. Instead, he hit the shot with great power — and put it high over the bar. It was a let-off, but Borota's positioning was so bad it seemed hard to understand why Valok didn't replace him; Yugoslavia, it seemed, were effectively playing without a goalkeeper.

"Of course we were asking ourselves on the bench whether to substitute Borota," Valok said. "I was considering it, but at the same time I hesitated because I felt that we would need two fresh players later in the second half. So, I decided to continue with Borota and later [Velemir] Zajec and [Momčilo] Vukotić turned the rhythm and pace of the game in our favour.... So, eventually it proved that it was the right decision that we didn't hurry with the substitution."

Borota was left out of a friendly against Greece in Thessalonikki three days later, which ended 0-0, and didn't play against Spain in the final qualifier. A year later, he was selected again, winning a fourth cap in a Euro 80 qualifier — again against Romania in Bucharest. This time Borota was blameless as Yugoslavia lost 3-2, but he was never picked again.

The warning was there, but it wasn't heeded and Romania levelled five minutes before half-time. A long ball caught Yugoslavia out, Hatunić failed to clear and Anghel Iordănescu, collecting the ball on the edge of the box, swept his finish past Borota, who had come charging too quickly from his goal-line.

And by half-time Romania were ahead. The speedy right winger Zoltan Crisan beat two defenders and, as the ball bobbed up, he headed it on to Bölöni on the edge of the box. Stojković went to block the shot, but the ball deflected off his heel and into the net. Borota was left flat-footed on his six-yard line, unable to react. To blame him would be unfair, but he didn't look good. "It was the strangest match I've ever played in," said Nenad Stojković. "There were those constant switches from joy to sorrow and vice versa. At the end we were not only exhausted and happy about the victory, but we also felt somehow lost and confused."

Romania had been perhaps a little fortunate but half-time brought a decisive change as Kovacs was forced to replace the injured Sătmăreanu with Vasile Dobrau. "In the moment Sătmăreanu was injured," Kovacs said, "I feared we would have problems. Our defence underperformed in the face of the mighty attacks from the Yugoslavs."

Still, the first chance of the second half went to the home side, Yugoslavia's defence dithering and allowing Iordănescu the opportunity to shoot from the edge of the box. This time, Borota made a decent save, intercepting the strike as it arrowed towards the top corner. It was a vital stop, as was emphasised two minutes later when Yugoslavia levelled.

Šurjak took a quick free-kick near the halfway line, passing to Sušic who received it around 40 yards out to the left of the Romanian box. He accelerated through two challenges and as Moraru came out, he slipped it past him. Bölöni got back to attempt a clearance but couldn't prevent it crossing the line: 3-3.

Any sense of caution disappeared. Both sides ripped into each other, trading attacks, blow for blow. A draw was of no use to either side: there could be no points decision, only a knockout would do. Georgescu put two good headed opportunities wide. Filipović, with a fine chance after 58 minutes, opted to try to lay in Zungul, who was offside. Iordănescu missed another good opportunity a minute later.

It was then that Valok made his first substitution, introducing the Partizan forward Vukotić for Zungul. His fresh legs quickly made an impact. With his first touch, Vukotić dribbled past Stefan Sames who tripped him a couple of yards outside the box. Šurjak ran over the free-kick, Trifunović rolled it to Sušić, whose ferocious shot beat a partially unsighted Moraru. It was the 22-year-old Sušić's hat-trick and meant he had scored five goals in his first two internationals. He went on to become one of Europe's most feared forwards, a legend at Paris Saint-Germain, who enjoyed a swansong at Italia 90 at the age of 35. His 54 games for Yugoslavia brought 21 goals and he is now coach of Bosnia-Herzegovina.

That was 4-3, but with half an hour to go the game was far from over. Both sides made changes in midfield. Mihai Romila came on for the disappointing Ion Dumitru, then Zajec was brought on for Nikolić. "We had nothing to lose," Nikolić said. "Practically nobody gave us any chance. Nobody thought that we could win in Bucharest, let alone with such a spectacular result and get back in the race for Argentina. But we played a real attacking game, without fear and when we conceded the goals, we encouraged ourselves to go on, to keep on fighting and playing. When I was substituted, Moca [as Vukotić was nicknamed] came on for me. This showed that we wanted to keep on attacking, that we were looking for the victory. It was a weird game."

Three minutes after Romila's introduction, Romania equalised. Bölöni, having been fouled 30 yards out, took the free-kick himself, knocking the ball to Vigu who helped it on to the left winger Zamfir. He crossed to the back post where Georgescu headed in unmarked. Again the Yugoslav defence was at fault, Stojković, Zajec and Boljat all drawn to the near post while nobody picked up Romania's main goal threat.

With a quarter of the game remaining, the scores were level at the result neither side wanted. Yugoslavia came again. The tireless Šurjak escaped on the left-hand side and put in a hard low cross that a stretching Flipović couldn't quite get on the end of. A one-two between Bölöni and Georgescu broke through the Yugoslavia defence, but Borota saved from the midfielder. Then Zajec, in characteristic style, dribbled through only to hit a weak shot from the edge of the box that Moraru saved comfortably.

Another goal was coming and it arrived with 11 minutes remaining. Šurjak took a throw on the left, finding Mužinić, who passed it on to Trifunović. He played a one-two with Sušić and then hit a fearsome shot from a narrow angle 12 yards out. It flashed under the crossbar. "It was a difficult position, a tight angle, for a shot on goal," Trifunović said, "but I hit the ball well. The goalkeeper probably didn't expect such a strike and also it was quite close, so he had no chance for a save." A lucky punch, maybe, but it was a phenomenal goal and Yugoslavia led 5-4.

This time Romania couldn't rally. They seemed dazed as Yugoslavia swarmed over them, looking for further goals that would reduce the magnitude of their task against Spain. With six minutes remaining, Vukotić played a pass with the outside of his foot into the path of Flipović and he hit a first-time shot past Moraru. As Trifunović, Sušić and Mužinić jumped on the tired but happy scorer they were joined by a Yugoslav fan waving his flag deliriously.

It could have been an even more decisive scoreline. Šurjaka had a free-kick well saved by Moraru and the keeper then made another excellent block to deny Sušić. But 6-4 it finished. Had they got a seventh perhaps it would have changed things, for then Yugoslavia would have played Spain in the final qualifier needing only a win to qualify for the World Cup rather than having to win by two goals.

As the Belgian referee Fred Delcourt blew the final whistle, the Romanians looked stunned and left the field to the celebrating Yugoslavs. Even Petar Borota, who had had an awful day, ran around with his arms in the air and when Nikolić came towards him, he lifted him up and carried him around with a big smile on his face. A few minutes later Milan 'Raki' Arandjelović, Yugoslavia's legendary physiotherapist who had worked at over 300 international matches, went into the Romanian dressing-room, bumped into Kovacs and asked him if he could have a Romanian shirt as souvenir. "Kovacs's face was completely pale, almost white," Arandjelović said. "You could see that he was disappointed and angry but he acted well and brought me a shirt.

Still, when he handed it over to me, he mumbled something in Romanian, which I couldn't understand, but I can bet that he said something like, 'Here's the bloody shirt, and now get the fuck out of here.'"

Valok, his thoughts perhaps already on the Spain game, tried to give an impression of calm. "Congratulations to the blue giants," he said. "They held out in a fiery atmosphere, they came twice from behind and found strength to attack for the victory. I congratulate everybody. I wouldn't single out anybody, still I have to mention the shining Safet Sušić. Also I want to congratulate the hosts for their fair play."

César Luis Menotti was also impressed. "To see so many goals in one game is really unusual," he said. "Before the game I predicted that Yugoslavia would qualify for the World Cup finals. Now they are much closer to achieving that."

But they didn't. Two weeks later, in front of a packed Marakana in Belgrade, Yugoslavia lost to Spain, Rubén Cano scoring the only goal in the 70th minute of a frenetic and often ill-tempered game. So Spain went to Argentina and Yugoslavia were left with nothing but the memories of the thriller in Bucharest. Ⓑ

164

Five Rings

"It was the typical head-in-the-sand
attitude that has kept the brakes on
British football for so long..."

Olympic Stories

Five tales from the rich history of Olympic football

By Marcus Christenson, Steve Menary, Jonathan Wilson, Colin Udoh and Joel Richards

 Sweden at London 1948

George Raynor only accepted the role as Swedish national coach because he had been rejected at home. He didn't want to go to Gothenburg in 1946 to start work for the 1948 Olympic football tournament; he would rather have worked with a club side in England. He was English and he was a good football coach. The problem was that no one in his home country was prepared to offer him a job. He was admired abroad, but viewed with suspicion at home. He was, in a sense, the Roy Hodgson of the 1940s (at least before the latter's successful spells with Fulham and West Brom).

During the Second World War Raynor had organised physical training and sport with the British Military Mission and toured the Middle East with a football team from the Iraq Military College. When he returned home in 1945, he was told by Sir Stanley Rous, the Football Association secretary, that there would be plenty of jobs as a coach. But having played his last game for Aldershot in 1945, he quickly realised that there would be no offers. He was distraught.

"Nobody wanted any system. Coaches were regarded as cranks who would soon fade away from the scene so that the game could continue," he wrote in his 1960 autobiography, *Football*

Ambassador at Large. "I found people believing that it would take at least two years for football to get under way again [after the war], and until that time coaching was quite out of the question. It was the typical head-in-the-sand attitude that has kept the brakes on British football for so long... What a different history of football might have been written if Britain, like the continent, had realised in those early post-war days the true value of the right coaching."

After finally giving up on Britain, Raynor accepted the invitation from the Swedish FA. He arrived in Gothenburg one rainy morning in 1946 at the age of 39. The chairman of the Swedish selection committee, Putte Kock, was initially taken aback by Raynor's unassuming character but was soon won over by Englishman's intelligence and enthusiasm. Raynor, for his part, quickly realised, to his delight, that there was "a tremendous thirst for football knowledge" in Sweden. "Everyone," he wrote, "was willing to take advice, anxious to learn." After a few months in his new country, Raynor accepted a two-year contract, turning the job into a one-man crusade to prove the British wrong at the 1948 London Olympic Games. He would show them what they had missed.

Sweden's neutrality during the Second World War meant the country and its football were in good shape compared to the rest of Europe. Raynor did, however, have some Olympic baggage to deal with. At the previous Games, in Berlin in 1936, Sweden had suffered one of their most humiliating defeats by losing 3-2 to Japan. The Asian nation went on to lose their next game 8-0 against Italy and when the Swedish squad arrived back to their own country some players reportedly wore signs saying "I did not play against Japan" around their necks.

There was embarrassment too for Raynor when Birmingham City visited Sweden a month after his appointment. The Swedes, who had proudly put the new national coach at the head table, realised that no one from the visiting team recognised the Englishman. It was a blow to the Swedes' (and Raynor's) self-esteem and the papers in Sweden wrote that their FA had hired "a nobody". Luckily, an RAF side came to Stockholm soon afterwards, with players such as Stanley Matthews and George Hardwick, who knew Raynor very well from his time at Aldershot. His pride was restored.

Raynor soon realised he had to make some tactical changes. He felt that some of the players were not "manly enough". He wrote, "That isn't to say that the Swedes were scared. Far from it. But while they were technically very good when they got the ball, the breakers-up, the men who could go into a fierce tackle and get the ball, were few and far between." He also decided to change the formation to include a so-called "G-man", something he had picked up at Bury. The G-man was a deep-lying centre-forward in the style of Hungary's Nándor I lidegkuti.

Slowly, Raynor's (and Kock's) plan started to come together. He picked Knut Nordahl as his G-man for his first match, against Switzerland, who had beaten the Swedes 3-0 the previous year, and Nordahl roamed to great effect with Gunnar Gren[1], who had been told to stay upfield, scoring four in a 7-2 win. There was much still to be done, however, and Raynor worked relentlessly with the Swedes to get them to mix the short game with the long. He also felt that the centre-half-back attacked far too much and consequently left huge gaps in defence.

Then, however, he spotted Bertil Nordahl play and immediately realised that Knut's brother was the answer to the centre-half-back problem (the third brother, Gunnar, was in the team as an inside-forward). "I was told that his [Bertil's] true role was that of a full-back," he said. "But I wanted him at centre-half-back because he was a player with some bite and I knew he would be complementary to Sweden's overload of delicate ball players."

However, the national team met so infrequently that the only way Raynor could transform Bertil Nordahl into a defensive centre-half was to visit the player's club, Degerfors, and work with him there. He did the same with several other players he felt he needed to work with. He travelled the country, staying for a fortnight or so in each part. There were only 12 clubs in the first division and they were not too far apart. Importantly, Raynor had also won over the selectors, with whom he had what he termed a "give-and-take relationship".

[1] For more on Gren's early years, see Gunnar Persson's piece on Motala in Issue One of The Blizzard.

They once rejected his suggestion of a player but he did not let irritation become bitterness. Equally, they realised that they could not push him around. Raynor wanted Sweden to play a more direct style — and so they did. In six internationals in 1947, Sweden scored 31 goals and conceded only eight, winning every game. But in November of that year they lost narrowly to a full-strength England side. The defeat signalled a change in form and the problems started to pile up. Time was running out before the Olympics.

The penultimate game before the tournament was a disaster, with Sweden losing 1-0 to Holland in Amsterdam and playing terribly. Jesper Högström writes in his excellent book *Blågult — fotbollslandslaget genom 100 år*, that "Henry 'Garvis' Carlsson had lost his form and his place in the national team and the experiment to try him on the right wing in Amsterdam had been a failure. The sensitive Gunnar Gren had become embroiled in an argument with his club, IFK Göteborg, and developed gastric ulcers. Gunnar Nordahl, too, had lost his form and his teammate from IFK Norrköping, Nils Liedholm, had also been a disappointment."

One problem seemed to have been solved, however. Gunnar Gren, who would later be nicknamed *Il professore* and play for AC Milan, Fiorentina and Genoa, had a tendency to showboat and Raynor struggled for a long time to make him play more responsibly. Gren, in the very first game Raynor had seen in Sweden, had "dribbled round three men, round the goalkeeper and then turned round, beat the goalkeeper again, and back-heeled the ball into the net,"

making the English coach "hopping mad". Raynor told Gren that every player had to play for the team, not show off for their own benefit, but the player continued with his crowd-pleasing tricks and was dropped. Gren responded by saying that Raynor "had his knife in him". Eventually, the two reached a compromise and Gren was re-instated in time for the Olympics.

Given all the other problems, it was a concerned Raynor who took charge of the final warm-up game. He knew he needed a good send-off from the Swedish public in order to complete a successful return to Britain. Raynor still had to tell the players to tackle more and use physical contact, such as "fair shoulder-charges". The Englishman also convinced the selectors to take a punt on Bian Rosengren — a man with "great drive" — and he had a wonderful game against the Austrians. Sweden won 3-2 and set off for their pre-Olympics get-together, meeting up at the beautiful spot of Hindås, near Gothenburg. There, Raynor had to "remove some of the cockiness" that had emerged during the unbeaten run in 1947. "They had got into their heads that they were world-beaters because they had not been beaten for some time," he wrote.

During the Olympics, Sweden had their headquarters near Richmond Park in south-west London. There the players faced a rigorous training routine: even the players' tournaments in badminton and head tennis were supervised by the coaching team. However, they were permitted shopping trips to Kingston upon Thames to sample the English culture and the players fell in love with the famous Bentalls store. When they ate,

Raynor reflected that "it might surprise those of you who remember those days of shortage to learn that our players thought the portions 'rather large'".

Sweden, who were one of the favourites to win the Olympic tournament, faced Austria in the first round. The Austrians were beaten easily at White Hart Lane as the tactics — to start furiously and so shock the opponents — worked perfectly. Sweden were 2-0 up within nine minutes after two goals from Gunnar Nordahl. Kjell Rosén added a third to complete the victory. The next opponent, South Korea, were portrayed as a banana skin in the Swedish papers, considering what had happened against another Asian team, Japan, 12 years earlier. Korea, having been occupied by Japan between 1940 and 1945, even had a player who had been on the pitch in that famous upset in Berlin. But in the end Sweden crushed Korea 12-0 at Selhurst Park. Gunnar Nordahl got four, Carlsson three, Nils Liedholm and Rosén two each and Gren one. Afterwards, the Swedes were less than complimentary about the Koreans; Rosén saying, "They had put on some kind of shitty lotion, so they smelt bloody bad."

There was disruption, though, before the semi-final, against their arch-rivals Denmark at Wembley. Agents from an Italian club had offered Raynor £500 to get Carlsson and Liedholm to sign for their club. He was horrified. "Here I was in charge of an amateur team in the Olympic Games and people thought that I would take money to break up my own side," he wrote. "I told the Italians they could get away from my players ... and stay away. But then, before the semi-final, the two Italians tried to get into our dressing-room, so I had to show

them the door and tell the guard that on no account must anyone be allowed to come in without a pass or without reference to me."

Against Denmark, Raynor had to play without the important Knut Nordahl, who was injured. After two minutes the Danes took the lead, running circles around Nordahl's replacement, Börje Leander. The Danes continued to attack and seven minutes later John Hansen hit the crossbar with a tremendous effort. But then the Swedes started to show the mental courage with which Raynor had been trying to infuse them throughout his tenure. Carlsson equalised after 18 minutes and Sweden gradually began to wear the Danes down. Rosén scored twice and Bertil Nordahl was so forceful in breaking up the Danes' attacks that the Danish radio commentator, Gunnar 'Nu' Hansen, said that the Swede should never be allowed to enter a football pitch again. The game ended 4-2 to the Swedes after another strike from Carlsson.

The opponents in the final, also at Wembley, were the physically strong and technically excellent Yugoslavs. And, predictably, the Swedes struggled early on. Gunnar Nordahl remembered afterwards how Sweden had been indebted to the brilliant Gren, who had been the only Swede who had dared to keep hold of the ball — who had, of course, nearly been dropped because of his showboating a few months earlier. Gren gave Sweden the lead, although Yugoslavia equalised just before half-time. Nordahl then made it 2-1 before his brother Bertil suffered a horrible-looking injury. He was white with pain and could hardly walk according to Raynor, but miraculously, when urged by the coach to get back on, he managed to do so. He soon broke up a Yugoslav attack and set up the third goal, from which the Balkan side never recovered.

The Swedish papers reported the next day that the Yugoslav players had called the Swedes "fascists" and "gangsters" on the pitch and that one of the Yugoslav officials spat Raynor in the face after the game and said, "Ah, English referee. English coach. Communist. It is bribery." But Gunnar Nordahl also said that the Yugoslavs came into the Swedish dressing-room after the game and congratulated them.

The radio commentator Sven Jerring, who had become famous during the debacle against Japan in 1936, told his audience that "big, strong, Swedish men cried and kissed" after the final whistle. The Swedish king sent a congratulatory message and there was a party at the Harrow Tavern near Wembley on the night of the final. It was reportedly a calm affair but there have been suggestions that the papers chose to focus on the behaviour of the tee-totallers Torsten Lindberg and Erik Nilsson, rather than Rosengren and Rosén, who did not hold back when it came to alcohol.

The success in London is still Sweden's only win in a major football tournament but whether the achievement outstrips finishing second at the 1958 World Cup and third in 1950 and 1994 is debatable. At the London Olympics, the opposition was far from the strongest possible. The IOC had let each participating country decide how to deal with the amateur rules. Sweden had found a compromise in their "half-amateur" status but the fact was that only Sweden, Austria, Denmark and Yugoslavia sent their best teams. The British teams did not have their best players, and neither did the south Europeans and South Americans. The Soviet Union and Hungary were not even there.

The repercussions of victory were, initially, very different for the coach and his players. The players finally gave in to the urge to play abroad while Raynor stayed at home. The English coach described how he picked up a newspaper in early 1949 to see that Gunnar Nordahl, arguably the best centre-forward in the world at the time, had signed for Milan, becoming a professional and thus ineligible for the national team. And so the exodus had started. Garvis Carlsson went to Bordeaux and then Atlético Madrid. Bertil Nordahl moved to Atalanta while Nils Liedholm and Gunnar Gren joined Gunnar Nordahl to form the fabled 'Gre-No-Li' forward line at Milan. Other, less famous, players moved too.

For Raynor this was problematic. Sweden could have been a force in world football, but Raynor was not able to use his best players in subsequent tournaments. Raynor turned down an offer of £10,000 from an Italian club in 1951, which led his wife to call him "foolish", but, three years later, after Sweden had failed to qualify for the 1954 World Cup, he finally left his adopted country. He managed Lazio and Coventry City (for five months) before returning to Sweden to help the national side finish second when they hosted the World Cup in 1958. But the one thing he wanted, an offer from a big English club, never came his way.

"This story is not going to be overloaded with sour grapes," Raynor wrote at the start of his autobiography. "It won't even contain one, for I am not going to complain because football clubs at home have never been too anxious to engage me, even though I have spent my time looking after the leading sides on the Continent — not without success either. True, I am sorry that it has been impossible for me to get fixed up at home, even after the 1958 World Cup, when I managed the Swedish side to second place, because I have reached the age when I have had enough travelling and want only to settle down in my home country and live the life of a normal Englishman. The thought of combining that with a job whereby I could put my knowledge and ideas to work helping English and British football attracts me. Apparently, however, it does not attract English and British football."

 Great Britain at Rome 1960

"I remember the time I found out I was going to the Olympics," recalled Brian Wakefield. "I was on the Tube with my wife and got hold of the *Evening Standard*. That's how I heard. I probably got a letter later, but I knew the squad being named was imminent so I bought the paper."

The nature of that call-up typifies Britain's previous Olympic efforts. Wakefield and the other 18 British players that went to the 1960 Rome Olympics — Great Britain's last appearance in the finals — were, like all their predecessors, amateurs. Today, the notion of an amateur footballer conjures up images of hung-over parks players kicking each other rather than a ball. To be amateurish now equates to

being hopeless but the maximum wage of £20 a week was still in place in 1960 and so many gifted players preferred to earn a living by other means; with Britain rigorously enforcing the amateur ideal, the Olympics was their tournament. A handful of players like the late Jim Lewis, a First Division title winner with Chelsea in 1955, featured in the Football League, but for most players viewing a life outside the game, or those going to university, there was an alternative; a thriving amateur scene offering a higher standard than many today realise.

"Players like Jim who remained amateur... it was because they were financially better off," explained Hugh Lindsay, who played in midfield in the Rome Olympics. "It was also difficult to break through as an amateur at a later age like 21 or 22 because you were not proven and had not been involved with a club since you were 16. My fear about turning pro was that I loved the game so much that if I turned pro and didn't make it, there was nowhere I could get a game. Maybe Sunday football perhaps, but in those days Sunday football was frowned upon. A lot of the amateurs played Sunday football but it wasn't even under the auspices of the FA then."

In Scotland, Wales or Northern Ireland, the top level of the amateur game focused on single clubs playing in professional leagues, such as Queen's Park or Cliftonville. In England, the showpiece Amateur Cup Final remained popular, while the Isthmian and Northern leagues were amateur competitions, though shamateurism — the practice of players taking secret payments — was rampant.

It was from this hinterland that the Great Britain manager Norman Creek sourced his players as he attempted to halt the slide in Britain's Olympic fortunes. Since winning gold in 1912, Great Britain's Olympic efforts had been hampered by rows over amateurism or between the Home Nations and typified by poor performances, a brave run to the semi-finals on home soil in 1948 under the young Matt Busby aside.

At Helsinki in 1952, Great Britain were humiliatingly eliminated before the start of the Games after a 5-3 thrashing in the preliminaries by Luxembourg. In 1956, Great Britain were forced to qualify and were knocked out by Bulgaria. After a swathe of withdrawals, a Great Britain squad comprised solely of Englishmen were invited back to Melbourne only to be hammered in the second round, again by Bulgaria.

Jim Lewis played and scored in that 6-1 defeat. Despite leaving Chelsea in 1958 and returning to his original club Walthamstow Avenue, he was very much part of the Olympic set-up. Lewis would be joined by another Melbourne teammate, the goalkeeper Mike Pinner, who also eschewed England's amateur leagues. Pinner preferred to play for Pegasus, the side of Oxford and Cambridge University graduates that had won the Amateur Cup in 1951 and 1953. Pinner was too young for those finals and his glories came through *ad hoc* appearances for Football League clubs like Aston Villa, Manchester United and Sheffield Wednesday, who called up the Lincolnshire amateur when their first choice keepers were injured. Pinner, who was turning out occasionally for Queen's Park Rangers as the 1960 Olympics came around, and Jim Lewis were certainties for Creek's squad.

A member of the Flying Corps in World War One, when he was awarded the Military Cross, Creek had played for Corinthians during the 1920s, when the Oxbridge side's FA Cup performances showed amateurs could still compete with professionals. A number of those Corinthians earned full England honours, including Creek, who nearly four decades later would have to achieve what no other British Olympic manager had ever done before or has ever done since: win a qualifying competition.

Throughout all the rows over the definition of amateurism in football, the Home Nations — led by England — were steadfast: no player who took money — for a cup of tea, for boots, for time off work — could ever be amateur, although the clubs frequently bent or simply ignored the rules.

In the communist bloc, however, there were no professionals. Top players were state functionaries or in the military, doing 'jobs' that meant they played football virtually full-time. Elsewhere, rules on amateurism varied widely. Italian footballers could not turn professional before the age of 21. So the 1960 hosts would be represented by Italy's Under-21 team. But before Creek's side could join the Italians in Rome, they had to overcome the Netherlands and the Republic of Ireland in qualifying.

All four Home Nations had featured independently at the 1958 World Cup finals and when, in early 1959, committeemen from each met at the St George's Hotel in Llandudno to discuss the Rome Olympics, the Scots, Welsh and Northern Irish were initially reluctant to allow their players to compete under a united banner.

A request to the British Olympic Association to consider entering four teams had been dismissed; a joint side was the only option. But the main sticking point was an estimated £3,700 bill for sending a team to Rome. After some debate in north Wales, agreement was reached and Creek, who led England's amateur side, was confirmed as manager.

The English held trials, while the other Home Nations nominated players. Before the first qualifier on November 21, the Great Britain XI played three warm-up games. A touring West Indies side were beaten 7-2 at Portman Road, then Creek's side visited Turf Moor for a game with the reigning First Division champions Burnley. On the bench for that game was the Loughborough University undergraduate Bob Wilson.

"Burnley were champions, this was the time of [the infamous chairman] Bob Lord and they had players of the quality of John Connelly, Ray Pointer and Jimmy McIlroy, and Adam Blacklaw in goal," said Wilson, who would go on to win the double with Arsenal. "OK, it finished 5-1 but there was a huge crowd and the amateurs competed against the best team in England. There was huge quality in the time I was associated with the Olympic squad."

Great Britain then went down 4-1 to Chelsea at Stamford Bridge. That may have seemed unpromising, but in the first qualifier the Irish were beaten 3-2 at Brighton's Goldstone Ground through a strike from a Scotsman, Hunter Devine

of Queen's Park, and a brace from Paddy Hasty, a Northern Irishman playing in the Isthmian League for Tooting & Mitcham. Hasty's Welsh club mate Dave Roberts also featured, making the side representative of all four Home Nations.

Before the return in Dublin, the friendlies against top club teams continued. Brian Wakefield shone in a 5-2 defeat to a strong West Ham side at Upton Park. Mike Pinner returned for a routine 3-1 win over the Irish in Dublin, but Wakefield was now his number two.

One of the goals in Dublin came from the Streatham teenager Bobby Brown who was beginning an amazing journey that would take him from south London parks football to a glimpse of Serie A. Brown, whose trademark was playing with a handkerchief in the pocket of his shorts, had not been at Barnet long when he scored both his side's goals in a 3-2 defeat to Crook in the 1959 Amateur Cup final, a performance that had caught Creek's attention.

On 2 April 1960, Creek's team sealed Olympic qualification with a 5-1 rout of the Dutch in Zwolle. Jim Lewis had missed the previous two matches after breaking his leg but returned in style, notching a hat-trick. Bobby Brown, by then the amateur game's rising star, again found the net. Thoughts were already on Rome for the return and Great Britain were fortunate to draw 2-2 with the Dutch at White Hart Lane.

Before the squad was named, a Caribbean tour by Middlesex Wanderers, an amateur touring side of some repute, was used to look at potential Olympians but Lewis and Pinner were seemingly guaranteed places."Mike Pinner seemed to have such possession that he never needed to turn up to training sessions," Wilson recalled. "He seemed to be automatic choice and it should never be like that. It was the one thing that needled us."

Lewis and Pinner did not need to take time off their day jobs — as a salesman for Thermos and trainee solicitor respectively — but there were still 17 other Olympic places up for grabs and the Caribbean was the place to make an impression. The only Welsh tourist, Llandudno's Alan MacIntosh, had a poor trip and no Welsh players made the final squad.

Neither did the Great Britain captain. Barnet's Alf D'Arcy put in some decidedly un-Corinthian challenges during the Wanderers' only tour defeat, a 3-0 loss to Martinique. "Norman Creek started having a go at me afterwards, saying we can't take players like you to the Olympics," D'Arcy said. He was left out of the squad for Rome and dropped from the England amateur side.

Bob Wilson's high-risk approach to goalkeeping involved diving at players' feet, which did not go down well with the conservative Creek. Wilson was later capped by Scotland but missed out in 1960. So did another future full international. A teenage Terry Venables was on the bench in Zwolle and delayed signing professional forms at Chelsea in the hope of becoming an Olympian but his place went to the Barnet draughtsman Roy Sleap.
Before the Olympic squad was finalised, Great Britain were routed 5-1 by the Italians in Brescia. That result augured

badly for Rome, where Creek's side would again face the hosts, Brazil and Formosa.

They began on August 26 against Brazil. Their players were mostly amateur under-20s but included Gérson, who a decade later would score in the World Cup final against Italy, and Roberto Dias, one of the few players Pelé believed capable of marking him. For Paddy Hasty, there was only one way to win. "Play all 19 of us," he joked to his fellow striker Hunter Devine.

The opposition were tough for Great Britain, but the game's location was tougher still. The players had already been told that after being eliminated they must fly straight home. The opener was in Livorno, so far from Rome that Great Britain's players would miss the opening ceremony. Unless they reached the final, Great Britain's footballers would miss the closing ceremony as well. That dampened the mood. "I was only 21 years old," said Bill Neil, a defender from the Scottish side Airdrie. "Not being at the opening or closing ceremony was disappointing. We weren't even in the village that much at the start and had to watch the opening ceremony on the TV."

A minute into the actual match, Roy Sleap fouled the winger Waldir and Gérson sent the resulting free kick past Pinner. Brazil dominated the opening stages but what Great Britain's draughtsmen, carpenters and trainee solicitors lacked in Brazilian flair they offset with British resolve and superior fitness. Since 1959, the Great Britain squad had met regularly in London for weekends at RAF Uxbridge before playing friendlies with club sides. For players like Devine and his fellow Scotsman David

Holt this involved lengthy weekend trips to the south, where they and the rest of the squad were put through exhausting fitness regimes by military instructors.

In Livorno, this paid off. Brazil knocked the ball around, but the closest they came to scoring was when Holt twice cleared off the line. After 22 minutes, Bobby Brown nipped between two defenders to equalise. Two minutes after the kick off, Jim Lewis astonished the Brazilians by putting Great Britain ahead. Moments later, Great Britain hit the bar. Suddenly seeing the closing ceremony was not such a crazy dream.

Then the defender Tommy Thompson was hammered by a Brazilian challenge so shocking that half a century later his surviving teammates are still convinced of its intent: to reduce Great Britain to 10 men. With Thompson's leg broken and no substitutes allowed, Great Britain were a man down. Norman Creek's Corinthians would have removed one of their own players rather than play on with a man advantage, but that world was gone. Despite outstanding work from Pinner, Holt and the Bishop Auckland joiner Laurie Brown, Great Britain were worn down, losing 4-3.

With only the group winners going through, Great Britain needed to beat Italy in Rome's Olympic Stadium to have any chance of progress. On August 29, 45,000 fans — the biggest crowd for any sport at that stage of the Olympics — created an atmosphere that unnerved even the experienced Pinner. Their opponents were more used to such conditions. Players like Gianni Rivera, Giovanni Trapattoni, Tarcisio Burgnich and Giacomo Bulgarelli had big-match

experience that belied their years, but team spirit can go a long way.

"We got a real hammering in Brescia but in the Olympics we were not over-awed," said Hugh Lindsay. "We had a number of players who played in professional football or football at that level. They might have had slightly more skilful players, but our application was sufficient to make sure it was a pretty even match."

In the opening stages, Bobby Brown had a shot blocked and the defender Sandro Salvadore produced a spectacular diving header to cut out a Hunter Devine cross. But after 11 minutes, the 18-year-old Rossano, who had just been signed by Juventus, scored. Italy dominated possession but brave tackling from the diminutive Lindsay and strong defending allowed Great Britain to regroup.

When Bill Neil won possession midway through the half, he was surprised to find Italy backing off. Advancing up the field unchallenged, he laid the ball off to Jim Lewis, whose deflection found Bobby Brown. He was under pressure, but managed to squeeze in an equaliser and it was still 1-1 at half-time. The BBC screened the second half live with commentary from Kenneth Wolstenholme. He was full of praise of Creek's team, who soon received another refereeing set-back as Lindsay was hammered by a brutal Italian foul. His team-mates waited for the inevitable free-kick but were stunned when the Belgian referee gave the decision to Italy. Rossano took the kick quickly, sending a low hard shot past an unprepared Pinner. With the crowd behind them, Rivera urged Italy forward, but there was no breaching a Great Britain defence heroically marshalled by Brown. As Great Britain began to counter, Wolstenholme's pitch of excitement — which had already led him to refer to Great Britain as "England" and then apologise — surged as Hasty met a Devine corner to equalise from six yards.

Already restive, the Italian crowd hurled cushions onto the pitch but Great Britain were dominant. Sleap was clattered by another bad tackle that was ignored by the referee. There was no protest. Sleap limped back into position, ignoring the referee's error as he helped Great Britain launch another attack. The future stars of Italian football had no answer to Great Britain's joiners and students, who couldn't quite find a winner. "A great British side" that "everyone back home can be mightily proud of" Wolstenholme said at the final whistle.

A dozen years earlier, after Great Britain had lost in the Olympic semi-finals to Yugoslavia, Busby gave those players yet to feature a start in the final match, a bronze medal play-off with Denmark. Norman Creek made some changes for the meaningless final game but Arnold Coates, Brian Wakefield, Les Brown and Hubert Barr remained on the bench. A crowd barely in three figures saw Great Britain labour to a 3-2 win over Formosa. Bobby Brown scored again, taking his total for the finals to five, but Creek's team were on their way home. Most players left immediately. On national service with the RAF, Mike Pinner stayed an extra couple of days but only the Scottish striker Hunter Devine remained in Rome. "We were told that you could stay on at your own expense, which was three guineas a day," said Devine. The actuarial student saw

Yugoslavia claim the football title, Don Thompson win gold in the 50-km walk and watched athletics with another gold-medal winner, the young Cassius Clay, but even Devine had to leave before the closing ceremony.

But that wasn't quite the end of it. After returning home, Great Britain's top scorer Bobby Brown was visited by envoys of the AC Milan manager Gipo Viani, who had managed Italy's Olympic side. The Barnet teenager was offered a contract with Milan but had already committed to an FA tour of Australasia and so delayed making a decision. On his return, Brown discovered that Viani had suffered a heart attack while he was away. Brown's chance of Serie A glory was gone; he never heard from Milan again. Brown briefly joined Fulham and later played in Europe with Cardiff City only for injury to bring a premature end to his career.

None of Bobby Brown's 1960 team-mates emulated Jim Lewis in winning the title, but many demonstrated their prowess. David Holt and the Northern Irishman Hubert Barr joined Hearts and Coventry respectively and won full international honours. Laurie Brown played for Arsenal then won the FA Cup with Spurs, Paddy Hasty joined Aldershot and Tommy Thompson recovered to enjoy a long career with Blackpool. Even Mike Pinner belatedly went semi-pro to help fund his solicitor's training and played in the First Division for Leyton Orient. Hugh Lindsay was once on Arsenal's books and made a handful of appearances for Southampton but, apart from playing for the Olympic side and the England amateur team, his career was restricted to what is today known as the non-league game.

Along with Jim Lewis and another Olympian, Bob Hardisty, Lindsay is probably the best post-World War Two player never to turn professional. He has no doubts about the quality of his Rome team-mates, saying: "Every single one could have been a professional and probably would have played in the Premier League today, but that was the way it was then."

③ Brazil at Munich 1972

When Brazil's footballers were knocked out of the 1972 Olympics after a draw against Hungary and defeats to Denmark and Iran, the players decided to make the best of it. For the goalkeeper Nielsen and the defender Fred, a few days of letting their hair down in Munich led to an unlikely involvement in the Black September terror plot that killed 11 members of the Israeli Olympic squad.

"We'd been knocked out of the Olympics so the whole delegation had a week's holiday," Nielsen said. "Every night we went out drinking beer on Marienplatz. We went to the cabaret. The owner saw our jackets with Brazil badges and was very nice; he told us to come every day. So one night my friend Fred and I missed the last U-Bahn. We slept at the station while we waited for the first U-Bahn the next day. Maybe at five in the morning Fred wakes me up. 'Come on,' he said, 'the U-Bahn's here.'"

When they got back to the Olympic village, though, they found it still locked up for the night. "Fred and I tried to get in the gate, but there's nobody there. So we walked around the fence looking for a low place to climb over. We find one and we see three guys with beards already there — dark hair, dark skin, dark tops. I said, 'Good morning,' but they didn't answer. One of them talks to another one — you could tell they were nervous and talking about us. They look at our jackets and realise we're athletes. So they do nothing.

"They were already going over the fence when we got there. They clearly weren't happy to be seen doing what they were doing and didn't want to let us past, but when we got into the village we went a different route. It was a long way round to the Brazilian section and when we got there I heard a noise: pfft, pfft, pfft.

"When a new delegation arrived they would raise their national flag and let off fireworks and it sounded like that. But I knew there couldn't be a team arriving at that time in the morning. But the night before an Italian fencer had won her third Olympic medal [Antonella Ragno-Lonzi, having won bronze in 1960 and 1964, took gold in the women's foil]. They'd been celebrating with fireworks and champagne, so Fred said, 'I can't believe the Italians are still celebrating.'

"We were a bit tired and the worse for wear. Fred wanted to go to sleep, but I said, 'Let's take breakfast.' He said, 'No, no, after.' So, OK, we go to sleep." When they woke up, the atmosphere in the Olympic village had changed completely. "It was about 11 when I woke up," Nielsen said. "The camp was going crazy. There were helicopters overhead, guards with guns. Something was happening in another part of the Olympic village so we went to see what was going on. In the window of the

Israeli section, we saw a man with a mask on and Fred and I realised it was the guy we'd seen before and we knew the noise we'd heard wasn't fireworks at all but gunshots. They shut up the village — nobody in, nobody out."

The three men Nielsen and Fred had seen were part of an eight-strong faction of the Black September terror movement, known as "Ikrit and Biram" after two Palestinian Christian villages whose inhabitants were killed or expelled during the creation of the state of Israel in 1948. Carrying assault rifles, pistols and grenades in duffel bags, they scaled the chain-link fence and used stolen keys to break into one of the apartment blocks being used by the Israeli team.

The wrestling coach Moshe Weinberg and the weightlifter Yossef Romano were killed in initial scuffles and nine other members of the delegation were taken hostage: the wrestling referee Yossef Gutfreund, the shooting coach Kehat Shorr, the track and field coach Amitzur Shapira, the fencing coach Andre Spitzer, the weightlifting judge Yakov Springer, the wrestlers Eliezer Halfin and Mark Slavin and the weightlifters David Berger and Ze'ev Friedman.

The hostage takers demanded the release and safe passage to Egypt of 234 prisoners held in Israel, along with two German radicals held in Germany, Andreas Baader and Ulrike Meinhof, the founders of the German Red Army Faction. The Israeli government refused to engage in any negotiation.

When attempts by the German authorities to buy the release of the hostages failed, it was decided to feign agreement to the Black September demands. A bus transported terrorists and hostages to two military helicopters which took them to the Nato airbase at Fürstenfeldbruck, where an ambush was planned. Five snipers were hidden around the airport with further armed police disguised as flight crew inside a Boeing 727 that was positioned on the runway.

The number of terrorists, though, had been underestimated and it was only as they transferred from bus to helicopter than the authorities realised there were eight of them. The German police inside the Boeing 727 voted to abandon the mission but didn't consult with central command, leaving just the five snipers to combat better-trained and better-armed terrorists.

The result was a bloodbath. Two terrorists were killed by snipers and another hit in the thigh while a German policeman was killed in a firefight. As German armoured personal carriers arrived at the airport, the terrorists seem to have panicked. All nine remaining hostages were killed: at least four were shot by their captors; one died of smoke inhalation after being shot twice in the leg; whether the other four were gunned down by members of Black September or caught in friendly fire remains unclear. Five of the terrorists were killed at the airport; the other three were jailed but released after the hijacking of a Lufthansa jet the following October.

Nielsen, meanwhile, seemed remarkably unflustered by the whole affair. "When it was over," he said, "all the players went to cabaret again." He was never interviewed by police and, although the Steven Spielberg film *Munich* shows two athletes jumping the fence with the terrorists, the goalkeeper's part in the incident remained unknown until a chance remark in a TV programme earlier this year.

 Nigeria at Atlanta 1996

Legends were made that year. Folklore was written. A fairy tale came to an inevitable happy, golden conclusion. And Africa stood proud, rallying behind 11 of their finest football warriors.

Few could believe that Nigeria had won Olympic gold. As a young man at university, I joined plenty of others in going totally, absolutely, bananas. We jumped on *okadas* (commercial motor bikes), waving flags, breaking bottles on the road, beating empty paint drums and generally raising an almighty din. All this, in the early hours.

The night went in a blur but it also seemed to carry on forever. I woke up in the morning, beer bottle in one hand, flag in the other, sprawled in front of my door, totally plastered. Hanging round my neck was a length of twine from which dangled a top from a beer bottle. How it was made or how it got there, I have not even a sketchy memory.

But that was my own gold medal. We ruled the world and I had my own little memento. Well, that was what I thought at the time.

We were Nigeria. We were champions. We were Olympic gold medallists. The world was at our feet. And we had done

it by conquering two of the world's greats, Brazil and Argentina.

To this day, the picture of Kanu on his knees, eyes closed, arms stretched high to the heavens, remains one of the most iconic images of Nigerian sport.

But, typical of Nigeria, this was a triumph born out of chaos.

Nigeria looked in danger of not qualifying for the Games after a 0-0 home draw against Kenya with a team made up of players from the domestic league and one or two journeymen from Europe and Asia. The Kenyans left Lagos celebrating their qualification and promising to hand a humiliating defeat to the Nigerians in Nairobi.

Neither fans nor administrators could countenance the prospect. National football was already at a crossroads.

Nigeria's military dictator General Sani Abacha had stunned the nation by withdrawing the Super Eagles from the 1996 African Cup of Nations in protest at the hosts South Africa's condemnation of the execution of the novelist Ken Saro-Wiwa. In response, the Confederation of African Football hit Nigeria with a two-tournament ban.
No African Cup of Nations for three consecutive tournaments had Nigerians writhing with the pain of football withdrawal. To miss out on the Olympic Games on top of that was beyond contemplation.

Drastic action needed to be taken. The bulk of the squad that had won the African Cup of Nations in 1994 were within the Under-23 age bracket. The likes of Jay-Jay Okocha, Sunday Oliseh, Daniel Amokachi and Victor Ikpeba were available for selection. Added to that mix was a talented squad of young, gifted players who had conquered the world at U-17 level in 1993 and were now ripe for graduation to the next level: Nwankwo Kanu, Celestine Babayaro, Wilson Oruma, Mobi Oparaku and more.

They were all called up by the coach, Jo Bonfrere. The media took one look at the Nairobi-bound squad and dubbed them the Dream Team, after the 1992 US Olympic basketball team

They proved to be exactly that. Kenya were handed a masterclass in front of their home fans. A final score of 3-0 flattered the hosts, and such was Okocha's magic on the day that a Kenyan commentator claimed that "by the time the Harambee Stars realised what was happening, Okocha had left the building."

He was duly fired for such unpatriotic impertinence.

Next up were Zimbabwe, led by Nigeria's 1994 African Cup of Nations-winning coach Clemens Westerhof. The Dream Team dispatched the southern Africans on the pitch, but an even bigger battle awaited. The Zimbabweans claimed they had documents proving that Nigeria's goalkeeper Abiodun Baruwa was overage. Their claims looked genuine. It took months for the protest to be considered by Fifa. It decided in Nigeria's favour, and a nation breathed a collective sigh of relief.

Anyone who thought the troubles were over at that point was either not a Nigerian or did not understand what it meant to be one. A final tune-up friendly against Togo in Lagos ended in an unbelievable 3-1 defeat, prompting panic. From Dream Team, the squad was rechristened the Dreaming Team.

To assuage a restive public, another friendly was hurriedly put together against the local club Shooting Stars. That finished 2-0 in favour of the Dream Team as they headed out to their training camp in Tallahassee.

The goalkeeper Joseph Dosu recalls how things went from bad to worse there. "We were first taken to a hostel where the Brazilian women's team were lodged," he said. "And then told we would have to take the rooms that they didn't occupy. We said we were not staying there and they would have to find us better accommodation."

The squad spent five hours outside before alternative lodgings were secured. But that was no better. "It was a motel," Dosu said. "The type where people just come in, do their business for one hour or so and leave. The rooms were so dirty we had to clean up by ourselves before we could check in."

Not exactly ideal preparation to win Olympic gold, but there was worse to come. After settling in, the players went on strike. "They owed us match bonuses and camping allowances and owed the coach about three-months salary," Dosu said. "The players decided we would not train until it was all settled."

Rather than settling, the federation decided to go behind Bonfrere's back and ask his Nigerian assistants to appeal to the players to come out and train.

They were met with an unyielding brick wall. "We were a strong, united group," the striker Daniel Amokachi said. "If we took a decision, we all stood by it." And stand by it they did, until the FA was forced to ask the embassy for money to pay up and training resumed.

It was within this cauldron that the ultimate conquest was forged. "We were one. We had our fights, we had our quarrels and our disagreements. But we always sorted ourselves out and we knew it was all for the good of our team," Amokachi said. "We had a good bond. The oneness in that team really won us the gold medal. We fought. Positive fighting. We get upset, and then we make you smile and keep going on."

Within such unity there is often a need for an eccentric character; the right-back Oparaku provided light relief. One day, he disappeared for nearly an hour. Bonfere was livid. When Oparaku returned, though, he shook his head and smiled as the full-back hauled a juke box into the hotel. The party was on.

But there was no smile when the Dream Team were beaten by Brazil in their last game of the group stage. The Dutchman was incandescent. In the dressing-room, he lashed out, kicking out at everything in his path and ended up peeling the skin on his big toe. "He wanted us to beat Brazil and eliminate them, but we lost and allowed them back into the tournament," Dosu said.

Brazil were the one team the squad agreed they would have to beat to win the gold and when they met again in the semi-final, Bonfrere's "I told you so" rang all over the dressing-room.

Additional inspiration came at the stadium. The Nigerian team bus arrived just ahead of Brazil's. But officials wanted the Nigerians to stand aside while Brazil drove in first. Amokachi and the others were having none of that. "Daniel was not the captain," Dosu said. "But he was a real leader. He told them we were going nowhere and warned the driver that if he moved aside, he would never drive that bus again."

Nigeria went in first. Amokachi believes the incident solidified their belief. "We knew we could beat them, but to be treated like that made us feel insulted and we were determined to prove them wrong on the field."

They were 3-1 down at half-time. Spirits were flagging. Damage limitation was the major concern for the players. But not for their coach. Bonfrere tossed in the attacking midfielder Wilson Oruma, switched to three at the back and told the players to believe in themselves and attack.

The result was amazing. Amokachi looked like a man possessed by a thousand demons. He appeared to terrify his teammates nearly as much as he did the opponents and the match officials. His drive spurred the team to a stirring comeback. Ikpeba pulled one back with 12 minutes to go and Kanu, latching onto Teslim Fatusi's mishit shot as Brazil failed to clear a long throw from Okocha, flicked the ball up to knock in a close-range finish to level in the final minute. Four minutes into extra time, reacting smartly as Oruma's pass bounced off the back of Fatusi, he added the golden-goal winner. "We knew we could do it," Amokachi said. "After that first game, we looked at their team and man for man, they were no better than us. We just needed to believe in ourselves and I tried to push the players on."

Once the Brazil hurdle was cleared, belief was cemented. "Defeat was not an option," Amokachi said. "You don't get to the final expecting to be second best, especially not after beating Mexico and Brazil."

The Argentina of Hernán Crespo, Ariel Ortega and Javier Zanetti awaited in the final. Again the Dream Team went behind — twice — but again they came storming back. "Amokachi was telling us that we didn't come here to lose. Uche was pushing the players forward. Kanu was saying, 'Come on boys,' and we knew we had to do it," Dosu said. Amokachi, chipping a superb finish after Kanu had missed his kick, made it 2-2 with 16 minutes to go before another last-minute goal, this time from the substitute Emmanuel Amuneke who hooked in the winner unopposed as Argentina's defence went vainly looking for offside.

When the final whistle went and an entire nation realised that Amuneke's goal had written African football history, goose bumps prickled across the continent. "It made me immensely proud," said the Ghanaian journalist Michael Oti Adjei. "You know what that means as a Ghanaian. The manner of the victory against the likes of Brazil and Argentina was unbelievable."

It felt like a coming of age for the entire continent, a rite of passage that put Africa among the ranks of the power players. "It meant a lot," said the South African journalist Joe Maluleke. "Africa was now on the world map and there would be greater opportunities for players. The inferiority complex was gone."

It was no surprise when, four years later, Cameroon provided an African encore.

The stars of that Nigerian squad became legends, recognised all around the mother continent and indeed the world. "I knew we had done something special," Okocha said. "But we didn't quite understand the full implication at the time. These days, so many years after, people still remember things that even you who played have forgotten. It is a blessing to have been part of that team."

It was a blessing even to have watched it.

 Argentina at Athens 2004

Scores of bubbly teenagers crammed into the small chapel at the Colegio Sagrado Corazón in Rosario to hear one of the school's most esteemed former pupils speak. The only condition laid down by Marcelo Bielsa, on accepting the invitation to address the students, was that there be no press.

On taking over as Argentina national team coach in 1999, Bielsa had installed an egalitarian approach to media access — his experience in Mexico with Club América, owned by TV executives, had made him reflect on the relationship he wanted with journalists. Powerful television channels broadcasting across the continent would have the same opportunity to speak to him as reporters from a provincial newspaper. That opportunity would be in a press conference which, if need be (and as was often the case), lasted hours in order for him to respond to all questions. It was not an entirely popular measure.

Despite his request to the school, the content of his speech at the Colegio Sagrado Corazón was made public as *La Nación* acquired a transcript. The paper published his words two years after the event, just as Bielsa was at his lowest ebb after Argentina had been eliminated from the 2002 World Cup at the group phase.

In 2000, Bielsa had told the young students that success "distorts, relaxes and tricks us," adding that failure is "formative and brings us closer to our convictions." He said "the moments in my life when I have grown the most have been the failures; the moments in which I have become a worse person have been in success."

Nowhere else is Bielsa more closely linked to success than in his hometown of Rosario. Having grown up six blocks from the Newell's Old Boys stadium, which has now taken his name, he became the youngest coach to win the Argentinian first division when, aged 36, he led the club to the 1990 Apertura championship. 21 years later, a similar surge of *Bielsamania* erupted when he took over as coach of Athletic Club of Bilbao.

 Bielsa in the Basque country was, after all, perhaps the perfect match. Newell's *mística* is largely built on teams that were made up of players who graduated from the club's youth system in the late 1980s. Bielsa carried that forward in the early 1990s. Athletic's transfer policy needs no explanation here. Jorge Griffa, who oversaw the Newell's youth system for over 20 years and essentially groomed Bielsa as a coach, inadvertently underlined why he is a perfect coach for Athletic. "He is a man who thinks like a youth team coach," said Griffa,

pointing to how Bielsa is constantly teaching his players. The admiration between the two is mutual. For Bielsa, Griffa ranks alongside Mahatma Gandhi and Che Guevara as a leader.

Decades before he had taken over at Athletic, Bielsa's eccentric touchline personality had attracted attention. It almost verges on the caricature —the Catalan TV3 show *Crackovia* recently portrayed him replying to Pep Guardiola's touchline greeting with a five-minute lecture in which he analysed and dissected Guardiola's words.

The fixture between Athletic and Barcelona this season triggered a series of articles discussing the "Argentinian connection" in Guardiola's formation as a coach. High on the list of influences on Guardiola, along with meetings with Ángel Cappa, Ricardo La Volpe and César Luis Menotti, was that of Bielsa. Falling just short of the first meeting between Freud and Jung, the *asado* at Bielsa's home in Rosario lasted 11 hours.

Guardiola is the most successful coach to state his admiration for Bielsa, although his approach is clearly in line with the Barcelona tradition. Gerardo Martino, Jorge Sampaoli, Mauricio Pochettino, Eduardo Berizzo, and to a lesser extent Diego Simeone, are among those who openly revere *El Loco*.

His nickname is a subeditor's quick fix. Indeed, the journalist Ariel Senosiain named his biography of Bielsa after the Charles Bukowski story, "Mad Enough." His meticulous and exhaustive preparations are well known. It was widely reported that before taking over at Athletic, he watched 55 of their games from the previous season, 42 of those twice. On taking over Newell's in the early 1990s, he was viewed as a pioneer when he asked the club to buy him a video recorder, a camera and large television. When Newell's lost the return leg of the Copa Libertadores final against São Paulo in 1992, he watched the match back twice before even leaving Brazil.

For his first coaching job, at the age of 27, he watched 3,000 players before selecting his 20-man squad. The players at the University of Buenos Aires football team slowly adjusted to the coach, barely a few years their senior, appearing on the training pitch with a thesaurus in hand and speaking to them using the formal pronoun *usted.*

His commitment to attacking, and one formation in particular, is another trademark. The famed 3-3-1-3 dates back to the 1992 Copa Libertadores campaign, in which Newell's lost the first match 6-0. The following weekend Bielsa tested his innovative formation and sent Newell's on a 26-match unbeaten run, stretching up to the return leg against São Paulo.

Regularly sent off as coach in his first years at Newell's, his temper is also legendary. On the day when Martín Palermo missed three penalties for Argentina against Colombia in the 1999 Copa América, Bielsa had been already been banished from the dugout. His message for Palermo not to take the third penalty — to protect the striker — did not arrive in time.

Beyond the eccentricities and his dedication to attacking football, he is naturally only judged on results. "I am only interested in winning," he said in 1992 while at Newell's, "although I understand there are thousands of formulas to achieve that." Although he accepts other schools of thought exist, Bielsa's vision is non-negotiable. Repetition on the training ground translates into constant pressure and attack in matches.

This intransigent philosophy transformed him into a deity at Newell's and also won titles at Vélez Sarsfield. As national coach, he transformed Chilean football, but his six years as Argentina coach continue to divide opinion. His only tangible success came in the 2004 Olympic Games, while his teams fell short at the 1999 and 2004 Copas América and more spectacularly in the 2002 World Cup.

From the 2004 Copa América squad, Bielsa named Roberto Ayala as his captain for the Olympics and added Kily González and Gabriel Heinze to make up his quota of three over-age players. Much of that squad — including Carlos Tévez, Andrés D'Alessandro, Lucho González and Javier Mascherano — had played in the 2001 Under-20 World Cup winning side.

For a coach like Bielsa, who shuns so many aspects of the modern game, the Olympic arena was perhaps the perfect setting. As he told the students at Colegio Sagrado Corazón, "I am absolutely convinced that fame and money are insignificant values. I think that the amateur spirit, the love of the task at hand, is the only thing that makes work a satisfying task."

For many of the players who travelled to Athens, the tournament was, precisely, a return to *fútbol amateur,* as youth team football is called in Argentina. At the Olympic village, they had no television, no computers, no air conditioning. They had to make their own beds and queue up alongside other athletes to use the facilities.

Out on the pitch, Argentina were clinical. 11 minutes into the opening match against Serbia and Montenegro, Cesar 'Chelo' Delgado skipped through the defence and fired past Nikola Milojević. Six minutes later, a driving run from Kily González followed by a one-two on the edge of the box with D'Alessandro created the second. Tévez added two, and Mauro Rosales and Heinze finished the 6-0 rout; the result was repeated when the sides met again at the World Cup in Germany two years later.

Tévez and Saviola scored the goals that defeated Tunisia 2-0 and D'Alessandro finished a swift attack against Australia to win 1-0 and take Argentina into the quarterfinals. With Tévez, still making his name at Boca Juniors, in imperious form, Argentina breezed past Costa Rica — the Apache hit a hat-trick after Delgado's opener - setting up a semi-final clash with Italy.

Ahead of the match, as Román lucht writes in his biography of Bielsa, *La vida por el fútbol,* the coach gave specific instructions to Mascherano, who had made his debut for Argentina under Bielsa before even making his first

division debut at River Plate. Ordering the midfielder to police Andrea Pirlo, Bielsa told Mascherano that if he performed, they'd make the final. If not, they would be playing for bronze.

An acrobatic volleyed finish by Tévez put Argentina in front and, with Pirlo effectively neutralised, two breakaway second-half goals from the Gonzálezes — Lucho and Mariano — finished off an impressive 3-0 win.

Argentina faced Paraguay in an anticlimactic finale, winning 1-0. Tévez scored the winner — his eighth of the tournament, leaving him the competition's top scorer. With 17 goals, Argentina were the highest-scoring team and did not concede a single goal. Bielsa's side had gone a step further than the 1928 and 1996 teams that lost in the final and delivered Argentina's first gold medal in 52 years. It was the only piece of silverware lacking at AFA's headquarters, and they brought home the Fair Play award to boot.

Bielsa accepted the Olympics lacked the same tension as other competitions, but he was content with the win for what it meant back home, he said. Two weeks later, he stepped down as Argentina coach. Ⓑ

Stroke is the third biggest killer and the leading cause of severe adult disability in the UK.

A lasting gift in your Will to **Stroke Association** will help us lead the fight against brain attacks.

To find out more about leaving a legacy and for details of our Free Will Scheme please call us on **020 7566 1505** or email **legacy@stroke.org.uk**

www.stroke.org.uk

Registered as a Charity in England and Wales (No 211015) and in Scotland (SC037789). Also registered in Isle of Man (No 945) Jersey (NPO 369) and serving Northern Ireland.

Contributors

The Blizzard, **Issue Four**

David Ashton is a playwright, TV and film screenwriter; creator of the BBC Radio 4 series, *McLevy*. He has written three novels, the latest being *A Trick of the Light*. Also an actor, he played Dr McDuff in *Brass*. His website is **www.david-ashton.co.uk.**

Philippe Auclair is the author of *The Enchanted Kingdom of Tony Blair* (in French) and *Cantona: the Rebel Who Would Be King*, which was named NSC Football Book of the Year. He writes for *France Football*, *Offside* and *Champions* and provides analysis and commentary for RMC Sport. He also pursues a parallel career in music under the name 'Louis Philippe'.
Twitter: @PhilippeAuclair

Steve Bartram is contributing editor at Manchester United's official club media, writing features for the club website, magazine and matchday programme. He has written or co-written eight books about United since 2007. The ninth and tenth — the diary of the 2011/12 season and an anthology of the club's 50 greatest games — are due to hit shelves in the coming months.
Twitter: @stevebartram1

Marcus Christenson was born in New Jersey to Swedish parents and lived and worked in Sweden, Italy and Germany before settling in the UK in 1995. He has been writing about football for the *Guardian* and the *Observer* since 2002 and also contributes to *WSC* and the Swedish football magazine *Offside*.
Twitter: @m_christenson

James Corbett is a sports correspondent and award-winning author who has reported from 20 countries across five continents for outlets including the BBC, the *Observer*, the *Guardian*, the *Sunday Times* and *FourFourTwo*. Most recently he has worked with Neville Southall on his autobiography and his *Everton Encyclopedia* will be published this autumn.
Twitter: @james_corbett

Misha Domozhilov was born in Leningrad (the USSR). He specialises in long-term documentary projects and sports photojournalism. He has won honours at the Grand Humanity Photo Award, Sony WPO, PX3 and the Atlanta Photojournalism Contest.

Luca Ferrato is the Italian football correspondent for the *BBC Radio World Service* and he writes for Insidefutbol. com, *World Soccer*, *Champions*, *The Green Soccer Journal*, *Football World India*, *Gazzetta dello Sport*, and the cycling magazine *Peloton*. He has written two books (in Italian), one about Subbuteo and the other on football in the nineties.

Ian Griffiths is a football writer who follows the game in Asia. Based in Singapore, he is the Senior Editor for espnstar.com. In the past, he has written for *Football Asia* and several of the Asian Football Confederation's official websites.
Twitter: @IanGriffiths67

Simon Kuper is author of *Football Against the Enemy*, a winner of the William Hill Sports Book of the Year, and *Ajax, The Dutch, The War*. His latest book, *The Football Men*, was published by Simon & Schuster in May 2011. He is a columnist with the *Financial Times*. A new expanded edition of *Soccernomics* (previously called *Why England Lose* in the UK) will be published this summer.

Sergio Levinsky is an Argentinian sociologist and journalist. He is the author of three books and the editor of a World Cup encyclopaedia. He is a columnist for *Jornada* (Argentina), the Chinese website www.163.com and Yahoo in Japan. His website is **www.sergiolevinsky.com.**

Ben Mabley is an Osaka-based writer/translator and the presenter of the Football Japan Minutecast, a short weekly podcast on Japanese football. He is also currently compiling the English-language version of the official Japan Soccer Archive. **Twitter: @BenMabley**

Steve Menary is a regular contributor to *World Soccer, When Saturday Comes* and playthegame.org. He is also the author of *Outcasts! The Lands That Fifa Forgot*, which was shortlisted for the NSC Football Book of the Year award, and *GB United: British Olympic Football and the End of the Amateur Dream.*

Vladimir Novak is a freelance journalist based in Belgrade. He writes for *World Soccer, Titan Sports* (China) and *World Soccer Digest* (Japan).

Brian Phillips is a staff writer for Grantland and the editor of the football blog *The Run of Play*. His writing has appeared in Slate, Deadspin, *Poetry,* and *The Hudson Review,* among other publications. **Twitter: @runofplay**

Igor Rabiner is the author of *How Spartak Has Been Killed* (in Russian), winner in the Sports Investigation category at *Knizhnoe Obozrenie*'s Sports Book Awards. His latest book is *Did Russia Buy the 2018 World Cup?* He has written for *Sport-Express* since 1994 and has been Russian Football Journalist of the Year four times.

Joel Richards is a journalist based in Argentina working in TV, print and radio. He has written for *FourFourTwo*, the *Guardian* and *When Saturday Comes.* **Twitter: @Joel_Richards**

Dominic Sandbrook is a historian. His most recent book, *Seasons in the Sun: The Battle for Britain, 1974-1979*, accompanying his BBC2 documentary series on the 1970s, was published by Allen Lane in April. **Twitter: @dcsandbrook**

Lars Sivertsen is a Norwegian writer and radio presenter. He writes for *Josimar* and *When Saturday Comes* among others. **Twitter: @larssivertsen**

David Tryhorn is a TV director/producer who has made a number of documentaries on Brazilian football. His latest film, *A Fragile Dream: Hope and Football on the Streets of Rio* has been released by Pipe Films. **Twitter: @pipefilms**

Colin Udoh is an award-winning Nigerian football journalist. He works as a studio pundit for SuperSport and writes for *Kick Off.* **Twitter: @ColinUdoh**

Jonathan Wilson is the author of *Inverting the Pyramid*, a winner of the National Sporting Club's Football Book of the Year, *Behind the Curtain* and *The Anatomy of England*. His biography of Brian Clough, *Nobody Ever Says Thank You*, was published in November. He writes for the *Guardian, World Soccer, Foxsoccer, ESPN Star, Sports Illustrated* and the *Irish Examiner.* **Twitter: @jonawils**

Blizzard Subscriptions

Subscribe to the print version of The Blizzard, *be the first to receive new issues, get exclusive Blizzard offers and access digital versions of all back-issues FREE*

Subscription Options

Set Price for Four Issues

Get a four-issue subscription to *The Blizzard* — for you or as a gift — for a flat fee including postage and packing (P&P):

UK:	£35
Europe:	£45
Non-Euorpe:	£55

Recurring Pay-What-You-Like

Set up a quarterly recurring payment for each edition of *The Blizzard*. The recommended retail price (RRP) is £12, but pay what you like, subject to a minimum fee of £6 plus P&P

See www.theblizzard.co.uk for more

Digital Subscriptions

If the cost of postage is prohibitive, or you just want an excuse to use your new iPad or Kindle, you can set up a subscription to digital versions of *The Blizzard* for just £3 per issue.

See www.theblizzard.co.uk for more

Information for Existing Subscribers

Free Digital Downloads for *Blizzard* Subscribers

Whether you have taken advantage of our set price or pay-what-you-like offer, for the duration of your subscription to *The Blizzard* you are entitled to download every issue FREE.

See www.theblizzard.co.uk for more

We very much value the commitment of our print subscribers and have a policy to make available new issues, special offers and other limited access events and benefits to print subscribers first.

About *The Blizzard*

Distribution & Back Issues
Contact Information
About Issue Five

Buy *The Blizzard*

We want as many readers as possible for *The Blizzard*. We therefore operate as far as we are able on a pay-what-you-like basis for digital and print versions.

Digital Version (Current & Back Issues)

All issues of *The Blizzard* are available to download for Kindle, Android, iOS and PC/ Mac at: *www.theblizzard.co.uk*.

- *RRP: £3*
- *Pay-what-you-like minimum: £0.01*

Printed Version (Current & Back Issues)

Purchase a physical copy of *The Blizzard* in all its luxurious, tactile, sensual glory at: *www.theblizzard.co.uk*. If you haven't felt our rough textured cover-varnish and smelled the inner genius, you haven't properly experienced its awesome true form. Read it, or leave it on your coffee table to wow visitors.

- *RRP: £12 (+P&P)*
- *Pay-what-you-like min: £6 (+P&P)*

Contact *The Blizzard*

All advertising, sales, press and business communication should be addressed to the Central Publishing Office:

The Blizzard
Ashmore Villa,
1, Ashmore Terrace,
Stockton Road,
Sunderland,
SR27DE

Email: info@theblizzard.co.uk
Telephone: +44 (0)7934 780 488
Website: www.theblizzard.co.uk
Facebook: www.facebook.com/blzzrd
Twitter: @blzzrd

About Issue Five

Editor Jonathan Wilson
Publisher The Blizzard Media Ltd
www.theblizzard.co.uk
Design Azure
www.azure-design.com

Copyright

Style-Style-Style!

Our range of top-quality T-shirts and hoodies are perfect as gifts or for Blizzardistas wishing to broadcast their footy-geek status to like-minded weirdos

Blizzard Dog

Blizzard Bitch

Football Theory

Men's Fitted T-Shirt

The Blizzard's canine compadre, resplendent in crisp, three-colour screen print on an Oxford Blue, 180gsm, 100% cotton, Jerzees Colours Fitted Crew Neck.

- Fitted body shape.
- Tubular constucted body for shape retention.
- Extra-reinforced shoulder seams.
- Available in S (36/38), M (38/40), L (40/42), XL (42/44), 2XL (44/46).

£16 + (£1.45 P&P - UK)

Ladies' Fitted T-Shirt

Sidney Duncan, founder of the 1893 *Blizzard*, detested the company of an "intelligent" woman. Display your lack of intelligence by sporting Dog on a Sky Blue, 100% pre-shrunk cotton, 155gsm Gildan Softstyle Ladies' tee.

- Seamless twin needle collar, taped neck and shoulders, twin needle sleeves and bottom hem.
- Available in sizes 10, 12, 14, 16 and 18.

£14 + (£1.45 P&P - UK)

Men's Fitted T-Shirt

The average human brain is 97% full of football trivia and song lyrics. Fact. Wear your brain on your chest with this French Navy, 180gsm, 100% cotton, Jerzees Colours Crew Neck.

- Fitted body shape.
- Tubular constucted body for shape retention.
- Extra-reinforced shoulder seams.
- Available in S (36/38), M (38/40), L (40/42), XL (42/44), 2XL (44/46).

£16 + (£1.45 P&P - UK)

Order Online at
www.theblizzard.co.uk

The Blizzard

Men's Hooded T-Shirt

Like to layer? This stylish, long-sleeved, Heather Grey skinnyfit hooded tee is sure to become your favourite wardrobe staple. Perfect for summer with its 100% 140gsm lightweight cotton.
- Twin needle hem and sleeves with drawcord
- Note: this is not traditional sweatshirt-style hoodie material.
- Available in S (36), M (38/40), L (42), XL (44/46), 2XL (48)

£20 + (£1.74 P&P - UK)

Blizzard Hoody

Men's Hoody with zip

Keep out the chill with this stylish grey Blizzard zipped-hoody. Perfect for those long winter nights when you're curled up with your favourite football quarterly.
- Full length concealed zip
- Front pouch pockets.
- Twin needle stitching, rib trim with spandex at cuffs and hem
- 270 gsm
- Available in S (34/36), M (38/40), L (42/44), XL (46/48), XXL (50/52)

£25 + (£1.74 P&P - UK)

Overrated

Men's & Ladies T-Shirt

Are you into the finer nuances of football, or just a man with few ambitions? Either way, scoop this subtle White, 180gsm, 100% cotton, Jerzees Colours Fitted Crew Neck.
- Fitted body shape.
- Tubular constucted body for shape retention.
- Extra-reinforced shoulder seams.
- Available in S (36/38), M (38/40), L (40/42), XL (42/44), 2XL (44/46).

£16 + (£1.45 P&P - UK)

HOME TAPING IS
KILLING MUSIC

AND IT'S ILLEGAL